CW00349264

Abby Lee, aka Zoe Margol... ...
pundit. She is a frequent con...
Observer among many oth...
guest on Sky News. Her boo... ...
Confessions of the Seductress Next Door was an international bestseller, translated into sixteen languages.

Zoe's blog, *Girl with a One Track Mind*, which began in 2004, has had over 7 million visitors, and it won the Bloggie Award for 'Best British or Irish Weblog' in both 2006 and 2007. The *Observer* ranked *Girl with a One Track Mind* as the 24th 'most powerful blog in the world' and *nerve.com* named it 'the world's most famous sex blog'.

Zoe has also been the subject of a Channel 4 documentary, *The Sex Blog Girls* and her book is being adapted into a screenplay and stage play.

Praise for Abby Lee and *Girl With A One Track Mind*

'Witty, moreish and incredibly explicit' *Guardian*

'A radical new voice . . . a publishing sensation' Channel 4

'[A] shining star' *Time Out*

'Insightful' *Sun*

'Fearlessly frank' *Independent*

'Cheerfully neurotic, unapologetically political' *New Yorker*

GIRL

with a

ONE
TRACK
MIND

ABBY LEE

PAN BOOKS

First published 2010 by Pan Books
an imprint of Pan Macmillan, a division of Macmillan Publishers Limited
Pan Macmillan, 20 New Wharf Road, London N1 9RR
Basingstoke and Oxford
Associated companies throughout the world
www.panmacmillan.com

ISBN 978-0-330-50969-5

1 3 5 7 9 8 6 4 2

A CIP catalogue record for this book is available
from the British Library.

Illustrations by ML Design

Printed by CPI Mackays, Chatham ME5 8TD

Visit **www.panmacmillan.com** to read more about all our books
and to buy them. You will also find features, author interviews and
news of any author events, and you can sign up for e-newsletters
so that you're always first to hear about our new releases.

ACKNOWLEDGEMENTS

I very much appreciate the guidance, suggestions and most of all the patience offered by all the wonderful people at Pan Macmillan. Thank you especially to Ingrid Connell, Natasha Martin, Helen Guthrie, Naomi Berwin and Toni Byrne for all your wonderful contributions to this book.

A big – indeed massive – thank you to my agent Simon Trewin at United Agents for making it all happen, and to Ariella Feiner for her assistance.

I also owe a debt of gratitude to David Bloom – thank you for always being ready to spring into action on my behalf (but luckily more cautiously than me).

To all my friends/colleagues/acquaintances who offered support when I needed it – thank you. Your care and loyalty means more than I can say. If you recognize yourself in the book, I hope you'll know that you're there because you mean a lot to me.

Thank you to Mike Atkinson, Sasha Frieze, Darren Shrubsole, Darryl Chamberlain, Diamond Geezer, Gordon McLean, Jonathan Swerdloff and countless other bloggers from back in the day. Internet friends FTMFW.

Special thanks to Alex Marsh for always being a trusted, listening ear and putting up with my rants. Also to Steve Sparshott for being my – very patient – touchstone and never boring of my use of the semicolon.

I am grateful, and incredibly proud, to be the daughter of my parents: their love, support and advice has been unwavering, and I can only thank them profusely for sticking by me unconditionally. I still hope they'll never read beyond this acknowledgements page though.

Finally, I would like to offer up my thanks and appreciation to all the people who read the blog and book, left comments, sent emails, contacted me on Twitter and Facebook, and especially those bloggers who rallied round when it all turned to shit. I'm eternally grateful for all your kindness and support. Thank you.

'This is a message for Zoe Margolis,' the woman's voice said. 'I'm a reporter for the *Sunday Times* and we're running a story on your being Abby Lee, the author of the anonymous sex blog and book *Girl with a One Track Mind*.'

I barely made it into the bathroom before I vomited.

(o)

A few months prior . . .

MARCH

Friday 17th March

I slept over at Tim's last night after going to the pub. Tim and I are old college buddies: it's been some years since we ended up in bed together and concluded from that we were better suited as friends. Nowadays we just talk about everything related to dating, rather than acting upon it; handily this enables me to get the no-holds-barred low-down on blokes and shagging: something all straight women would like to have, I'm sure. It's so nice to have a male friend like Tim to whom I can put my explicit questions, and to be able to converse about sex with him without any threat to our friendship.

During the night I woke up and had to pop to the loo. On the way to the bathroom I encountered something rather surprising: Tim sitting on the living-room couch in the dark, naked, with the TV on.

'I was just watching the game,' he said defensively, as he grabbed a cushion and covered himself with it, quickly switching the channel as I entered the room.

I laughed and pointed to the pillow. 'So, you normally watch football nude, then?'

Embarrassed, he clutched it closer to his groin. 'I know what it looks like, but I was just watching the game, honestly.'

I raised an eyebrow at him. 'How long have we known each other? C'mon, Tim, there's no need to be shy; if you were bashing one out, that's fine by me. Go right ahead.'

As I spoke, I was recalling a faint memory of him stroking his cock next to me in bed. I remembered how he used to grip his shaft in his left hand and gently tug his balls with his right and I wondered whether, ten years on, he still used the same technique.

I stood there looking at him continue to blush and realized that my thoughts were inappropriate; we are just friends, and the days of sexual experimentation between us are long gone. Time to get that thought out of my head, pronto.

'I'll just pop to the loo – you go right ahead and do whatever it is you were doing before I interrupted you,' I said, stifling a giggle.

'I wasn't wanking!' he exclaimed. 'I promise.'

'Yeah, right,' I snorted.

I walked off towards the bathroom, leaving him to get on with it. But, admittedly, in the back of my mind I was wondering what it might be like to watch him wank again.

// posted by thegirl @ 1:44:00 PM

Saturday 18th March

It's not easy being a Girl with a One Track Mind, you know. Not only am I preoccupied with sex, with a libido that exceeds most men I meet, but being the anonymous author of a popular blog based on my sex life really does take it out of me. Keeping up the façade which I have had to create in my life, in order to be able to maintain the secrecy of my blog, wears me down.

I began writing my blog a few years ago because it was a space for me to express myself freely, truthfully and honestly; where, as a woman talking about sex, I would not be judged. That's not to say that I don't attract some horrid, hateful responses to my blog, because there are many, but being anonymous means I can avoid personal attacks. Given some of the vitriol I receive, I'm thankful for this shield of protection. Not all the emails and comments are cruel: in fact the majority are supportive, and people genuinely seem interested in thinking about and debating sex, rather than just being titillated. What's been nicest of all are the supportive emails I receive from women: so many of us, it seems, are Girls with One Track Minds.

Sometimes, I wish I could tell my friends just what it is that I do at home, after meeting up with them; I wonder if they'd be more surprised by my immediate hopping online to post something new on my blog, or by my incessant post-martini wanking. I'm guessing the former would shock them most, but I dread to think what they'd make of the latter. The thing is, I'm not ashamed by the things I've done or written about, but I'd hate my nearest and dearest to read my innermost thoughts and feelings about sex, in addition to reading all the explicit details. Nor do I want to be judged by my colleagues on the lifestyle I lead: no doubt I'd never be taken seriously at work again, which would make my job in the tiny community of the film industry almost impossible.

So I keep up a pretence with my friends, I lie to my family

and I creep around at work; no one suspects that I'm leading another, very busy, but secret, anonymous life online. And I do love that life: I enjoy the response my blog receives, I like the contributions and comments people make after reading something I've written; I find it cathartic being able to write about the sexual adventures I have had. But as the blog becomes ever more popular and interest in it grows – in a few months it's going to be published as a book – I worry that it risks people finding out who I really am. 'Girl with a One Track Mind' has been the place where I've truly opened my heart, and laid everything bare, but behind the 'Abby Lee' sexblogger online persona lies me, Zoe, an average thirty-something woman who just wants the normal things in life: a career I'm passionate about; a happy, fulfilling relationship; and great sex.

Obviously I'm most concerned with the latter. Well, for now, anyway.

'I think it's great that we're not having sex any more,' I remarked nonchalantly, sipping my beer.

Amidst the hubbub of the busy north London pub, Blog Boy took a slow swig from his pint and then leaned back, a bemused expression on his face. I watched him for clues, waiting for the familiar laughter lines to appear around his bright blue eyes, but they didn't, and suddenly the atmosphere around our table seemed quiet.

'What I mean,' I clarified, stammering a little, 'is that with all that happened, I'm relieved we've managed not to have sex and remain friends over this last year.'

And I truly was. With him knowing all about my blog – after all, he's an anonymous blogger too, and naturally we first met online – I have always felt relaxed with him. I guess it was inevitable that I would fancy him – and god, did I. We ended up seeing each other over many months, during which time I developed feelings for him and wanted us to enter into a relationship. Sadly this wish wasn't mutual: evidently we weren't a match. But I was OK with how things were left between us because despite my disappointment, we still stayed in touch, and I'm really happy we are able to be friends now. Not to mention we also enjoy each other's company – hence our outing tonight to hear some live music.

'But,' I continued, treading carefully, 'I think the sex thing between us will always be there: I'll probably always feel attracted to you.'

Blog Boy smiled at me, finally. 'Yep, and me too with you. You can't just switch that off . . .'

I relaxed and smiled back at him. 'We just have to make sure we don't act on it, not give in to our desires: that way our friendship will be fine.'

Blog Boy grinned in agreement and we raised our beers in a mock toast. At that exact moment, a pretty thirty-something blonde woman approached us. A little tipsy, she grab-bed the table for stability and leaned in towards me.

'Is he your boyfriend?' she said softly, with a suggestive wink.

I looked over at Blog Boy, our gaze meeting in a mutual ironic smile, which led me to reply, 'He might be,' as I grinned back at the woman flirtatiously.

'How long have you been together?'

I paused, trying to think of an accurate answer. 'We've known each other a few years . . .'

'You look very happy,' she said, wobbling slightly in her high heels.

'We're just fine, thanks,' I replied, stifling a laugh and throwing Blog Boy a look.

'Well, then, I don't want to interrupt your evening,' she said, smiling, 'but could you please spare a cigarette? I'll pay – whatever it costs. Anything you want for it, I'll give you.' She swayed a little in Blog Boy's direction and I raised my eyebrow at him to see what his response would be.

Because he's sweet-natured, unlike me, instead of stating a reasonable demand, he simply reached into his packet of cigarettes. 'Here you go,' he said, offering her one. 'Enjoy.'

'Oh, it's not for me, it's for a friend,' she replied, but took the cigarette anyway. She stroked each of us on the arm, thanking us profusely as she did so. Then she bade us farewell and wished us a pleasant evening together, squeezing us both on the shoulders as she left. At this, Blog Boy and I exchanged a brief look of surprise; instinctively I knew we were both thinking the same thing.

I quickly turned to watch her shapely figure move away from the table and felt the blood rush to my head and my heart begin to thud loudly. I wasn't sure if it was the excitement of having just seen the band The Bravery perform live not even half an hour before; or if it was due to the large amount of beer I had drunk; or whether it was being faced with a sexy voluptuous woman quite obviously flirting with us both, but whatever it was, I suddenly felt impulsive.

'Do you realize you could have asked her to do anything

for that cigarette and she probably would have?' I said, smirking at Blog Boy mischievously.

With a stupefied grin on his face, Blog Boy laughed. 'Yeah, I guess . . .'

'I mean, honestly, she would be up for it, I'm sure.'

Blog Boy smiled again, but this time more hesitantly.

'Seriously, she is. I know it.'

I swung round for another peek at the woman and turned back to Blog Boy. 'Jesus,' I whispered to him conspiratorially, 'if I had noticed what nice breasts she had when she was standing next to us, I would have asked her to press them into my face in return for that cigarette.' I turned to look at her again.

'Actually,' I continued, even more enthusiastically, 'I would have asked her to rub them against your face. She's got great boobs, look at them!'

We both fixed our gaze on the woman: her tits were indeed great. In fact, all of her was great: just my type, actually. Rubenesque, a big bum, buxom: the exact kind of woman I go for. (Given I only have Sapphic leanings about 2 per cent of the time, I am extremely fussy and quite shallow about the type of women I find sexually attractive.) Unable to tear my eyes away from her curves, like some kind of drooling character in a cartoon, all sorts of sexy thoughts entered my head and the pounding in my chest became almost unbearable.

'I could get her to do it,' I said to Blog Boy, eagerly and with sudden confidence. 'I know I could. If you want me to, I will. Honestly, if you want her tits in your face – and, quite frankly, I wouldn't mind seeing that – I bet you she would do it if I asked her.'

Blog Boy shifted in his seat a little. 'No, don't. It'd be embarrassing.'

'You don't want me to ask her? Don't you think she's sexy?'

'It's not that. I mean . . . She's very nice, yeah. It's just, well, oh, I don't know . . .' He trailed off and I knew the potentially heated moment would be lost unless I acted on it quickly.

'I won't embarrass you, I promise,' I reassured him. 'I tell you what: how about a kiss instead? Would you like that? I know she'd be up for it; I guarantee it.'

He smiled shyly at me and bit his lip. 'OK, I suppose . . .'

Before he had even finished speaking I had turned to look at the blonde woman who was now standing just a few feet from our table. I observed her chatting away with her friend and I tried to think clearly, but my mind was racing with adrenalin and excitement. A few seconds later, she saw me staring at her and smiled at me. I immediately gestured to her to come over; as I watched her sashaying in my direction, I took a deep breath and hoped for the best.

When she arrived at the table, she bent down and rested her hand on my shoulder. She was so close to me, her silky blonde locks grazed my face and I could smell the arousing, yet subtle, scent of her skin. Her large breasts, tantalizingly, were just an inch from my face and I fought off the temptation to lift my hands and cup them gently.

'Hello again,' she breathed and leaned in closer so her ear was against my mouth. Electricity rippled through me. Didn't she know what effect she was having on me? As if she read my mind, her hand, still resting on my shoulder, travelled smoothly to the nape of my neck; I could feel each of her fingers delicately pressed into my skin. I took this as a sign it was OK for me to touch her too: I rested my fingers on her hip and as I began to whisper in her ear, my fingertips lightly traced a small circle into the exposed flesh above the waistband of her jeans.

'You know before, when you said you would do anything for a cigarette?'

'Yes?'

'Well, there is something I would like you to do.'

'What?'

'My friend: he likes you.'

She pulled back from me slightly and fixed her eyes on mine, searching my face for clues. 'I thought you said he was your boyfriend?'

I shook my head. 'No. We're just friends – good friends.'

'Oh. I see.' She seemed relieved and she readjusted her position closer to me, once again allowing me a whiff of her.

'Yes. And, well, he thinks you're really sexy.'

She giggled. 'Oh really?!'

'Really. I do too: you are very sexy.'

'Well, so are you.'

I paused, taking in what she was saying. 'Um, thanks . . . Would you kiss him?'

'Kiss him?'

'Yeah.'

'Just a kiss?'

'He'd really like that, yeah.'

'I don't want to do anything else.'

'No, of course not. Just a kiss, that's all.'

'Well . . .' She shifted back and hooked me with her smile. 'If I get to kiss you too, then I will.'

'Of course, that goes without saying.'

The words came out of my mouth before I even had the chance to think them. And a split second later, her lips were on mine and her fingertips were softly caressing my face. Time stopped and all I was aware of was the faint taste of mint from her mouth.

Fuck, I thought, I'm actually kissing her: it's this easy. This is how you get to kiss a sexy girl: you just proposition her! Out of the corner of my eye I quickly peeked to see if anyone in the pub was watching: not even an eyebrow raised. But then this is Amy Winehouse's local, so I guess they're used to people drunkenly snogging in public.

With her soft mouth pressing firmly against mine, my mind raced. What exactly did I want her to do? I mean, I knew my objective, but faced with it actually happening, I suddenly questioned my motivation. That I fancied her there was no doubt, but why on earth was I proposing that she snog Blog Boy? Was it because he was my mate and I was doing him a favour? Was it because some part of me – the old me, when I had fallen for him – wanted to witness his pleasure, because it would give me pleasure? Or was it just that I, a Girl with a One Track Mind, am obsessed by all things sexual?

My conscience ached. I felt like I was objectifying her, taking advantage of her drunken state for our titillation, and 'lezzing it up' for Blog Boy: this was definitely a porn cliché I couldn't subscribe to.

With these thoughts spinning around my head, she moved away from me and over to Blog Boy, planting a large, brief kiss on his bemused smile, whilst I watched, equally confused and aroused.

Suddenly she resumed her position in front of me and, in one quick move, leant down to kiss me deeply again. All anxiety and worry I had was immediately dispelled by the intense throbbing between my legs. This wasn't about exploitation, or sexist objectification, or even pleasuring Blog Boy. This was about me and her and how turned on I was, and at that moment I didn't give a fuck about anything else: I could have very happily kissed her all night.

But the kiss ended as it began: swiftly. Grinning at me, with a glint in her eye, the blonde woman turned and left our table. I found myself in a state of shock, looking over at Blog Boy, whose face clearly matched my own stunned expression.

'What just happened there?' he asked.

I shook my head. 'I don't know. I really don't.'

He laughed. 'You just made a girl kiss me!'

I slowly nodded.

'And you!'

'Evidently . . .'

Blog Boy and I continued musing on the events and drinking our beers until closing time. Then we said our goodbyes and separated with a smile: the perfect way to end an evening with an ex-lover, especially given how painful it had been for me when things didn't work out.

But it wasn't until later that a sudden, frustrated thought struck me: something more might have happened tonight – but not with Blog Boy. I might be a bit crap with men, but you can multiply that by a thousand when it comes to women: if only I didn't have such shit 'gaydar' perhaps I wouldn't have been making my way home alone on the night bus . . . Damn it.

// posted by thegirl @ 0:12:00 AM

Sunday 19th March

I've been thinking that some of my blog readers might assume that I'm well versed in girl-on-girl action: a sex diarist should be successful in all sexual ventures, right? I'm really not; I may have a one track mind, but I've had as many crap shags as good: I'm not always successful in sex. So, with the events of last night ringing in my (hungover) head, I'm reminded about the first ever lesbian experience I had: what a nightmare that was.

I was always bi-curious, I think, but have felt very hesitant about pursuing that aspect of my sexuality. For starters, I much prefer to fuck men. And I neither represent, nor am I attracted to, either the 'butch dyke' or the 'lipstick lesbian' stereotypes, so I've always been rather sceptical about exploring another woman sexually.

However, the desire to experiment was there, so when Claire, a friend from the writing class I took in my early twenties, suggested I go to a lesbian bar and offered to help me try to pull, I jumped at the chance. Claire was a lesbian, so hopefully she would know the ropes and point me in the right direction; she said she'd give me some tips on chatting a woman up – 'Just talk to her!' – and on making the right approach at the right time. Given my previous attempts at chatting up women had only resulted in my managing to smile at a pretty girl from afar, it was clear my picking-up-women technique needed some assistance.

After settling down into a prime position in a Soho lesbian bar, I hoped we would spot some talent. It was odd being in an all-female environment: I felt strange, even uncomfortable, ogling women in the same way I usually ogle men. But Claire and I gulped down copious amounts of wine, which helped me relax a lot, and before I knew it I was distracted by an intense conversation about a writing assignment. I was excited about being there, of course, and wanted to scout around and catch a few girls' eyes, but I was trying not to be rude and ignore Claire: after all, she was a good friend and had generously offered to assist me – the least I could do was give her eye contact and converse properly.

As the evening went on, though, and the early hours neared, and I was no closer to looking at another girl, let alone chatting her up, I found myself getting drunker and more frustrated: why was Claire so intent on having a deep discussion about writing projects with me? Surely she wanted to advise me about chat-up lines and how to approach cute girls? She was there to help me pick up a woman, right?

Wrong.

Over time, I had always tried to ignore the way Claire's eyes frequently dropped to my breasts as I talked. I put this down to the fact that, yes, my tits are big, and yes, it might be hard for her not to notice them. But I dislike people staring at my breasts when I am speaking and, given the situation in the bar, was now feeling pretty uncomfortable that Claire's eyes were glued to them. She barely gave me eye contact as her gaze continually fell to my nipple line. Fine, she likes my breasts. I can deal with that. But at some point she leaned across the table and grabbed hold of my arm, stroking it from my shoulder down to my hand, clasping my fingers in hers, saying, 'You're so fucking sexy, god, I like you so much. I want you.' And then she pulled me to her and kissed me deeply.

I was so shocked I didn't know what to do; this was entirely out of the blue. We'd been friends for a year: I had no idea she might fancy me. But at this point, analysing it was irrelevant: Claire had her tongue down my throat.

The thing is, I just didn't fancy her. Although Claire was very pretty – luscious, sleek auburn-red hair, deep green eyes, trim, svelte body – she just wasn't my type. There I was, being snogged by a girl who I didn't find sexy, and who also happened to be my friend, and at that point I should have pulled away, had some strong moral words with her about us not getting sexually involved, said goodnight and made my way home.

But by now – and in public, I might add – she was running her hands across my breasts, making my nipples rock hard. With her deft fingers stroking and cupping my tits, I felt my body respond to her touch and between my legs I began to ache, yearning to have something to relieve the pressure building up there. I felt my breath quicken and looked at her, this slender, petite woman I wasn't particularly attracted to, and tried to think.

With a combination of alcohol and the heat between my legs, I selfishly didn't end it right there. OK, so her tits are non-existent; and she is skinny; and she has no arse. Not to mention that she is my friend. But she is a woman; and she wants me; and my pussy is soaked and needs attention; and I am drunk. And if I close my eyes and concentrate really hard, maybe I can just pretend she is Salma Hayek.

So – I am ashamed to say – I pulled her to me, kissed her deeply and started caressing her breasts, teasing her nipples like she was doing to me. And when she then suggested having sex in one of the toilets, I followed her downstairs enthusiastically.

It wasn't long before we were stood in front of each other naked, her slender body appearing tiny next to mine. It suddenly struck me why I dislike skinniness in my sexual partners: I need them to have a strong physical presence like me, or else I feel like I dominate things. And because I like to switch roles in bed – being both submissive and dominant – similar body shape and size are preferable.

Or, in other words, I don't want to feel like a huge gallumphing cow having sex with a flimsy flower – that just doesn't turn me on.

But I was trying to ignore all that. After all, I was horny as hell, a pretty girl was naked in front of me and I was finally about to get intimate with another woman. So, shallow selfish person that I am, I concentrated instead on the task at hand: moving closer to her so she could press her tits against mine.

Finally, porn gets it right: this is as great as it looks!

I rubbed my nipples against hers, feeling the throbbing between my legs increase as I did so. She slid her thigh in between mine and we ground our hips against each other. It felt so good – even if it was a little frustrating because I kept wishing she had a cock to slip in between my legs, rather than just her slim thigh.

Still, moments later, I had a bit of relief: she slipped her fingers between my legs and I did the same with her. It was a miniscule celebratory moment for me: the first time I ever felt the inside of another woman's vagina and I was struck by the wetness, heat and tightness – it's just not the same when you touch yourself.

With her fingers rubbing me frantically and my orgasm approaching, I leaned in to kiss her, and that was when she whispered the magic words in my ear, 'I'm so in love with you. I want you. Come back with me, I want to make love to you all night.'

Which of course made my climax disappear spontaneously.

There was I, selfishly enjoying having drunken sexual liaisons with a woman I didn't fancy, who was also a close friend, and she had the audacity to be in love with me. Great. I couldn't have hoped for a better introduction to lesbianism.

It certainly wasn't like that in the porno.

My horniness deflating like an erection caught out by a ripped condom, I pulled out my fingers from deep inside her and tried to explain that I just wanted to be friends – which was a bit contradictory, given that my fingers were still soaked with her juices. But she deserved honesty from me, and although she was upset about my abrupt ending of our heated embrace, I know it was better to have nipped things in the bud, so to speak, than to let anything develop any further.

You see, it's one thing to have drunken sex with a mate, but it's another thing entirely when they are in love with you: the sex becomes loaded with anger, people get hurt, friendships get damaged. Claire and I fell out some time after our dalliance, and I've not seen her in over a decade, so having sex with another friend is not something I plan to rush into again.

I'm happy to say that most of my ex-lovers are friends of mine now: we've realized that we're better suited as mates who don't have sex. Even though, admittedly, it can be a bit frustrating sometimes if you're both gagging for it.

Thank god for vibrators, is all I can say.

// posted by thegirl @ 10:21:00 PM

Wednesday 22nd March

Thinking about my night out with Blog Boy, and the snog off that gorgeous girl, made me realize something: I don't believe in luck.

Let me rephrase that. I don't believe luck can be made, as if some people have a knack in striking lucky and some people don't. No. I believe in chance. Taking chances. Putting yourself in a position where there is an equal chance of failure or success, and accepting whichever comes your way.

I do this regularly, though I am often not aware of it till much later. People who know me ask me how I have the balls to:

Demand a refund due to the terrible projection of a movie in the cinema?

Send food back in a restaurant when it's not exactly what I ordered?

Greet Ken Loach as if he were an old mate (he's not)?

Ask for a job from someone I have just met?

Walk up to a stranger and ask him out for a drink?

And when I think about it, I really don't know how. I mean, it's not that I am not scared to do all these things – I am. I have a delayed reaction, I guess; the fear doesn't hit me till later, usually when I get home, and then I think to myself, 'What the fuck did I just do??' – just like I did with that woman and Blog Boy.

I understand that to others I may seem super confident, outspoken and flirtatious, but inside, I am shitting bricks like everyone else.

It is in my nature to be outgoing and assertive, and I think I also enjoy taking chances and putting myself on the line, especially when it comes to men. Maybe I like the thrill of it. I mean, as well as the possibility of failure, there's also the chance of success – and both get the heart racing. Take the following examples over the last year:

asking the sales assistant who was helping me try on ski trousers out for a drink (he had a girlfriend).

walking up to a guy I had seen on the studio lot where I work and asking him out to dinner (he had a girlfriend).

chatting up one of my gym instructors (he had a wife and kid).

meeting a guy from a newspaper personal ad (we ended up shagging).

chatting up a guy on the bus (we ended up shagging).

following a cute guy around in the supermarket (he had a boyfriend).

flirting with a guy in my local newsagent (both of us with the *Guardian*, him with a smile, me in a hurry – haven't seen him since).

asking a total stranger out for a beer (haven't heard back from him).

All of these situations have made my heart beat a little faster, which must be good for my soul, if not for my nerves. And even though I have been gutted (to say the least) about the ones that didn't work out, at least I have taken chances and put myself 'out there'.

Without risk, there is no serendipity. Life would be exceedingly dull. And a dull life is one not worth living, I reckon.

Even if I do cringe on a regular basis, wishing I hadn't been so forward . . .

// posted by thegirl @ 9:33:00 PM

APRIL

Sunday 2nd April

I don't talk about my job on my blog, for fear of discovery, but it is something that is a hugely important part of my life – alongside sex, of course. I love being a runner in the assistant director's department on feature films. It may be the bottom rung in the department, but when you're on set you're an 'A.D.' just like all those above you, and people come to you with questions about the running order of the day. So I primarily take care of the actors (and their egos), and co-ordinate action on set, whilst trying not to collapse from exhaustion doing 70+ hours a week, month in, month out. It sounds tough – and it is – but I love it: once you have the movie buzz in your blood it never leaves you.

I do struggle, though, especially being one of the few women on the film set, and the only woman in my department.

But there are some advantages to this:

1. No one forgets my name, even with a shooting crew of 100+ people.
2. Many of the crew feel protective towards me and look after me like I was their sister or daughter.

3. Guys jump to my aid with any favours I need (tasks to be done; heavy things to be carried, etc.).
4. I am frequently offered cups of 'builder's' (very strong) tea.
5. Cakes from the afternoon break on set are always saved for me.
6. I get a lot of attention from other crew members.
7. All the guys flirt with me, which helps to relieve the boredom on set.
8. I get chatted up by various crew members; given that many of the guys on set are young, fit and strong, this can be quite enjoyable.
9. Being surrounded by blokes means I get to ogle bums and crotches all day and fantasize to my heart's content.
10. Whilst the men's banter on set can be graphic and full of innuendo, I have an unending supply of sarcastic replies that soon shut them up.

But there are also some disadvantages to being the only female on the set of a film:

1. As soon as a pretty actress walks on set, all the blokes ogle her, leaving me ignored – not helpful when my job hinges on my ability to issue instructions to the crew.
2. Many of the crew are threatened by me and undermine me at every opportunity.
3. Some guys will obstruct the tasks I need to do just to show that I am less competent than them.

4. I get asked, 'Make us a cup of tea, love,' every five fuck-ing minutes by any number of random blokes on set. (See p21!)

5. I rarely eat cake (or any of the other stodgy, high-fat food we get provided with at work), so end up offending the kind-hearted men who are trying to fatten me up at tea-time.

6. Being the focus of attention is not always appreciat-ed: when you look rough from working so many hours, or are feeling down, it's exhausting having to project happiness all the time – women are expected to look beautiful in my industry, and if you don't, you basically don't exist.

7. Having to deal with constant flirtation distracts me from my work, plus it makes working relationships on set less professional.

8. I dislike being chatted up by middle-aged married men; I have no interest in being their 'bit on the side' (a frequent occurrence in the industry). Sadly, they are in the majority on the film-set floor.

9. Being surrounded by fit blokes all day can be frus-trating because I don't have time to relieve the ten-sion between my legs.

10. Dealing with constant sexual innuendo and harass-ment can be exhausting, and I regularly have to fend off personal attacks.

But really, I suppose I'd just be happy at work if:

a) I was doing fewer hours.
b) I was treated with more respect in general.

c) I had a boyfriend who was willing to turn up during the ten minutes I get for lunch and sort me out with a quickie in the toilets.

I'm back at work tomorrow, on a quick commercials shoot, and somehow I doubt that any of these are going to happen – but I live in hope.

Tuesday 11th April

Over the years I've had some weird emails from readers of the blog. Many of these are nice – in fact most of the emails I receive are supportive and friendly – but a few are disturbing, either because they're abusive, or graphic, or just plain odd. I guess it comes with the territory, writing so openly about sex and my sex life; it also doesn't help that I am a woman doing so: I'm sure male sexbloggers don't get emails from people threatening to rape them.

I received such an email tonight, and it made me cry. I desperately wanted to tell one of my close friends about it – Fiona, my old college friend; Kathy, a childhood school friend; even Tim, my sex-gossip partner-in-crime – but to do so would destroy my anonymity. I would lose all the security I feel, and the freedom of expression that I have in my writing. God only knows what they'd think about my broadcasting every last detail about my sex life on the Internet; I shudder at the thought of them reading my blog. It's not that they're prudish, but it's so personal it'd be like them reading my diary.

Ironic that I don't care if millions of people read my blog – because they don't know who I am – but it would destroy me if my nearest and dearest did. I hope they never do.

Monday 24th April

I'm back on a feature film for a few weeks of shooting, and this means one thing. I'm not referring to the early mornings, or the stroppy diva-like actors demanding frequent cups of tea, or being given mundane tasks to do by my boss. No, I'm talking about chatting up cute men on the new crew; it's one of the (few) perks of the job.

So I was delighted that a flirtation with a sexy special effects man – I'll call him Adam – on another film set has now transferred to the new movie I'm working on. Our banter has become increasingly sexual – as conversations are wont to do on a film set – and I have really been enjoying our chats. Until, that is, he began to argue with me, this lunchtime.

'The main advantage to being a man,' Adam said, 'is the fact that I don't need to take off my work belt when I go for a piss.' He tugged on his radio holster to emphasize his point.

I couldn't disagree: our work belts are cumbersome, heavy and especially inconvenient when needing the loo. A well-practised balancing act is required if you need to sit down on the toilet, so as not to drop your walkie-talkie in it. And if you're horny and needing some release, you've got five minutes of negotiating with holster-removal just to be able to gain access: not good, if you're in desperate need of a quick frig.

It was true – being a woman on a film crew is a disadvantage. I nodded at him and shrugged in agreement.

'And,' he continued, 'we don't get periods or childbirth or anything like that, so really, you've got the bad end of the stick being a woman.' He looked at me triumphantly and I suppressed my desire to hit him. Hard. Annoyingly, though, what he said was valid: it's a struggle just to get past basic discrimination like bosses not hiring you because you might, at some point, get pregnant. Even once they're hired, women are paid less, treated with disrespect and suffer regular harassment on film sets, so it seems women can't win.

Then it occurred to me: one female quality that beats anything men have; that there is one skill that, were they to have the chance of experiencing it, would make men beg and plead to be a woman just for one day.

'Well,' I said, fixing him with a steady gaze, 'there is one area where women have the advantage. And nothing men have comes close to that.'

He stared at me, a confused look appearing on his face. 'What's that, then?'

'Two words. One of them is multiple.'

'Multiple what?'

'If you have to ask, then clearly you are missing out,' I said, flatly.

As it dawned on him what I was insinuating, he glared at me. 'Well, I've got two words for you too.'

'Oh yeah? Which two?' I replied, and expected him to say, 'Fuck you.'

He looked at me jubilantly. 'Every time.' He shot me a sarcastic grin.

I burst out laughing.

'What's so funny?' he demanded. 'You're the one missing out: at least men come every time.'

I couldn't help but utter, 'If it's only the once, then it's definitely you who's missing out, my dear.' I carried on laughing as I walked back to the office, turning to see him still staring at me, even more confused.

For the rest of today I had a smile on my face, thinking that if he knew just how many times I normally climax during sex he would be eating his words.

As well as possibly eating something else – but he's definitely blown his chance for that now: chauvinism's my number one turn-off.

// posted by thegirl @ 8:45:00 PM

I want to talk about orgasms.

Granted, it's not the first time I have talked about them, but I feel it's an important subject. This is because I regularly get emails (from both women and men) asking me advice on how women can achieve better (or any) orgasms. When I hear that supposedly around 25 per cent of women never climax during sex, it makes me sad, as well as angry: surely it should be a woman's right to always come? It bloody well is mine, I can tell you.

But I'm no sexpert, so I'm not going to suggest techniques to help women get off. However, being quite partial to the odd orgasm or five, I'll put my two pence in – for what it's worth.

I haven't always been multi-orgasmic – far from it. In fact, the first couple of years I had sex, I never climaxed at all; the men I was seeing were far more skilled in achieving their own climaxes than helping me obtain my own. With them fucking like jack-rabbits, it was all over and done with in two minutes, leaving me horny – and unsure what to do.

At the time, I remember complaining to an older friend of mine that I didn't know what an orgasm felt like. She replied, somewhat incredulously, that if I never explored myself with masturbation, I would have difficulty climaxing, regardless of how good in bed my partner was. 'Mama knows best,' she said, winking, and suggested I should get to know my nether regions better, with my fingers or a vibrator.

So I did. Whilst I'd masturbated before, it had always been half-heartedly – and never resulted in an orgasm – but now I had an objective. I took my friend's advice and attempted to master the art of self-exploration, dipping my hands between my legs at every opportunity – I was a keen student, you see. I learned a lot from my constant playing:

1. That I could climax easily.
2. That certain types of stimulation get me off quickly.
3. That I love orgasms.

When I discovered just how easy it was to give myself pleasure, I felt robbed: all those times I had had sex and not climaxed – not enjoyed the divine goodness of an orgasm – and yet the guy had always come. How unfair was that?

It wasn't the bloke's fault, though. It's too easy to lay the blame on men for women's lack of orgasms. Sex is an interaction between two people (usually), not just one 'giving' another pleasure. That's not to say that some men aren't responsible for some lame sex (and believe me, I have shagged a few crap lovers in my time), but in my opinion, the reason most women don't climax is because:

1. They lack confidence in bed.
2. They are insecure about their bodies.
3. They feel 'dirty' somehow about their enjoyment of sex.
4. They are uncomfortable with asserting their needs.
5. They are unfamiliar with their bodies.

It is the latter point that I am concerned with here: how can women expect to climax if they don't even know their own bodies? There's no point expecting men to know what turns us on if we don't even know ourselves.

I am saddened reading comments from women on my blog who complain how they just 'lie back' because they 'know' they're 'not going to come' or how they just 'don't feel comfortable' about sliding their own hand between their legs, whilst in bed with a partner, to ensure they climax too. Or, worse, that they fake a climax so that their partner won't feel 'inadequate'. It depresses me immensely to hear this from women: not only are they missing out, but their partner is too – what man doesn't want to feel a woman come (around his cock, over his fingers, under his tongue)?

I say to the women who have difficulty climaxing: go and fiddle with yourself. Immediately. Discover what your vulva feels and looks like; become familiar with your arousal and what turns you on; focus on your pleasure. Every woman is different: clitoral stimulation might work for you; G-spot pressure for another; penetration might get you off; perhaps labia rubbing is your thing. Whatever it is, you won't know it until you've tried it, so grab a toy and have a play. At the very least, you'll have fun trying, so why not get stuck in?

Being knowledgeable about their own bodies allows women to be more active in their pleasure, as well as increasing their confidence: a clued-up woman who frigs a lot is far more likely to grab her lover's hand/head/cock and stick it between her legs in just the right place than one who doesn't masturbate and rarely (if at all) climaxes. And a woman in touch with her body – and who has developed self-assurance (and self-esteem) through self-pleasure – will have no problem reaching between her legs with her own hand whilst in bed with a partner. Whilst she might do this because it turns both of them on, she also might do it to ensure she will climax – which always helps if the bloke lacks these skills.

I think it's time women took the pressure off men; removed the expectations of them being responsible for 'giving' us orgasms. Instead we should become more active in our own pleasure, taking charge of ensuring that we too will get off, regardless. Because not only will that mean women will enjoy sex more, and feel more relaxed, but as a result, men will too – a win/win situation.

So, ladies, get busy and get those fingers sticky. Just make sure you have enough batteries.

// posted by thegirl @ 11:21:00 PM

Tuesday 25th April

I could be getting a little paranoid, but after my conversation with Adam at work yesterday, he has been giving me strange looks today, and it made me wonder: has he read the blog? I mean, it's unlikely that he has, but with its ever-increasing popularity, it could just be a matter of time before one of my colleagues skims over it, and wonders if they know who Girl with a One Track Mind is. I've tried to be careful online, never alluding to my job role on set, or using real names, or even which actors I might be working with, but it's possible that if I talk about sex at work and then write about it on my blog, then someone could put two and two together and realize that Abby Lee is me, Zoe.

I don't know, perhaps Adam's odd glances were just because I've been ignoring him since his ignorant 'women can't come' statements, and maybe my worries are all in my head. Still, what with the book coming out soon, I can't take any risks: I'd better be quiet about sex and keep my mouth shut at work a bit more, I think.

Although, saying that, I would open it again given the chance to suck the new camera assistant's cock: he's a sexy bastard and it's been bloody ages since I had a shag, damn it; I'm not exactly an 'active' sexblogger right now.

Wednesday 26th April

On set this morning, I got into a very deep conversation with one of the grips – I'll call him Alex – and, in contrast to

Adam, it showed me another side to the whole blokes-at-work stereotype.

We'd been watching a gorgeous baby being filmed in a scene, and I made a comment to him about how cute it was and that seeing it had made my heart melt a little.

'I'm broody too, you know,' Alex volunteered, and he looked at me mournfully.

I gazed back at him, raising my eyebrows in mock sympathy. 'Oh, of course; and being twenty-four, you'd know all about desiring kids.' I shook my head in mild exasperation.

'Actually, I've wanted kids since I was nineteen,' he said. 'So the last five years have been quite frustrating for me, still being single and all.'

I studied his expression for a moment, trying to detect the usual film-set sarcastic banter. His face was serious; too serious. I couldn't figure out if he was for real.

He continued. 'Look, I know it's probably not cool for me to say it, but I do want kids. I want to settle down. I want to meet someone special and share my life with them. I'm not getting any younger,' he added.

Yeah, try being a woman with a ticking biological clock, I wanted to say to him. There are only a few years left for me before my ovaries go on strike; if I don't get my eggs fertilized soon, they'll end up useless, like some old battery-farmed hen being killed for cat food.

'Well,' I replied, 'you still have plenty of time. You've got ages yet before you'll be an old, incapable dad, who's too tired to play footy with his kids. So don't worry about not meeting someone; it'll happen.'

He smiled at me and I wondered what he would look like

naked. Granted, he was very young and I would probably tire of his childish ways quite quickly, but perhaps I should be bedding someone like him, rather than the men I have fallen for over the years who wanted nothing to do with commitment and children. Admittedly, neither did I, but I tended to be attracted to a particular 'type' when I was much younger and that type are generally known as 'bastards'.

He interrupted my train of thought. 'The girls on this film, they're a bit young, aren't they?' He pointed at the few females on the set, caked in foundation and mascara (make-up department) and tight jeans and high heels (costume department). Then he looked at me and I became aware that my trousers were still muddy from filming outdoors and that my T-shirt had stains over the nipple area where I had accidentally managed to drip oil from a smoke machine I was helping carry. I suddenly felt embarrassed and self-conscious with this young man's eyes all over me.

He smiled at me again and I realized that perhaps he was trying to make a point: I've become a confident woman at ease with who I am; I have no need to prove my sexuality to men by covering myself in make-up and sexy clothing at work; I now want something more than just a succession of random fucks lined up in my future. And this was attractive to him.

For a moment, I fantasized about what it might be like, were he and I to be a couple. What would we talk about? What things would we have in common? What would we do with our spare time together? What would sex with him be like? What would our kids look like?

As I watched him grin at me and awkwardly run his hands

through his hair, I felt a desire to reach out to him, to touch his face and tell him that everything would work out, given time.

Fuck around, I wanted to say. Enjoy your youth; experiment; discover what it is that you enjoy; who it is that you can be. And when you've done that, when you've come full circle and know you're finally ready, that's when it will be the right time to meet someone like me.

I looked at him and in his unwrinkled smile, saw my own youth reflected in his face. There was a time when I would have been jealous of that; wanted my unlined face back. Not now. I don't want to look back any more; I'm ready for my future.

// posted by thegirl @ 09:52:00 PM

'He's fit.' *He certainly is.*

'Tall, muscular physique.' *Agreed.*

'A nice arse: well rounded.' *That's true.*

'Good strong features and a full head of hair.' *Yup.*

'You want him.' *Well . . . I wouldn't say no.*

'You do. Come on – look at him: he's perfect.' *He's OK, yes.*

'You, him: it'd be great.' *Let's not jump to conclusions . . .*

'He'd be ideal – and you know it.' *I don't think so . . .*

'Go on. Seize the day!' *Look, I don't even know him.*

'Quick, before it's too late!' *OK, enough already.*

'Tick tock.' *Shut up.*

'You're running out of time.' *I'm not listening.*

'Yes, you are. Lately you've been listening a lot.' *Well, I'm not listening now. Lalalalalala.*

'Come on! You're ripe! Do it!' *Shutupshutupshutup.*

'Oh, but you are. You've said so yourself. Your periods have never been as regular: every twenty-eight-and-a-half days – you're in synch with the moon, for fuck's sake – now's the time!' *I'm not ready.*

'Who says? You're in your mid-thirties and you're at a good place in life. The time is now!' *No, it's not; I'm not ready yet.*

'What about the fact that you look at guys, imagining the combination of your features. You can't tell me that's not meaningful.' *It isn't meaningful.*

'Ah, but you look at babies in the street and your heart pangs.' *I'm telling you, if you even hint at Baby Hunger . . .*

'You said it.' *Look, fuck off, all right?*

'Go on: get fertilized! You know you want to.' *It's not as simple as that. Anyway, I'm not ready for children yet.*

'But you want them, don't you? And look: see how you're staring at his crotch and imagining what his cock would feel like – that's a tell-tale sign.' *Yeah, a sign that I wouldn't mind fucking him.*

'No. It's a sign that you want his babies!!!' *Oh, for fuck's sake. No, it's not. I'm just feeling horny.*

'Horny because you want his sperm!!!' *No. Horny because I want an orgasm.*

'But your orgasm is linked to wanting his babies!' *No. My wanting an orgasm is not connected to my wanting his children. It's connected to the fact that I'm horny and need some release. Anyhow, I don't even know his name, for fuck's sake – why would I want his kids?*

'Because you want to have children.' *That might be true.*

But I don't want his children. Anyway, I want a relationship first.

'Aha! So you do want them?!' *And? So fucking what?*

'So that would explain why you're always horny!' *How so?*

'Because you want kids!' *Oh Jesus. Please tell me you're not going down the biological determinism route with this; you know my feelings on that.*

'It's the truth, ain't it?' *What? My sex drive must somehow be an evolutionary directive, with the sole purpose to procreate?*

'Yup, exactly: it would explain everything.' *No, it fucking wouldn't; that's a simplistic argument and you know it.*

'Whatever . . . But look at him: you want him!' *Just shut up, please.*

'Go and get his sperm! Quickly! Before we dry up and there's no healthy eggs left!!!' *Look, ovaries, I've had enough of this. I'm going home for a wank, and when I've climaxed, I can tell you that the thought of having this bloke's children will be just a distant memory. So ditch that thought right now.*

'OK. Maybe he's not the one . . . Speak to you again next month, then.' *Yes, unfortunately it would seem so . . .*

Thursday 27th April

Thinking about my conversation with Adam the other day, I realized that it's been ages since I was involved with someone from work. Mostly because we do such long hours and there is just no time to get intimate with someone. But also, it's always better not to mix business and pleasure, and certainly not if I'm going to write about them on my blog.

However, the last time I shagged someone from work that I fancied – a sound guy I met on a low-budget film years ago – it was before I began writing the blog.

It had been a short day, perhaps only twelve hours' of shooting on location, and, after some weeks of flirting, we finally ended up in my hotel room that night. We began snogging furiously and it didn't take long for our clothing to be removed: I was horny as hell and dying to fuck him. As I made my way down his body, slipping my finger under the waistband of his underwear with the intention of pulling the rest of his pants off with my teeth, I caught a whiff of something. Of him, to be exact. It wasn't a fresh male aroma – it didn't smell of clean sweat, or working-day staleness, and certainly not delicious sexual arousal – it stank of pungent, acrid dirt: calling it rancid would have been an understatement. He reeked, and I almost gagged.

Now, at this point my fingers had just begun circling around his cock, and I found myself in a difficult position. Did I continue what I was doing and – risking projectile vomiting – slide his smelly cock into my mouth? Perhaps it would it be best to just politely toss him off inside his pants in the hope of avoiding the dreadful stench coming from his groin? Or, should I show my disgust, stop groping his penis, and tell him to go and wash it pronto?

I did none of the above. It gives me little pride to describe what I did next: I promptly removed my hand from his underwear, pushed him onto his back, sat on top of him, and dry-humped his pants-covered hard cock until I had an orgasm.

And then I threw him out of my hotel room, full-blown erection and all.

Selfish I might be, but if there's one thing I cannot stand it's a man who lacks personal hygiene: there are no excuses for a bloke who can't keep his cock clean – even if he's working long hours on set. If I can keep myself clean and smelling nice, then so can he. So if a guy thinks his stinky schlong will get some action with this girl, he's got another thing coming.

As, in this case, me.

// posted by thegirl @ 9:34:00 PM

Saturday 29th April

Stuck in traffic last night after work, I was hit with déjà vu. It wasn't just that the surroundings looked familiar – green spaces, posh houses and wankers in 4x4s are aplenty in this part of south-west London – but there was something else about the place that was making my memory synapses spark.

Then it hit me. A bloke I shagged ages ago lived just a couple of streets away. This got me thinking: which parts of the city am I similarly familiar with? How well do I know London? Who have I fucked in this metropolis, and where? A quick memory jog produced the following:

- There was that guy in Croydon all those years ago: what a fucking shithole that place was. Unsurprisingly, he was also a complete arsehole.
- The bloke in Tottenham was fun: we fucked in my office, me grabbing hold of my boss's desk, imagining his reaction if he knew of my getting rammed from behind.

◉ Then there was the chap from Morden. He had a thing for cunnilingus. I didn't object.

◉ Twickenham man was great in the sack, but his obsession with constantly sticking a finger up my bottom began to annoy me.

◉ The man from Acton was eager, but dull as fuck. Boredom and shagging don't go well together.

◉ Kensington bloke probably thought I was a bit of rough, given his wealth and massive penthouse apartment. So I roughly fucked his cock till it hurt.

◉ The guy from Wembley likened his cock to a bicycle tyre: 'Pump it hard,' he said to me as I grabbed it, 'and then ride me.' I did.

◉ Harrow man was very sensual. He had a thing for fucking me during my period. 'You're even hornier then,' he reassured me. He wasn't wrong.

◉ The guy in Cricklewood thought that playing some R. Kelly songs would get me in the mood. How wrong he was.

◉ Highgate man was sweet, kind and a fantastic kisser. That made up for never having a climax with him.

◉ Euston bloke first fucked my friend, and then me. When we found out shortly after, neither of us spoke to him again. Plus, he was crap in bed.

◉ The guy from Finsbury Park was left with a hard-on as I exited his flat. Don't worry, I made sure I had climaxed. He wasn't worth my returning the favour.

◉ The man in Brixton loved my arse. Whilst I enjoy my bum being focused on, sometimes it's nice to have face-to-face penetration too.

◐ Woolwich bloke was too drunk to fuck. After wasting an entire box of condoms through unsuccessful attempts at penetration, we both gave up.

Funny that I can barely recall the names of some of these guys, but where they lived, what part of London we were shagging in, I can remember in detail, like some kind of mental roadmap of the city. Helpful for if I get lost, I guess. (Though I'm not going to be pinning up a map of London on the wall and sticking pins in the areas I have shagged in; that would just be silly.) (And I would most likely run out of pins.)

The one place in London that I have rarely had sex in? My own home. There are a few reasons for this:

First, I am a very private person and am reluctant to let a guy into my personal space unless I like him a lot, trust him and wish for him to get to know me better. If things are just casual, then it's going to be at his place, or a hotel, or, if needs must, a public toilet.

Second, my house is a tip – not that you would know it to look at me: I take great care over my personal hygiene and try to present myself well (give or take some flyaway, frizzy hair). My home, though? Constant mayhem. So when I do show a bloke just how many knickers I have lying all over my floor, it won't be on our first date: I wouldn't want to put him off me from the start.

Lastly, if there's going to be anyone leaving someone's flat first thing the next morning, with a bow of the head and an embarrassed, mumbled, 'Thanks,' it damn well is going to be me.

I shan't be one of those women who gets saddened by the

bloke exiting at first light (believe me, I've been her in the past, and I'm not doing it again). But I also don't want to be the woman stuck with a guy who just won't leave when you want him to (again, I've been her, and again, it's no fun). That's not to say that all casual sex ends in regret and a wish to be alone immediately, but it's easier to be the one who arrives and leaves on their own terms.

Admittedly, traipsing over to the bloke's place and back has cost me a small fortune in tube, rail and taxi fares over the years, but it has helped me discover – in the most fun way possible – different parts of this great city, so I think it's worth the outlay. Even if, once or twice, the sex was a bit shit.

// posted by thegirl @ 11:36:00 AM

DEL'S TAXIS
RECEIPT

AMOUNT £ 10

THANK YOU FOR YOUR BUSINESS

MAY

Monday 1st May

Another 6 a.m. start at work today, yuck. If it wasn't for the fact that I love the movies, there is no way I could manage these early mornings: I'm definitely a night owl when it comes to my body-clock.

Whilst standing around during one particularly long and boring visual-effects rehearsal that seemed to take all bloody morning, I got to thinking about sex – as you do – and I came to a conclusion:

I have one important rule regarding shagging and my job.

Apart from minor rules, e.g. limiting heavy sex sessions solely to the weekend to prevent exhaustion on set the next day; being more sexually graphic in my language than my male colleagues so they know I won't take any shit from them; and never getting caught wanking in the toilets.

The main rule I abide by, though, is this: never fuck actors. Simple.

But why not fuck actors? Surely given the opportunity, a Girl with a One Track Mind would jump at the chance to shag someone talented/famous/handsome, right? Not me: they are nothing but trouble.

Over the years, whilst I've been on set, I have been approached by various actors trying to get in my knickers, no doubt thinking that a lowly crew member makes for easy shag-pickings. Hollywood A-listers to no-name extras have all tried the come-on: from grabbing my arse to handing me their phone number. And to each and every one, I've smiled sweetly and politely declined their advances.

You see, regardless of how talented they might be on screen, when they're off-screen actors will undoubtedly be shallow, narcissistic and full of self-loathing – not qualities I admire. To get up on a stage or film set and be able to switch off the world, whilst also project realistic emotion and thought, requires skill and deftness in being artificial; an ability to convince others of sincerity is, after all, what makes an actor's performance believable. But every actor I have met carries this falseness off-screen as well as on, and I have zero interest in shagging someone like that.

It's not surprising actors relate like this, though; they are surrounded by unreal adoration from people who treat them as though they are special and different to the rest of us, making the actor lose touch with reality in the process. I am always mystified as to why people lap up the magazines and newspapers that have cover stories about some celebrity and which latest lover/diet/tragedy is occupying their life; it just bores me.

So when one of these shallow people chats me up, I don't swoon at their feet, even if they are drop-dead gorgeous. Instead, I am aware of the abuse of their position: with their status and power, they can make advances to any female on set without fear of the consequences. The risk to the female crew-member, however, is the loss of their job when the actor tires of them; I have seen this happen and don't plan on losing my job any time soon.

This puts things into perspective: at work I may be desperately horny and attracted to an actor's handsome physique, but with one small slip-up – a moment of weakness resulting in their cock inside me – I can wave goodbye to my future. So I won't be getting into bed – or a dressing room – with an actor any time soon.

Though it can be a little frustrating at work when faced with a hot bloke in a rubber superhero costume and I can't find the time to have a quick fiddle, it has to be said.

// posted by thegirl @ 10:34:00 PM

Friday 12th May

It's Friday night, I've now got some time off work whilst the main film crew shoots abroad, and it's been ages since I caught up with my friend Fiona. We've been mates since college and whilst our lives are quite disparate, whenever we get together it's like no time has passed at all: we always talk openly with each other. Saying that, there is one topic we don't discuss, which is the night she used her professional dominatrix skills on me, and we both ended up in bed with some poor bloke who was surely unable to sit down for a week. (She was very skilled with his belt, it must be said.) She doesn't do that work any more, and neither of us brings up that night in conversation: some things are best left unsaid, I think.

But when Fiona and I do get together, it can only mean one thing: cocktails. And talking about sex, of course; the two go hand in hand.

'There are two types of the men in the world,' I

announced, somewhat drunkenly, as I lifted another martini up to my lips.

'And which might those be?' Fiona replied, slurping loudly on her mojito.

I took a long gulp. 'Those who haven't found the clitoris; and those who have.'

Fiona laughed and placed her glass back on the table. 'Very true.'

'Thankfully,' I continued, 'the former are in the minority – it's been quite rare in recent years for me to meet a guy who just heads straight for penetration and then in-out rabbit-pumps me without even attempting some clitoral stimulation.' I paused, for dramatic effect. 'As much as I enjoy a rampant quickie, there is something to be said for some decent foreplay now and then, right?'

'Thank god most men seem to know it takes more than that to get a woman going,' Fiona agreed.

I nodded. 'But I'm not sure whether those men who know about the clitoris are much better.'

Fiona looked at me curiously. 'What do you mean?'

I leaned in to her conspiratorially and said, in a low voice, 'Just because they know where it is, doesn't mean they know what to do with it.'

Fiona laughed loudly and slapped me on my arm playfully.

I continued, on a roll now. 'Too many men seem to want a medal just because they know of the clitoris: "Look, darling, I've found it!" Well, no, I don't think congratulations are in order – especially if they aggressively attack it as if they were trying to rub out a stain on the carpet.'

Fiona roared and spat out her drink from laughing. 'God,

that's so fucking true! What is it with them? Don't they know about delicacy?'

'Evidently not,' I replied. 'They tug themselves so bloody hard, they probably think the same works for us.'

Fiona shook her head. 'No. Fuck no.'

'It's like once they've found the "magic button" all they can think to do is press it, pull it, tap it and rub it – they don't seem to realize that it can be very sensitive.'

Fiona nodded in agreement again and whispered to me. 'Mine can't be even be touched: it's just too much for me.'

'Me too,' I replied, whispering back. 'Too much pounding and it goes numb: then there's no hope in me coming.'

We both sighed and took deep swigs of our drinks. Then I perked up again. 'It's not all bad,' I said. 'I think there's a third type of bloke – even if they are few and far between.'

'Oh yeah?'

'Yeah. I've been with a few men who not only know where the clitoris is, but know just how sensitive it is too: they never ever touched it, but still made me come all the time.'

Fiona raised her eyebrow, quizzically. 'What did they do?'

'They teased me for ages; you know, touching or licking near it and around it, but never actually directly on it. It drove me fucking crazy – made me want to stick their cock in me pronto.'

Fiona laughed. 'That's definitely the way, god yes. I wish more men did that. Hey, maybe we should set up an information group – a way to educate men about getting a woman properly aroused?'

I sniggered. 'What a good idea! We could teach them all about the benefits of indirect clitoral stimulation, and as a result, they'd have women soaking wet, begging to fuck them. Then men would get shagged rampantly and women would get lots of orgasms prior to penetration. Win/win: fantastic.'

Fiona grinned and we both finished off the dregs of alcohol in our glasses.

I then thought about it some more. 'This group sounds like a great idea: we should do it. I would suggest calling it the Third Way, but it makes me think of politics and New Labour – hardly a turn-on!'

I got up to buy us some more drinks. On the way, I eyed up a handsome man in a suit who was standing by the bar, and wondered how I might get him into a conversation about equality in bed without sounding like I wanted to shag him, even though, obviously, that's exactly what I would like to do. But given it has been weeks since I last met up with Fiona, I didn't want to sacrifice our time together by running after some hot bloke, even though I've been single for a while now and could really do with a shag.

// posted by thegirl @ 11:57:00 PM

Saturday 13th May

Waking up with an immense hangover, and barely able to remove myself from my bed, the only thing I felt able to do this morning was grab my laptop from my bedside table and log on to the Internet. Well, a nerdy sexblogger like me has to get her priorities straight and you never know what delights lie online, right? My choice paid off: to my surprise, an unexpected email greeted me.

'Guess who's here?!' the message read. 'Long time no see! You busy? I'm in town tomorrow for a couple of days, be great to see you – feel like some fun?!'

It was from Derek, a guy I had a brief casual fling with last year. I recalled the last time I saw him: he had demanded I sit on his face most of the night. It was, I should say, rather delightful. What a coincidence, after my chat about foreplay with Fiona last night: Derek was definitely one of the 'Third Way'-type men; he certainly knew how to get me in the mood.

Being a Girl with a One Track Mind, it only took me a minute to go from thinking about that to remembering what his cock felt like in my mouth, and given the memory instantly made my pants wet, I emailed him straight back:

'Hey, what a nice surprise. I actually have some free time this weekend – let's meet.'

I hope he calls me soon.

// posted by thegirl @ 1:44:00 PM

BUTTERWORTHS CHEMISTS

DUREX PLEASUREMAX CONDOMS 12 PACK	£ 7.99
DUREX PLAY FEEL LUBRICANT 100ML	£ 5.49
WRIGLEY'S ORBIT SUGARFREE CHEWING GUM	£ 0.65
VASELINE LIP THERAPY WITH ALOE VERA 20G	£ 1.15
BUTTERWORTHS HOLD UPS 15 DENIER BLACK	£ 3.75
TOTAL	£19.03
CASH	£20.00
CHANGE DUE	£ 0.97

13/05/06   22.20

0669400145056706111109

Girl's Guide to:
Preparing for a date – women

1. Put a face-pack on.
2. Epilate your body. This ranges from armpits, legs, thighs and vulva to the arse. Plus other places we shall never mention.
3. Shampoo and condition hair.
4. Wash and scrub body (painfully) to remove (supposedly) dead skin.
5. Remove face-pack and cry, because you have a huge spot on your chin and you are in your thirties and for fuck's sake, it's supposed to only be teenagers who get zits, and now with this damn red mound you won't be getting any sex tonight.
6. Dab toothpaste onto your chin. You're going to stem the growth of this hormonal boil if it's the last thing you ever do.
7. Moisturize skin from face to feet with scented cream/lotion.
8. Rub extra lotion onto your breasts and groin area. Who knows: if you pay extra attention here, so might the bloke, with any luck.
9. Deodorize your armpits. And your feet. We shall never speak of the latter again.
10. Fix hair into a sexy style.
11. Remove all hair pins because you now hate the style you previously spent so long fixing.

12. Wrestle with your new 'do, but instead create a mad frizz.
13. Sit on the loo, crying.
14. Paint toenails.
15. Paint fingernails.
16. Put on some make-up.
17. Scream in frustration as you smudge your still-wet fingernails on your nose.
18. Find some sexy underwear.
19. Try not to weep when you discover that your expensive bra is now totally misshapen because you threw it in the washing machine by mistake.
20. Find a different bra from a not-as-nice set.
21. Do the bra up on the tightest fitting to enhance your cleavage. Struggle to breathe.
22. Slowly slide chosen outfit on without messing up hair/make-up/nails.
23. Slip on some shoes/heels/boots.
24. Try not to cry from the pain in your feet because NO HUMAN FOOT IS SHAPED LIKE A WOMAN'S SHOE.
25. Brush your teeth.
26. Spray breath freshener in your mouth.
27. Put on some lipstick and try to discover the balance between having 'moist lips' and 'Oh fuck, my lips have stuck together'.
28. Leave the house and attempt not to trip up.
29. Try not to sob as you realize you've left your purse/mobile/Oyster card/keys inside the house.
30. Depart, hoping that your date/potential shag goes well.

Girl's Guide to:
Preparing for a date – men

1.a) Shower. N.B. Optional, see 2.
1.b) Use a towel to dry yourself. N.B. Preferably not the one you use to dry your dishes.
2. Spray Lynx everywhere. N.B. If you've not done 1, then ensure you apply liberally to your genital region.
3. Brush your teeth. N.B. Optional. You can always pick up some chewing gum en route.
4. Get dressed. N.B. Think: comfort. Also: ease of access, should anything arise.
5. Leave house, hoping your date/potential shag goes well.

Sunday 14th May

I was delighted that Derek ended up calling me yesterday evening, suggesting we meet this afternoon. I was, it is fair to say, very much looking forward to getting fucked and couldn't wait to see him again. So I left the house fully prepared for the day: freshly showered, wearing a cute dress and with a selection of condoms and a sachet of lube in my purse.

Because it has been almost a year since we last saw each other, I was rather pleased to find that the chemistry was still there; as we sat drinking cocktails our body language matched, his arms finding their way around my waist, mine around his within minutes of our meeting. I fondly recalled how well we had fitted together, fucking with gusto; he somehow knowing just how I like it from behind; how I enjoy my ankles above my head; how I will come and come from three fingers inside me. I could barely wait till we got back to his hotel and I would get to feel his cock inside me once more.

That was until we had the following conversation in the hotel bar:

Me (making conversation): How's the dating? Seeing any nice women at the moment?

Him (blushing:) Yeah, kind of.

Me (digging slightly further, not hoping for details): Anyone special?

Him: I guess so.

Me (becoming slightly concerned that my shag may not happen): Is it serious?

Him: You could say that.

Me (hoping they're not 'exclusive'): Long-term, then?

Him: Yeah, a couple of years now.

Me (hesitating): . . . So you were with her when we were fucking last year?

Him (slowly): . . . Yes.

Me (stunned): Why didn't you tell me that then?

Him: I thought you knew.

Me (incredulous): No. I didn't know. If I had known, I wouldn't have fucked you.

Him: Oh. Sorry.

Me: I can't believe it. That's really low, you know that?

Him (nodding): Sorry. I really thought you knew; I figured you were OK with it.

Me (in disbelief): No, I am not OK with it. I'm not that sort of woman.

And I'm not. Some years ago, I was party to another woman being cheated on: I had an affair with her boyfriend. It was not something I had planned on getting into, but before I knew it, I had feelings for a man who was otherwise involved. Each time we met up and he pretended his girlfriend didn't exist, my conscience ached with guilt. I swore I would never – to the best of my knowledge – do it again. Not only because it caused me heartbreak – I was in love with Russell and was devastated that he didn't leave her for me – but because I don't want to be the sort of woman who shits on other women. Call me an old-fashioned feminist, but I actually feel some solidarity with other women: I want to stand shoulder-to-shoulder with my sisters, not fuck their men behind their backs.

I may have been sitting in the bar with wet pants, absolutely dying to shag Derek, but faced with a man who was interested in having secret sex outside of his relationship there was no choice for me to make: I wasn't going to fuck him and that was that. I have some principles, after all, and whilst horniness has led me to some bad decision-making in the past, knowingly fucking an attached man (even just in a casual sex situation) is not something I want to do, drunk, horny or whatever.

So we sat there, still sipping our cocktails, and I told Derek what I thought of him: how selfish I felt he was; how upset his partner would be, were she to find out about his dalliances. To his credit, he agreed with me, saying that he's unsure why he wants to cheat on his girlfriend and we discussed ways of him confessing. Whether he'll tell her or not, I don't know, but what I do know is that when I rested my head on my pillow tonight (after having a frig, it must be said), I felt that at least my own conscience was clear.

But I need to ask myself: either in relationships or a casual situation, why do I seem to have such misfortune with men? I think I'm overdue some good times – and they can't come soon enough.

// posted by thegirl @ 11:21:00 PM

Wednesday 17th May

After the unsuccessful meeting with Derek, I have been going out of my mind: frustrated beyond belief; totally desperate. It is quite clear that I am displaying the classic symptoms of Irrational Horniness:

1. I have been thinking about sex all the time.
2. I have downloaded porn to watch every time I've been at the computer.
3. I have gone through three sets of watch batteries from usage of my vibrator.
4. I have got repetitive strain injury in my wrist from constant frigging.
5. I have gone through my address book and considered

calling old fuck-buddies for a shag, even though I
promised myself I wouldn't see them again because
a) they weren't that good in bed
b) they bore me intellectually, which made the sex
   mundane
c) they have girlfriends now.

6. I have considered contacting men I have recently
   dated – but not wanted to take things further with –
   and asking them to fuck me.

7. I am thinking about perusing online dating sites and
   debated contacting some random stranger for a
   quick no-strings-attached shag in a hotel.

8. I have wondered about going to the swingers' sex
   sauna I discovered with my old college friend Tim
   some time ago, and propositioning a cute bloke to
   eat me out in the steam room.

9. I have considered calling a platonic male friend who
   I am not even attracted to and asking him to 'do the
   honours'.

10. I have even been tempted to sit legs apart on a train
    whilst wearing a skirt and no knickers and hope that
    a sexy guy will notice and then make a move on me.

Clearly, something is awry: with my being affected by
Irrational Horniness, it seems obvious that I have not been
thinking straight; I have been worried by this.

That is, until earlier this evening, when I suddenly realized
why I also have an agonizing stabbing pain in my belly and
my breasts are swollen and sore: I've just got my period.

Thank fuck for that, is all I can say. It's quite a relief to know that it's all down to my hormones and that I will be thinking rationally again soon. That's not to say I won't still be horny, but just that I won't resort to any irrational or desperate behaviour to satisfy my urges. Instead, I'll just satisfy my urges with my vibrator, like any normal woman.

Speaking of which, I must obtain some more batteries.

// posted by thegirl @ 8:28:00 PM

Thursday 18th May

I am beginning to think something is wrong with me. Not because of my high sex drive or because I think about shagging all the time, or even because I am obsessed with all things erotic. No. What I am worried about is far, far worse:

I think I am the only woman in the world for whom the Rampant Rabbit vibrator does absolutely nothing.

I was – like many others, I imagine – impressed by the claims made about this well-known popular sex toy a few years back. 'As seen on *Sex and the City*!', the packaging shouted at me, and even given my cynicism about the completely patronizing marketing of the product, and the fact that it was pink and glittery and screamed 'girly rubbish' all over it, there was a little part of me that was curious about it. After all, it worked for the prudish character Charlotte in *Sex and the City*, and everyone else seemed to be raving about it, so I hoped that I too would spend all weekend locked in my bedroom gasping with delight.

I didn't. There may have been gasps coming from my

mouth, but that was the sound of incredulity, rather than of pleasure.

It's not like I didn't try to make it work for me. Every base was covered in order for me to have a productive frig:

1. I surrounded myself with a variety of porn (the male performers with body hair; the females with natural breasts).
2. I ensured my mind was clear for fantasy (my lips around his erection; him fucking me from behind; her breasts in my face).
3. I had a bottle of lube to hand.

Well, a girl likes to come, prepared.

Throbbing like mad and with a dampness threatening to breach the Thames Barrier, I was looking forward to a little pussy pounding, so I grabbed hold of the Rabbit with horny gusto and set it to work.

Funnily enough, that is exactly what it did: hammer away like some kind of roadworks, its noisy motor sounding like a drill inside of me. Not the sort of thing to get one in the mood. But, you know, I am persistent: when I need to have an orgasm, nothing, and nobody, is going to stand in my way. So I concentrated on the sensations the toy was providing, rather than the loud rattle it was making.

Unfortunately, these disappointed as well: having a rubber shaft speedily swivelling clockwise (or anti-clockwise) inside my vagina not only distracted me from feeling any pleasure, but actively turned me off too. Not that I had expected the Rabbit to provide the same motions as a penis, but one would hope that its sensations would be similar. At least, that's what I would have liked; I adore the feeling of a cock inside me.

But real cocks do not swivel. Not even slightly. True, if their owner has good bedroom skills and is aware of the advantages of circling their sacrum (rather than moving in and out with their hips), then their penis will move up and down and round and round, in a rather delightful way that will hit my G-spot just so. And it's also true that the guys who know about, and flex, their pubococcygeus (PC) muscle using Kegel exercises, can make their cocks bounce back and forth (and control their orgasms) – which is fun, and feels fantastic during penetration. But cocks doing a 360-degree turn? No. And thank god: I don't want a super-cock; a regular one will do just fine, thank you.

That wasn't even the worst of it, though: there was also a clitoral stimulator (otherwise known as the Rabbit's 'ears') to contend with. These sit either side of the clit and about which I can only say two things:

1. 'Aaaaaaaaaaaaaaaaaargh!'
2. If a bloke was giving me the same stimulation I'd be pushing him away and telling him to ease off.

With the 'ears' pulsing away with such intensity, my entire vulva went numb, and immediately I knew that there was no way I was going to be able to have an orgasm if I continued. For a woman like me this says a lot. If I wanted to feel like that, I'd call up Steven, the ex-boyfriend who cheated on me, but really, I'm not that masochistic.

Anyway, after a couple more failed attempts, my Rabbit

now sits unused at the bottom of my underwear drawer. I've resigned myself to the knowledge that I am – in terms of the supposed mass female approval of this toy – different to other women: the Rabbit just doesn't work for me.

I guess, though, given the marketing of this toy, it means more women are making themselves have climaxes, so who am I to complain? If there was a political party campaigning for women to have more frequent orgasms, I'd sure as hell vote for it. I suspect plenty of other women – and men – would too.

// posted by thegirl @ 9:36:00 PM

Friday 19th May

Sitting at home in pain today – thankfully, a day off from the shoot – I was reminded of a recent conversation I had with a work colleague, Kevin. We've always had a very open dialogue about sex – both bored on set, I suppose – so when he approached me as I was doubled up in agony on the side of the set, I didn't stint with the truth.

'What's wrong?' Kevin asked.

I pointed at my stomach. 'Cramps. Bad ones.'

'Time of the month?'

I nodded and then grimaced from the pain, holding a heat pad against my swollen belly in vain.

'Why don't you take some painkillers?' Kevin suggested. Seeing the angry look appearing on my face, he then quickly tried to make amends. 'Oh, they're not working? Bugger . . .'

'Yes,' I hissed, as another muscle contraction shot agonizingly through my stomach. 'You'd never know I took three ibruprofen, two paracetamol and one codeine tablet little more than an hour ago. Fuck!' I bent over and tried to breathe through the cramp.

Kevin moved towards me. 'What you need is a man to give you a nice massage, that'll take away the pain.'

I recovered briefly from the spasm. 'Well, that would be nice,' I agreed, 'but do you know what would really help with the pain right now – besides a gentle back rub?'

He shrugged. 'What?'

'A good orgasm. There's nothing like a climax to help with period cramps.'

He frowned at me and I remembered a similar conversation we had when we began working together a few years before, one where he expressed disgust about menstruation and sex. 'Oh Kevin, you're still not hung up about periods are you?!'

'Look, I'm just not into that . . . all the blood and stuff – yuck.'

'Yuck?!' I almost spat at him. 'Yuck? For fuck's sake, it's natural, women bleed. Are you telling me you won't shag a girl when she's menstruating?'

He shook his head. 'No, I won't.'

I thought about the men I've fucked; the ones who knew my body and the ways in which my appetite changed according to my cycle; the ones who liked how horny I become when I menstruate; the ones who didn't care about getting handprints of blood on their sheets because they got off on my deriving pleasure from their touch.

I stared at him. 'So what about your girlfriend? You've been together two years now: what do you do every month when she's on?'

He grinned at me. 'Well, I get a blow-job if I'm feeling horny.' He laughed.

'And her? What does she get?'

Kevin held my gaze and kept his mouth shut; knowing me well, he was aware that he was about to get a bollocking.

'Look, Kevin, I'm telling you, there is one thing – one major thing – that a woman wants when she has her period. Forget sympathy, understanding, back rubs and the rest; what she really needs is an orgasm. Aside from the huge pain relief she'll receive, it'll also assist her with her horniness – surely you'd want to help out with that?'

Kevin shrugged. 'But the blood – ugh!'

I fixed him with a stare. 'Do you mean to tell me that you've never taken advantage of your girlfriend's period-induced randiness?'

'I've never really thought about it,' Kevin replied. 'When she says she's on, I just give her some space and then go and have a wank if necessary.'

I shook my head. 'You're missing out, Kevin, you really are: a woman is at her most ravenous when she's got her period.'

'Really?' he asked.

'Really,' I said, and leant in to him, lowering my voice. 'She may be groaning from the pain, but she'll also be climbing the walls with desire. Like I am now: I am absolutely gagging for it.'

'Yeah, but that's you,' Kevin retorted. 'You love sex.

Maybe it's not the same for other women . . .'

'But you told me your girlfriend is a sex fiend; what have you got to lose by finding out just how rampant she gets from her period?' I asked.

'The blood,' he reminded me. 'I don't like the blood.'

I groaned. 'Yeah, but if your girlfriend was lying on her back, stroking her nipples and sliding a finger between her legs, saying, "Oh god, I'm so wet and horny, I need something inside me," wouldn't you forget about that and want to go and assist her?'

Kevin grinned. 'Maybe . . .'

'So, fucking try it; if you give her a few orgasms when she's in pain, she'll be so grateful, you might even get extra blowjobs out of it afterwards.'

He laughed. 'Well, now you put it that way, it does sound a little more appealing.'

I continued, 'I'm telling you, Kevin, you don't even have to fuck her: just finger her gently and she'll be in ecstasy. It's not asking for much, just a little orgasm or three. Then you'll get to have a horny, happy, pain-free girlfriend, who'll be less moody as a result. Plus, of course, you'll have a few extra orgasms yourself too. Win/win.'

He grinned at me. 'You know, you've got a valid point. I might have to investigate some more.'

'Do. I hope your girlfriend enjoys it.'

'She's a lot like you; I'm sure she will,' Kevin grinned at me and began to walk back towards the middle of the set.

With searing pain in my stomach and now a dull throbbing between my legs, I had no choice but to quickly visit the studio toilet to fix myself. A quick flick later and I was practically pain-free. I tidied myself before heading back to set and felt rejuvenated, ready to work again, my mind and my body unblocked.

Cheaper than drugs and more effective (not to mention pleasurable): perhaps it's about time orgasms were offered as pain-relief on the NHS?

// posted by thegirl @ 6:22:00 PM

Tuesday 23rd May

I'm over my period now, but sadly the horniness hasn't really ceased much. I think it's because it's been quite a while since I last had sex, and what with the anticipation and let-down with Derek, I'm even more desperate for a shag than usual. It's time to take things into my own hands.

So, I've been scouring through the Craigslist website, which has a 'casual encounters' personal ads section, in the hope that I might find a like-minded bloke who's up for some brief fun. Of course, there's always the risk of meeting an arsehole online, but no more so than in a local bar, and it's certainly less of a risk than hooking up with someone at work; at least via a website I can filter out the twats.

As luck would have it, I've found one ad that seems interesting: it's a guy who wants to try out a little BDSM* in bed.

---

* BDSM is an acronym relating to sexual practices, which is derived from the combination of the terms 'bondage and discipline' (B&D, B/D, or BD), 'dominance and submission' (D&s, D/s, or Ds), 'sadism and masochism' (S&M, S/M, or SM). But then you knew that already, I'm sure.

Now, ordinarily I wouldn't go for something kinky as my first choice for a casual fling: my preference would just be a good, hard fucking, any day. But this guy says he wants to dominate me; that he's inexperienced at BDSM but wants to experiment; and that – most importantly – he's looking for someone with a high sex drive. This seems perfect, because I've only had a couple of experiences with BDSM and loved having a paddle smacked against my arse: I'd certainly like to experience that again. Who knows – perhaps I could get a shag and a spanking too? Bonus. He looks quite sexy from his photo and because his open-minded attitude to sex also appeals, I've fired off an email to him suggesting we meet up.

Here's hoping: I really need some sex.

// posted by thegirl @ 10:12:00 PM

The Girl's Guide to:
Men: how to get laid when you place
an advert on a casual sex website

1. **Be grammatically correct.** Placing an ad that is badly spelled or with terrible sentence construction doesn't bode well to anyone reading it; it just makes you appear stupid. Plus, you'll look like you're typing with only one hand, which might be true but really won't assist you.
   Example:
   'cum smole weed with me today and let me get the munch where the sun don't shine,ill go down there for hours!'
   I'm not sure where you might be going down, darling, but it wouldn't be between my legs, that's for sure: I expect a man to be able to converse on at least a semi-intellectual level (when he comes up for air, anyway).

2. **Don't appear desperate (even if you are).** Have a wank, get rid of your excess horniness, and then post the ad. Do not, in any circumstances, be tempted to write something like this:
   'i have the whole weekend scheduled off for sex but have no-one to do it with as yet'
   Evidently. Looks like a weekend spent watching those new DVDs. Again.

3. **Don't appear too picky:**
   'I'm 35yrs, 191cm, 80kg, handsome, cultivated, suc-

cessful and am looking for female companion (younger than 35yrs, BMI less than 25) to have fun with.'

Specifying a particular ratio of a woman's height/size is not going to get you in her pants. Fact.

4. **However, don't appear not to be picky at all – and then contradict yourself (using bad spelling and zero punctuation):**

'can't accomadate no time wasters looks unimportant pic a must'

And if you're going to request a picture, it makes sense to offer one in return. Otherwise women will just suspect you're going to use their image to wank over and not take you seriously. (See below.)

5. **If you want to get laid, try offering more than just a soggy photograph:**

'I'm looking for a woman to email me a sexy picture of herself, that I can print off and wank over. I'll then take a picture of my cock over your cum soaked picture and email it back to you.'

Been looking at too much porn, me thinks, if a bloke cannot relate to a woman unless she is 2-D.

6. **Be thoughtful about what you are going to offer the woman:**

'Maybe you would just like to sit on top and ride me – I don't mind honest . . .'

Thank you – how generous of you.

7. **Don't be arrogant:**

   'Sex can be devastatingly bad or just devastating. Choose the latter and drop me an email.'

   You won't pull if you come across as a wannabe Casanova. Men who appear full of themselves generally turn out to be shit in bed. Most women know this, and those who don't soon learn – and spread the word.

8. **Conversely, a man who shows basic wit and intelligence, and who can be mildly self-deprecating, would probably appear more considerate of a woman's needs in bed. Thus, more women would reply to his advert, ensuring a higher probability of him getting laid:**

   'Watery eyed albino seeks large gins and absolutely no sympathy from women who aren't that bothered about the fact that, to me, you probably just look like a shapely, yet smudgy blob in the middle distance. Must be prepared to put up with my walking into doors, abusing people with 20-20 vision and never getting a sun tan.'

   I'm betting this guy has had a few offers.

9. **Don't bother putting pictures of your penis in the advert. Or, if you must, put a picture of your face alongside it. However nice your cock may be, in and of itself it isn't going to market your worth as a potential lover. If a woman was only interested in a phallus to play with, there are plenty of vibrators out there – and she'd be guaranteed a good orgasm with one. So**

please, be funny, be honest, show your face in the ad, and you're much more likely to get a response – and perhaps get lucky.

10. However, if your objective in the advert is not to get laid, and you don't mind women printing off pictures of your erection and using them to masturbate with, then please, feel free to post the cock pics – I need a few more for my collection.

Friday 26th May

'When you get a "no", get happy,' someone said to me many years ago, when I worked in sales. The idea being that every rejection you experience brings you closer to acceptance; for every person who turns you down, you'll get nearer to the one who says 'yes' to you.

The same can be applied to chatting someone up, I think, which is why I didn't worry about emailing the guy on Craigslist: if it happens, it happens; if it doesn't, it doesn't. It's not a big deal.

For years I have worked with this philosophy. When it comes to dating or sex, it's usually me who puts myself on the line, doing the equivalent of the cold-call. Men almost never approach me – I've had to rely almost wholly on my plucking up the courage to go and talk to a bloke, rather than waiting for him to come to me. I think more women should take the initiative and approach blokes: why should it only be men who take the first move?

I have, though, on occasion, wondered why men don't approach me; I decided to question Tim about this tonight, during one of our regular evenings that we spend moaning to each other about our sex lives.

'I want you to watch me as I go to buy us more drinks,' I informed him, midway into the evening. 'It's an experiment: tell me what you notice; I want to know if any men seem interested in me.'

He agreed and I sauntered to the long bar, ordered our drinks and tried to look relaxed amongst the thirty-something dressed-up crowd. A few minutes later, cocktails in hand, I made my way back to our seats.

'Well?' I asked. 'Anything?'

Tim nodded. 'Yup. I spotted two blokes checking you out.'

I was stunned that any blokes would have shown any interest. But I didn't believe him till he pointed each of them out to me. 'Why didn't either of them approach me? Is my hair a mess? Am I showing too much – or too little – cleavage?'

Tim shook his head. 'You look great; it's not about that. The problem is how you carry yourself. You look too confident.'

Not the first time I have heard this – I recall a boyfriend saying the same thing, some years ago. I sat there in silence and waited for Tim to continue.

'You see, that makes you unapproachable: many guys are intimidated by women who look so at ease as you do. Even the way you walked to the bar, you seemed so self-assured, it was like you owned the place. It's scary for the average bloke to deal with that – far easier to talk to the timid-looking girl sitting by the door.'

'But I wasn't confident,' I pleaded. 'Actually, I felt very self-conscious and couldn't wait to get back to my seat.'

'You carry off your insecurity well, then: you looked fear-less.'

'What am I supposed to do?' I asked him, exasperated. 'Pretend to be all meek and shy, in the hope that guys approach me? That just seems so pathetic . . .'

Tim shook his head again. 'Nah, you'd just come over like a twit: that's just not you. And women shouldn't change who they are just to fit in with what some men are comfortable with. Be yourself and do what you do; eventually you'll meet a bloke who sees through all that.'

I looked down at the table, sadly, thinking how I've been single for some time now. 'And if I don't?'

Tim slurped on his cocktail. 'And if you don't, then just continue to chat guys up: it's worked for you so far, so why change?'

He had a point: of all the boyfriends/dates/shags I have had over the years, I'd say a good 95 per cent of them were insti-gated by me. Clearly something about me, or something I do, works: so to coin a cliché, 'If it ain't broke, why fix it?'

But I don't always have success from my approaches – far from it. I have had more face-to-face rejections than I can count; I have given out scores of scraps of paper with my number on and never been called back; typed tons of ignored emails; sent dozens of unanswered text messages – being turned down is something I am used to and accept as part of the course of being single. Let's face it, if I was upset by every rejection I have ever had (and there have been many), I would be a quivering wreck by now (and never get laid), which clearly is not the way to go.

Still, sometimes the snubs I get do affect me. I'm not as strong as I think I am and every so often I take to heart the rejection. I then begin to question my approach to men: am I perhaps too aggressive? Too forward? Too honest?

Occasionally I wish that just once, some nice bloke would approach me and talk to me. Not some pick-up artist, or some arsehole wanting to tell me what great tits I have; but instead, some normal guy who just thinks, 'She looks interesting, I want to go and talk to her and find out what makes her tick.'

Do you know what they'd find out? That I am not as confident as I appear; that political issues and movies fire me up; and that I'm a hippie at heart, believing that 'all we need is love' for the world to be a better place. Of course they'd also discover that I have a high sex drive, am interested in group sex and that I would jump at the chance of being spanked in bed. (If they chatted to me for more than an hour, that is.)

Even though I'm sure that with the amount of 'no's I have had, I must be closer to that 'yes' I so wish for, I would love for a guy to take charge, make a move on me and initiate things. And maybe, for once, even do the same in bed. God, I would love that.

I really hope Craigslist Guy gets in touch.

// posted by thegirl @ 11:33:00 PM

Saturday 27th May

Today, for the first time in weeks, I went for a run. With my recent filming schedule preventing me from being able to train until now, it was with some relief that I finally got my trainers back on and headed out in the sunshine to my local park this afternoon. I really looked forward to feeling the air on my skin, my heart beating fast and my body becoming drenched in sweat.

Forty minutes later and all I had managed to run was four miles. Ten measly minutes a mile. That's crap. Especially so because the last time I went for a run, managing eight miles was not a problem for me.

I'm disappointed that my stamina has, as they say, gone to shit. This is bad for two reasons:

1. I am going to have to struggle to get back to a good level of fitness again.
2. If I get the opportunity to have a rampant shag with a guy, I might not be able to keep up with him.

Obviously, I am more worried about the latter.

The thing is, my stamina usually exceeds that of most men I meet. When sex is on the cards, I'm quite happy to fuck. And then fuck some more. And then fondle. And then fuck some more. Add in some more fondling and a bit more fucking and then multiply that by five and extend it over the course of a few hours and that is my level of sexual energy. Let's just say I like to fuck. A lot.

Given that I know most men do eventually get tired and I'm not one to want to make a bloke feel inadequate, I'm more likely to cuddle up to them after a handful of climaxes than tell them that, actually, I am still throbbing between my legs, and are they up for fucking me for a fifth time?

So it's not that often that I get so shagged beyond all recognition that all I want to do is drop off to sleep. But it is possible – even for a girl like me: I had a fling with a marathon runner for a while – damn, that boy had stamina. Stamina like you wouldn't believe. One night – eight orgasms in – I actually had to beg him to stop.

With his cock sticking out like a fucking flagpole, I told him that I couldn't physically have any more sex. My body was ruined: I couldn't move. I was well and truly shagged out. And do you know what this sadistic bastard did? Stuck his tongue between my legs, ate me out until I was on the brink of another orgasm and then screwed me hard until I had had two more, saying, 'Now I have fucked you good and proper.' Bastard.

But it just goes to show that there is a correlation between fitness, stamina and endurance in training, and the ability to last all night whilst shagging. I'm not saying that being able to run 26 miles will ensure your cock stays hard when you want it to – but surely it must help.

So with the pathetic exhaustion from today's run showing me how crap my stamina currently is, I am left worrying how I will manage if I happen to meet another bloke who can go all night. Right now, not very well, I imagine: I'd probably collapse after just one good hard shag.

But given my normally ravenous bedroom appetite, perhaps that's not such a bad thing.

Sunday 28th May

Craigslist Guy emailed me! I awoke this morning to a flirtatious message in my inbox, sexy photographs of him semi-clothed and an invitation to dinner. I emailed him straight back and luckily he was online too: we ended up conversing over IM (Internet Messaging: real-time online chat using text) – so much quicker than email – which resulted in some very heated talk. He also sent me dozens of pics – some BDSM ideas that he wants to try out. I'm definitely up for a little exploration and I like his experimental attitude, so if there's chemistry between us in the flesh, then I think we might end up doing something.

Perhaps I'm being overcautious, but I decided to give Craigslist Guy a fake contact name – Katie, because my pseudonym Abby Lee is being bandied about, given the book's impending publication, and I'm trying to keep me, Zoe, as far away from my online sexblogger persona as possible; I dread to think what would happen if someone was to connect the two identities. It's a bit confusing – I've even given him another phone number, from a new SIM I purchased – I really don't want to take any risks with my anonymity. I hope I don't get mixed up with names.

Anyway, perhaps it will make the sex more fun . . . We have agreed to meet up tomorrow evening; I can't wait.

INTERNET DATING:
Meeting in Real Life – Pie Chart

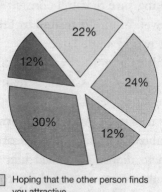

22%

24%

12%

30%

12%

☐ Hoping that the other person finds
  you attractive
☐ Hoping that the other person is as
  attractive as they look in their picture
☐ Hoping that the other person is not
  a psychopath
☐ Hoping that the date won't result in
  broken dreams and being convinced
  that online romances are just a myth
☐ Hoping that you'll get a shag

Tuesday 30th May

Craigslist Guy and I met for dinner last night and our conversation became explicit almost immediately: it was obvious that there was mutual attraction. Over a lovely French meal I was rather excited to hear how he wanted to handcuff me, try out a paddle he had just bought and 'force' me to endure multiple orgasms before 'allowing' me to have his cock inside me. Finally! A shag on the cards, hurrah.

As we sat drinking a lovely cabernet sauvignon, I felt myself become wet as he detailed our little S&M play, and I almost felt compelled to fuck him then and there. But I didn't. This was going to be planned-out casual sex: we were covering all bases, making sure that full consent was agreed upon, in the safety of a well-lit public restaurant; the hardcore fucking in candlelight would come later.

We discussed all aspects of sex and BDSM; likes and dislikes; interests and turn-offs. As well as telling him how much I wanted to experience being submissive, I also mentioned that I was happy to switch positions: I love to induce pleasure in another, teasing them until they cannot stand it any more – nothing gets me wetter, in fact, than a half-hour blow-job which ends up with my riding their cock. (The thing about 'spitting or swallowing' is irrelevant to me: 99 per cent of the time, my blow-jobs end in penetration for me. Win/win, I reckon.)

Anyway, I only mentioned my in-bed egalitarianism so that he would understand that it might be a little difficult for me to relax into the passive position of being submissive: being on top (literally) so frequently, it would take a confident, strong man to be able to take charge, spank me and fuck me with abandon. So, given all our IM discussions, I was rather hoping that he would assure me that that is what he wanted too: what girl doesn't want an occasional light spanking and rampant shagging from behind, I ask you?

What I wasn't expecting was for his eyes to light up as I said I also enjoy dominating a man, and then to get asked if I had ever considered using a strap-on. Now, admittedly, this is actually a fantasy of mine: it's long been something I have wanted to explore, because the inner pathways of a man's pleasure are somewhat foreign to me. Whilst I am fully aware of prostate pleasure in theory – a girl like me will certainly look up 'bum fun' on Google – in practice, I am unfamiliar with it, so I am very keen to get to know more.

As I saw the excitement in his eyes when he popped the question, I didn't think to hesitate replying 'yes': it's not every day you meet an open-minded man who wants a woman to fuck his arse, so given the opportunity, of course I was going to be enthusiastic about it.

I suppose I should have been suspicious when he emailed me scores of images, and a few of them featured men being fucked by women wearing strap-ons. Whilst I liked the pictures, I found myself thinking, 'This is all well and good, but what about MY getting fucked up the arse too, eh?' In retrospect, extended fantasies had been detailed, which looked suspiciously like it would be me dominating him and not the other way round.

But, you know, it's been ages since I've had sex, I was incredibly horny and definitely up for some BDSM fun, so when he suggested, after dinner, that I go back to his place, I went there (after texting Tim with Craigslist Guy's address, for safety) with an open mind: anything could happen and as long as it was all within our previously agreed limits, I was cool with it.

However, when he licked my stilettos, I began to have some doubts.

OK, look, I was wearing stockings, so if a man wants to kiss the length of my legs and caress my feet, I'm more than happy to oblige him. And if he then wants to suck a toe or two, who am I to complain? But lick the entirety of my shoe? Suck the heel? Roll his tongue around the in-step? I may not be experienced in BDSM-play, but as far as I know, I don't believe that foot-fetishism is a regular practice for a dominant man, and it was at this point that it hit home that tonight it wasn't going to be ME that got fucked.

The main reason I had answered his particular ad was because I wanted to try out being submissive in bed, so it was with some disappointment that I faced up to the reality of the situation. However, though gutted about it all, I'm a resourceful woman, and I figured, fuck it: I'm here now – may as well attack the situation with gusto. So I did.

I decided to get into a more dominant, active role and – to his rock-hard delight – stayed there all night, bossing him around and making demands on him. It wasn't particularly difficult to do: I am, after all, very assertive in my day-to-day life, especially in my job. Though I don't sit on many men's faces during the day, it has to be said. (Well, occasionally, but minus the suffocation factor I was doling out to him.) And, to be fair, it was turning me on too.

At some point – when I had had him on the brink of orgasm many, many times, and I could sense he really, really wanted to come – I told him that I was going to fuck him up the arse. I was planning to do this with a couple of fingers, but when he enthusiastically reached into a chest of drawers and then handed me a buttplug, I knew he had other ideas. (He'd probably been planning for that all night.)

I told him to play with himself as I lubed up the toy, and as he watched me, his cock leaked so much pre-come I knew he wouldn't last very long. I began to whisper to him, telling him what I was about to do, that he was going to get fucked by me and that his arse was mine, that he had no say in the matter, that I was going to fuck him and that was that. And as his breathing intensified, I slowly nudged the tip of the plug against his arse.

I didn't have to press it there for long: he spread his arse cheeks with his hands and pushed himself against the plug, allowing it to enter him with ease. I took my time inserting it; I didn't want to rush (or hurt) him. As the plug filled him in its entirety, he groaned and his eyes rolled back and I knew he wasn't far off.

'You're a good boy, aren't you?' I said, swivelling the plug inside him.

He nodded, biting his lip, groaning.

I smiled at him. 'You like me fucking you, do you? I'm fucking your arse and there is nothing you can do about it.'

He moaned and I felt his body shake.

'Come on,' I said, 'open that arse up – take it. Your arse is mine. Take it.' I pushed the plug into him as far as it would go and gripped his balls. And then I switched on the vibrator. As soon as he slid his own fingers around his cock, he began to spurt all over his stomach, his chest and his face; his entire body clenched up and he let out an animalistic groan.

'Good, was it?' I asked a few minutes later, when he had calmed down somewhat.

He nodded, grinning widely. Pleased with the result, I lay next to him and we made small-talk for a while. Then I demanded he finger me and lick me, which he did, eagerly, and soon after climaxing, I made my way home.

It was an interesting evening, but overall it was disappointing. I may have had a handful of orgasms, but I would have swapped all of them for one big one, induced via a good, hard rogering. This makes me sound ungrateful – and maybe I am – but when, after some months of no sex, a girl needs a good dicking, tongue action doesn't quite cut it: it just felt unfulfilling.

Still, I'm glad I now have some experience using a toy in a guy's arse: this will come in handy for when I meet that special man in my life, who will (hopefully) be into such playing. I pray that he will also be into dominating me, though: I can't think of anything more boring than my always being in control – sometimes even a feminist like me likes a man to take charge.

Only in bed, though – if a bloke expects he's going to order me around outside of it too, he's got another thing coming – and I'm not talking about him climaxing. If anyone's going to be having an orgasm, it'd better be me – at least the first three, anyway.

// posted by thegirl @ 4:53.00 PM

JUNE

Thursday 1st June

Thinking back to my sex with Craigslist Guy a few nights ago, I was reminded of when, some years back, a man offered to be my tongue slave.

Obviously, this wasn't about proving his linguistic dexterity. Rather, it was his suggesting – well, requesting, really – that he had the honour of lapping between my thighs for hours on end, with no need for me to reciprocate.

The first time he suggested it, I laughed out loud. Lucky for me he couldn't see or hear me because we were only chatting on IM.

The thought of a man offering to lick me, with no reciprocation expected (or wanted, even) was, at that time in my life, a first. In my ignorant youth, I was unaware of the pleasure to be had from just giving; I didn't know how enjoyable it could be sexually pleasuring someone else. Sex was, at that point, all about taking; in my case, men taking, and me not getting anything at all (such a lot has changed since then . . .).

So, to have a man actually ask to pleasure me, slowly, with no expectation I would return the favour, left me a little shocked. I was intrigued, and for a brief moment I did flirt with the idea, especially when he sent me emails like:

'I want to lick and suck you for hours. All you'd need to

82

do is lie there: my tongue would do all the work.'

I was very tempted to tell him to come round and bury his face between my legs, but something held me back. Besides the usual (Internet + sex + stranger = be extra careful), I think it was his increasingly enthusiastic requests that scared me a little:

'How about if I lay on the floor – a cold, uncomfortable floor – and you sat on my face? Don't worry if I have difficulty breathing: I like that. I want you to use my tongue for your pleasure: I will be your slave.'

Er, OK . . . You see, back then I didn't really understand; now, of course, it makes sense: he wanted me to dominate him, like I did with Craigslist Guy. This is partly why I never took him up on it: I didn't understand about the dynamics of power-play and BDSM in sex; I had yet to learn how enjoyable it could be – from both positions. The thought of dominating someone, or being dominated, made me nervous.

But fast forward to now, and things have changed; and over a quick coffee and gossip about Craigslist Guy with my friend Fiona today, I brought up the topic.

'I wish I hadn't been so naive back then,' I said. 'I really didn't realize what an opportunity that was . . .'

'Yup,' she replied. 'It'd be so nice to have a bloke like that on demand; one that'll just eat pussy whenever you want . . .'

We both sighed and sipped on our cappuccinos.

'You know, I'm not such a huge fan of cunnilingus,' I admitted.

Fiona looked at me, incredulous. 'Really? Why ever not?'

'Oh I like it, don't get me wrong. But I prefer penetration:

it always gets me off. I find it hard to let go being licked – so I rarely come from it.'

'It's the opposite for me,' Fiona said. 'Give me a licker any day.'

I laughed. 'Well, I'll never turn it down; I just prefer it when I'm in the mood . . . Like when I'm watching telly or something, he could just be sitting there, chomping away: that would be nice.'

Fiona giggled. 'Or when you're doing emails, he could be kneeling between your legs, giving you a good sucking.'

'It would help me concentrate, I think. I could probably get a lot of work done that way.'

'Me too.'

We both sat there, taking in the delicious thought.

'You know,' Fiona said, deliberating, 'if you fancied a bit of fun with no strings attached, I know a couple of guys who'd gladly be your tongue slave.'

'Oh yeah?'

'And they'd clean your flat afterwards too . . .'

'You're talking about actual slaves, aren't you?' I sometimes forget that Fiona used to work as a dominatrix.

Fiona grinned.

'Well, my flat is a fucking tip . . .'

'It's worth a thought . . .'

I laughed. 'I guess, but I'm looking for a sexual relationship that's a bit more balanced and meaningful than that, and a full-time slave isn't something that appeals to me: I want a man who'll throw me on my back and fuck me – not one who expects me to subordinate him.'

'Who ever said anything about full time? Once a week should do it.'

'Darling, with the state of my flat right now, he'd need to be eating my pussy every day for a month for it to have any effect.'

'Well, with the state of my sex life, daily licking sounds pretty good to me!'

'I suppose if he alternated tonguing me with using his cock to fuck me, then I might be willing to let him clean my place too . . .'

'And then you'll finally invite me over to dinner at your place again: result! Just say the word . . .'

We both laughed and continued chatting, and the topic soon moved on to less domestic matters. I sat there wishing I could tell Fiona about the blog, and that I've got a book coming out soon – it kills me to have to lie to her. But I just can't risk her knowing: no matter how open our conversations are about sex, I just wouldn't feel comfortable with her looking at the blog. It'd change everything for me if the people I wrote about knew I was doing so.

I hope that day never happens.

// posted by thegirl @ 10:53:00 PM

Friday 2nd June

Given that I have many more rest days off before the shoot restarts, I thought I'd meet up with Tim again and grill him some more about men – as well as tell him about Craigslist Guy, who's already emailed me, asking to meet up tomorrow. I'm not sure I want another night of me dominating him, but maybe a regular shag will be on the cards? I can only hope.

Upon arriving at the Stoke Newington bar, I could see Tim was eager to spill the beans about the date he'd recently had with a new woman.

'So, let me get this straight,' I said, after he'd finished describing their date. 'Because your cock got hard with her on the first date, then that means you will ask to see her again?'

Tim nodded. 'Yes: if something's there, then I'll want to follow it up.'

I pondered this for a minute. 'So, if you don't get an erection, you don't bother calling her?'

'Well, yes, I suppose you could say that,' Tim agreed.

'What if she's really funny or you have loads to talk about; doesn't that matter? Surely that should be taken into account, aside from you getting the horn for her?'

'You're not getting it,' Tim said, slightly exasperated, and took a long swig from his pint of beer. 'Having a hard-on isn't just about thinking she's physically attractive and wanting to fuck her.'

I was confused. I was certain that of all the times I have been alone and faced with a man whose cock is hard, it was because he wanted to fuck me; for what other reason would he be erect (bar a medical disorder)?

I questioned Tim further. 'So, if it's not about wanting to fuck her, why should a second date depend on you having an erection during the first one?'

'It's about chemistry,' Tim replied. 'I know it's good because I'll get a hard-on with a woman; if we're connecting – mentally – then I'm going to be attracted to her. Hence the erection: it's a good judge of the spark between us – if my cock gets hard, I know I like her and want to see her again.'

I thought about this for a moment and suddenly an image of the BBC's Peter Snow entered my head. I giggled out loud as I imagined Snow pointing out the Rate of Increase in Male Attraction via an Erection Swingometer.

'What are you laughing at?' Tim interrupted.

Not wanting to tell him about my Cockometer© (I've found it's best not to joke about men's genitalia except when with female friends), I was instead liberal with the truth: 'It just seems funny that you would be sitting there with a woman on a first date with a hard cock in your trousers and not be tempted to ask her to touch it.'

'Well, it's not like I'd be at full mast; it'd be a secret semi – just there for me to feel, not for her to see. Anyway, sometimes it's nice not to act on an erection – builds it up for next time.'

'Seems like a perfectly good waste of a hard cock to me,' I said, thinking about how frustrated I would feel, not being able to touch my date's hard-on, if I knew it was nestling between his legs on account of me.

Tim laughed. 'Don't worry, I still bash one out when I get home; no wastage there.'

I giggled. 'I should think not!'

'Anyway, it's not as if it's not the same for you – surely you get a little wet if you like a guy?'

'Well, of course I do, but I don't really think I am the best example of female sexual response – I'm not sure many women sit there on a first date imagining what the guy looks like naked.'

'You know, you'd be surprised: I bet lots of women are like

you – most, in fact. You're not alone in your desires.'

'Well, maybe,' I said, thinking about all the women who've emailed me or left comments on the blog saying similar things. 'I hope you're right, anyway, for your sake as much as mine.'

'I know I am; I've slept with enough women to know. And I know I'm definitely not the only bloke who gets a boner when he meets a girl he likes: all men get a semi if they're attracted to the girl they're on a date with.'

'All men? All men get a stiffy with a girl they like?'

'Yup. And those who deny it are lying, I guarantee it.'

I thought about this for a moment and wondered about all the dates I have had over the years. If Tim was right, there must have been at least a few erections that occurred that I never saw (not including the ones I had spent the evening trying to imagine of course, of which there were many).

What a shame I never knew about them; I could have had much more fun on those first dates had I been aware of the guy's predicament – even if it meant just verbally teasing him.

Clearly I enjoy using my tongue for other things too, but I do try to wait until at least the second date before sharing those particular skills.

Speaking of second dates, I'm thinking I should give Craigslist Guy another chance; I'm going to email him when I get home and tell him I'm up for round two.

// posted by thegirl @ 12:45.00 AM

The Girl's Guide to:
Rules for summer

MEN:

1. Wash your armpits and wear anti-perspirant deodorant. Stinking out a tube carriage in summer is just rude.

2. Wear a T-shirt. As much as I may like your bare chest to fondle whilst in bed, showing your nipples on the number 53 bus is too much, even for me.

3. Don't wear socks with sandals. Just don't. Unless you plan on being celibate for ever, that is.

4. Trim your toenails, file the dead skin off your feet and use talc between your toes. Visible fungus on your feet is not attractive: if you want your toes sucked, you'd better make 'em more appealing.

5. Go commando under your trousers/shorts when walking out and about. As well as keeping you (and your potential baby-making sperm) cooler, you'll also attract interested looks from women like me, eager to see the outline of your cock beneath. You may even get chatted up as a result.

WOMEN:

1. Limit the amount of perfume you wear. Stinking out a tube carriage in summer is selfish. A clean body smells much nicer than one doused in artificial chemicals.

2. Wear a properly sized and fitted bra. Flesh bulging out over the sides and top or nipples pointed down to the floor is not a good look, believe me.

3. Don't wear socks with sandals, like some sad fashion victim from the 1980s. That decade is over – and for a good reason too: Thatcherism, day-glo, yuppies – I rest my case.

4. Chipped toenail polish looks foul. Either touch it up, or wear none. And don't be shy of using the pumice stone: it is your friend.

5. Lose the thong poking out of your hipster trousers: a builder's bum is always unattractive – even if your pants are lacy. And if you're going to wear a skin-tight skirt, ditch the knickers altogether: better to go commando and show off your arse, than have thick seams digging into your curves. Plus, it makes for easier access, should you decide (with any luck) to sit on some nice boy's hand.

Sunday 3rd June

I'm pleased to report I finally got shagged by Craigslist Guy! After agreeing, at the last minute, to have me round again, he suddenly turned all alpha-male on me and surprised me with his boldness.

After fucking me, and giving me three orgasms, he said, 'I want you to watch me wank,' and then directed me to sit astride his legs, as he grabbed his cock in one hand and began to stroke it. I have to admit that I was aroused by his confidence; it was certainly a change from the other night, when the ball, quite literally, was in my court.

Not one to turn down a sexy opportunity, I shifted my weight and straddled him, ensuring that his thigh was in direct contact with my groin. I knew it would turn me on to watch him play with himself; I find it so erotic to be privy to a man's personal method of self-pleasure; what better way to learn new/better hand-job techniques than to watch a man giving himself some loving hand-action?

I sat there as he grabbed, tugged and pulled away, even though I was knackered after all our shagging and wanted to go to sleep. But three orgasms in, I felt like the least I could do was to assist him with his pleasure too, so I leant over him, pressed my breasts together and gently slid them over his cock.

'Fuck, your tits are fantastic,' he exclaimed, as my nipples rubbed against him. 'Sit up; I want to look at you.'

I leaned back and he groaned loudly. 'God, you're gorgeous; you have such a sexy body, do you know that?'

I grinned at him in silent thanks, and watched him tugging merrily away at his member. He smiled at me, and I could tell from his fast breathing that he was close. I thought he might need some help to send him over the edge, so I licked my finger and then teased his arsehole with it a little. He groaned again and lifted his hips off the bed, thrusting into both his hand, and my finger.

It wasn't long before he was shooting all over the place. I gripped his balls as he climaxed and watched the spunk rhythmically flying over his abdomen and chest.

'Ouch!' he exclaimed suddenly, and shifted his body away from my grasp; I worried that maybe I had tugged him too hard. 'Are you OK?' I asked, gently stroking him. 'Did I hurt you?'

'No, not at all,' he replied. 'I think I just got some in my eye.' I looked up and saw him wiping away the spunk he had managed to shoot all over his face.

I have to say that although facials are definitely not my thing, the sight of him covered in his own juices was a sight to behold; it made me want to have a little play myself. I'm all for more equality in the bedroom – especially if it's the guy getting spunked on.

When he'd finished cleaning himself off, Craigslist Guy wanted to curl up and snuggle with me, and suggested I stay over. I declined, politely, and made my way home. He's a nice guy, but I don't find him interesting enough as a person or feel enough chemistry to want to be more intimate with him. Somehow, though, I suspect that he's wanting more with me. If we're to have sex again I guess I'm going to have to talk to him about that.

// posted by thegirl @ 3:53:00 PM

Thursday 8th June

Last night I dreamt I went to Manderley again.

Actually, I didn't, but I did dream I was lying on top of Russell Brand, my naked body against his; the hardness of his cock pressing against my damp crotch; our lips entwined in a passionate kiss as we began to grind our hips together and fucked each other with intensity. It was a nice dream, and ended as all good ones should: with my fingers between my legs, and a smile on my face.

'Russell Brand: yes or no?' Blog Boy asked me the other night.

'Yes; definitely.'

He looked incredulous at my response. 'Why?! Please don't tell me you like him for what he does on telly?'

I shook my head. 'Nope, most of that irritated the hell out of me – but he is a very talented stand-up comic; you should check him out.'

'But he's a knob! He looks like a prat.'

I shrugged. 'Well, admittedly he's not my type: scrawny and lanky doesn't really do it for me; I much prefer a man with some meat on him. Plus he seriously needs to brush his fucking hair . . . But it's not his looks that make me want to shag him.'

'If not that, then what? Please, enlighten me . . .'

I took a sip of my drink. 'There's one reason, and one reason only, that I would fuck Russell Brand.'

'Because he's got a big cock?'

I groaned. 'Oh please, cock size is so fucking irrelevant. As long as it's visible, and works, I really couldn't give a shit what a penis looks like, or how big it is.'

'OK, then; he's supposed to be great in bed, right? Is that why you'd shag him?'

I shook my head again. 'No. Whilst I don't doubt he's probably a great lay, that's not the sole reason I would fuck him.'

'Why, then? Come on, I want to hear this . . .'

'Because, unlike most guys, Russell is not threatened by other men's sexuality. He is confident enough to be able to flirt with men, as well as women, and knows that by doing so, it doesn't undermine his masculinity – regardless of his sexual orientation. So by being relaxed about it, he's saying he's OK with other men and their desires, as well as his own. That's a very attractive trait to have. A man like that is going to be open-minded, and, almost by definition, will then be interesting in bed. Ergo, I want to shag him.'

'Hmm. I've never heard it put quite that way: that's a very interesting argument. So you're basically saying, he's got a David Walliams factor to him: i.e. could possibly swing both ways . . .?'

'I guess, though I don't think Russell does, but it's the fact that he doesn't give a fuck that people might pigeonhole him as gay when he flirts with guys that makes him so sexy. Him knowing – and playing upon – the fluidity of his sexuality with others makes him shaggable. So, yeah, I would. And I bet many other women would too – for those exact same reasons.'

'I can see your point now, yeah . . .'

We sipped our drinks and Blog Boy changed the subject. I decided not to mention to Blog Boy how much I'd love to see Russell fucking another guy up the arse. I guess there's a time and place for sharing my threesome-with-two-men fantasy, and it certainly wasn't then . . . Though last night's orgasm was pretty timely, if I do say so myself – even if it was just a dream.

// posted by thegirl @ 4:28:00 PM

Monday 12th June

The last few days have left me thinking a lot about man-on-man action: maybe it's because of that dream about Russell Brand, or maybe just because I've never been with two men and I can honestly say that it is my number one fantasy. I've got to fulfil it before I settle down with someone; call it the last item on my pre-marriage tickbox.

I'm still not sure when it was that I realized that the idea of two men having sex together was sexually attractive to me, but I am certain of one thing: I know it turns me on – a lot. Maybe the seed was planted many years ago, when my boyfriend Chris dropped it into the conversation one night:

Him (grabbing my hips, pulling me harder onto his cock): Do you remember that guy at work I mentioned? The one who winked at me?

Me (fondling his nipples): Yeah – the cute one?

Him (squeezing my arse): Him. I think he flirted with me yesterday.

Me: Oh, really? I bet you liked that, eh?!

I winked at him. He looked at me for a moment as I rode his cock hard. 'Yes, actually I did. It gave me a boner.'

For a moment, my brain flickered into gear and the reality of his statement hit me. I felt a tiny surge of jealousy, of insecurity, of anxiety. And then I became aware of another feeling; something much more overwhelming than the brief questioning in my head: the intense throbbing and wetness between my legs.

I carried on riding him, and, feeling his cock pulse inside me, I wondered how best I should approach this new information; whether I should coax out his feelings about it; or perhaps just tease him. 'It turned you on, did it?' I asked him, a slight smile on my face.

'Yes,' he replied softly, 'it did.' He pulled me even more deeply onto him and I was sure his cock felt harder inside me than it ever had before. Clearly he was enjoying the thought of another man. And, I was surprised to discover, so was I.

'So,' I continued, 'if he were here now, what would you do?'

He paused for a moment, looking unsure how to respond. I smiled at him and he visibly relaxed. 'Well,' he said, cautiously, 'I'd like to feel his cock against me.'

'And then?' I asked. 'What would you do then?'

'Then I'd like to stroke it,' he said, 'maybe feel it on my mouth.'

'Mmm,' I replied. 'Feel it rub against your lips.'

He nodded and pumped his cock harder into me.

'Would you like to suck it?' I asked. 'Run your tongue all over it?'

He nodded enthusiastically and we both ground our hips together until we climaxed simultaneously.

After we caught our breath, I tried talking some more about his desire to be with another man, but he kept changing the subject. It was only years later that he finally felt able to explore this side of his sexuality, and by that time, our relationship was long over.

A few years hence, I was offered a threesome with two

guys that I met in a nightclub. Stupidly I told my old school friend Kathy about it, thinking that she would be as excited as me by the offer.

'Yuck!' she exclaimed. 'What happens if they touch each other?! That would be disgusting!'

Of course, being a twit and somewhat insecure at the time, I turned the guys down, and regretted it for years. (I still do.)

But Kathy's response wasn't out of the ordinary: ask any of my mates, even the ones I consider 'liberated' – the progressive women, the open-minded men – and they'd all recoil if I suggested

1. that I would like to fuck two men, and
2. that it would turn me on if they touched each other too, and
3. that I would be happy just to watch the two men touch each other.

But, on the contrary, if I suggested:

1. that I would like to have sex with a man and a woman
2. that it would turn me on if me and the other woman touched each other
3. that I would be happy if the guy just watched me and the other woman touch each other,

I know for sure that my female friends would blush – and then say, 'I've always wanted to try that!' and my male friends would say, 'Go for it! Can I watch?!'

Whilst I wouldn't – and don't – say no to a little girl-on-girl action in my life, you would find me eagerly shouting, 'Yes, yes!' to a little boy-on-boy. Forget lesbianism: what could be better than more than one cock? Answer: two cocks. It's twice the pleasure; double the fun.

But it seems that if a woman admits that she likes homosexual sex – watching or participating – most people would assume that she's talking about lesbian sex; in fact, it's almost expected: a 'liberated' woman + healthy sex drive x open-minded sexuality = lesbian tendencies. And in straight porn, it's all directed towards men, of course, as the women smile coyly at the camera and beg the (off-screen) man to 'cum and join us'.

Yawn.

Why is it considered acceptable for women to dabble with other women, but not men to dabble with other men? Why should lesbianism be the only gender exploration in straight people's beds? Why is it so taboo for a man to want to explore another man?

I'm not going to even begin to explain this: it's heterosexist hypocrisy and unless I am plied with at least five whisky sours, I don't think I should delve into this topic – I'll only get annoyed.

But aside from these issues affecting society at large, I am more concerned with how they affect me. Or, in other words: will I ever find a bloke who shares the same interest as me in his being with another man?

I would love to meet another guy, who, in a relaxed manner says, 'Sure, I'd try a bloke; I've always wanted to know what it was like to suck a cock,' and then fuck me hard as we talk about how we might fulfil this mutual desire.

But I'm not optimistic about finding such a guy. Whilst I am very open about sex and my sexuality, I can honestly say that having a desire for my partner to fuck another man is not something I bring up in conversation with men that I meet with any regularity. I wish it was. But I think I would scare the majority of men off if I mentioned that

1. I think about cock all the time
2. I would love to have a threesome with two men
3. I want to settle down and have kids.

Which are the three things that have recently been occupying my mind on a regular basis.

Aside from my being a sex fiend and needing a shag three times a day, that is, but I think that can be dropped into the conversation a little bit more easily.

// posted by thegirl @ 10:22:00 PM

Saturday 17th June

I went over to Craigslist Guy's place again last night. The sex was great, but the suspicions I had the other evening seemed to be correct: moments after our all-night shag-a-thon he told me he wanted to see me again, tomorrow night. I'm now worried that he might be reading into things a little too much, so I thought it best to quickly establish some 'rules' whilst we had breakfast this morning.

'So, you're OK with us just being casual,' I said tentatively, as I took a big gulp of instant coffee. Not something I would ever buy, being a coffee snob; the cheap bitterness soured my mouth as I swallowed, and I struggled not to spit it out.

He nodded at me. 'Yeah, it's fine. That's all I was looking for anyway.'

I felt like I had to drive the point home – just in case. 'Great. But I just want to make sure we're both on the same page here: we're going to shag and nothing else – right?'

He nodded again. 'Absolutely.' Then he grinned at me. 'Although that arse of yours will get a thorough spanking next time I see you.'

My pussy throbbing at the thought of it, I smiled back at him, but continued. 'I look forward to it: that sounds fun. And that's what I want right now; I'm not looking to get into anything deeper at the moment.'

I watched his face for a response, and as I did, I was aware that what I had said was not entirely true.

Over the last couple of years, as well as fooling around with a few men, I fell for someone who didn't want me, and was smitten by another who was unattainable. Meeting these men made me realize that I did want to be in a relationship, and have something special, and be in love, and all that malarkey. I did want to settle down and partner up: I am no longer in denial about that.

I don't need the heartbreak from a man who doesn't want me, or to deal with the head-fuck from a man I can't have. Whilst I still want to explore and experiment, I do want more than a succession of one-nighters. If writing a sex blog has taught me anything, it's that shagging can be wonderful, but I do miss being in a loving relationship very much.

I believe someone I'd like to settle down with is out there somewhere and that serendipity will eventually make our paths cross. When it does, I'll meet my equal. But until then, I just want to have some casual fun: I'm not going to turn down an opportunity to enjoy myself, just because I am single.

So here I am, sitting opposite a nice bloke, who had fucked me more than substantially not even an hour ago, but I couldn't imagine getting any more involved with him. And, let's face it, he still didn't even know my real name.

I realized he was staring at me and waiting for me to break the silence.

'So, you're cool with us just fucking?' I asked, bluntly.

'Of course,' he replied. 'But I'm not really into that whole fuck-buddy thing.'

My heart sank; I waited for him to continue.

'Just so long as when we meet up, you're mine for the evening and you're comfortable with going out to dinner, having some good conversation and my grabbing your arse when we walk down the street, then I'm completely cool with us both fucking other people.'

A good compromise, I guess. 'Cool.'

'And,' he continued, 'I want to be able to fuck you all night long when we do get together.'

I smiled at him. 'That goes without saying.'

He reached over the table and grabbed my hand and stroked it. The action touched me, but felt too personal for the situation, given what we'd just talked about.

Things had to be clarified. 'Look, I need you to know, I'm not going to be intimate with you; I'm not going to massage you all night, or stroke you softly, or lie in your arms cuddling you, sorry.'

He shrugged, and I felt bad for being so brutal, but surely it was better that he knew the situation now?

'It's just that I don't need the head-fuck right now, OK? It's easier to be casual if there are no emotional ties; intimacy is for a relationship – I'm not looking for that at the moment.' At least, not with him.

'So you said,' he replied, somewhat shortly.

'And you're OK with that, right?' I asked. 'Because we both have to be in this for the same reason, or someone will get hurt and I really don't want that.'

'Come here,' he said, and stood up away from the table.

I pushed back my chair and walked over to him. He pulled me close and I felt his cock pushing against the thin bathrobe he had given me to wear.

'Look,' he said, firmly, 'I think you're fucking gorgeous. I really enjoyed last night; I want to fuck you again very much.' He pressed his erection against me to emphasize the point. 'But I know what this is, and it's fine with me: I am going to fuck other women too; let's just have some fun and enjoy ourselves.'

Relieved somewhat, I relaxed into his arms and we kissed for a while. Reminding me of the time, and my lunch-date with my friend Kathy, he pulled away from me and gave me a light spank on my arse as I walked into the bedroom to get dressed.

'That arse is mine,' he said as I re-emerged a moment later, adjusting my crumpled dress. 'Next time, I'll be leaving marks on it.'

I laughed. 'Good. I look forward to it.'

His face lit up in a wide grin, and I gave him a quick peck on the cheek as I opened the door and slipped outside. I walked towards the tube, appreciating the freshness of the mild summer air, and the space to clear my thoughts. I sat on an almost empty carriage on the train and smiled to myself about last night's events. But even though I felt happy and sated, there was a quiet, nagging feeling inside me and it somehow stayed with me the entire journey home.

// posted by thegirl @ 8:28:00 PM

Sunday 18th June

Looking in the mirror this morning I have discovered:

1. My shoulder is mildly dislocating (obtained through twisted positioning of our bodies).
2. Grazes on my elbow (from propping myself up on one arm).
3. Bruising on my knees (being clumsy means I knock against everything).
4. Cramp in my calf muscle (enthusiastically pulling his arse in towards me with my feet has its disadvantages).
5. A stiff neck (lack of sleep meant plenty of tossing and turning). (More of the former, naturally.)
6. A tired back (taking it from behind can be exhausting).

7. Sore inner thighs (my 'fuck muscles' don't get a workout as often as they should).
8. A throbbing vulva (rampant grinding against his hand has its drawbacks).
9. A pounding headache (the unfortunate payoff for my frequent, and intense, orgasms).
10. A large love bite on my neck –

'You've damaged me!' I yelped down the phone upon seeing the discoloured mark he'd left. 'I've got a massive bruise on my neck!'

Craigslist Guy laughed. 'Call it "marking my territory",' he growled.

I giggled when he said that, but it's struck me now that maybe he was being partly serious.

JULY

Monday 3rd July

After a rather intense few weeks of work, I have some free time again. I have quite a bit of preening/self-care to catch up on; it's been many months since I've been able to do so. Here are the things I need/want to do:

List One
1. Get my hair cut. Frizzy and me don't go.
2. Get my hair highlighted. It's summer! Yes, it is, OK?
3. Get my legs waxed. Furry and me don't go.
4. Get my bikini line waxed after I have had four vodkas, so that I don't shout at the beautician that she is a 'fucking sadist' and 'What are you doing? trying to kill me???'
5. Buy some new bras that
   a) fit properly and complement the shape of my boobs
   b) actually make my nipples point straight ahead and defy gravity entirely. They do exist, don't they?
6. Buy a couple of hip-hugging, arse-shaping, pencil-line skirts that are made for curvaceous women and not skeletal models. Easier said than done.
7. Buy some new jeans that don't advertise what underwear I am wearing to the world. Again, easier said than done.

8. Find a couple of tops whose buttons don't pop open at breast level, because they are designed solely for flat-chested women. A week-long chore, believe me.

9. Find some open-toe heeled sandals that
   a) fit my big feet
   b) are comfortable
   c) accentuate my calf muscles so I look as good as Jodie Foster in *Inside Man* (her legs are enough to make a girl switch sides).

10. Run at least three times a week so that I can trim up asap (and also then pluck up the courage to talk to the fit blond bloke at my gym).

List Two

1. Try out some new sex toys.
2. Go to a fetish night.
3. Be a voyeur at an orgy.
4. Have sex with two men.
5. Fuck a bloke outdoors.
6. Shag a total stranger.
7. Experience anal sex again.
8. Get handcuffed and spanked hard.
9. Be the plaything for a heterosexual couple.
10. Have an orgasm in a public place (again).

I don't know about other women, but I'm bored shitless by shopping. When it comes to how I'd prefer to spend my free time, I think having a good shag will always beat finding a sexy skirt to wear. And as for beauty regimes like going to a beautician every week for a facial and manicure, when you get the chance to have a cock in your mouth, who really gives a shit what you look like? Not me. I'd rather appear as if I've been dragged through a hedge because I'd just had a hard fuck than worry about the state of my hair. (No wonder it's always a mess.)

So I suppose that the things on the first list are just chores for me to get done; and those on the second are the reward for doing them. Here's hoping I churn through them all quickly.

Though really, I'd prefer number seven on the second list to be done as slowly as possible. Unless it's part of number four on the same list, in which case I'd be so excited, I'd probably forget about the pain it might cause.

Wish the same could be said for waxing.

// posted by thegirl @ 3:30:00 PM

Thursday 6th July

I've decided to try out a new beautician who Fiona recommended. Apparently she can 'get even the shortest, most stubborn fucking hair out of your pussy'. Well, if that's not a good recommendation, I don't know what is.

So there I was earlier today, legs askew on a table, trying to ignore the pain and the fact that my vagina was on display to a complete stranger, when the beautician initiated a conversation with me:

'I would.'

'What?'

'I would.' She gestured with her elbow to the TV on the

wall, and then pointed at the miniature on-screen Robbie Williams miming to his music video. 'I definitely would.'

'Really?' I watched the screen and wondered what Robbie might look like naked. Quite fit, I imagine.

She interrupted my train of thought. 'But it'd only be for one night – the guy has far too many issues for more than that.'

'How do you know?'

'He comes across like that in interviews,' she replied, assuredly. 'He seems like he's got more than a few emotional problems.'

I decided not to comment on her assumption that interviews reflect 'truth' of any sort, and instead wondered to myself if supposed 'emotional problems' were what attracts me to certain men in the first place; their dark, insecure side, a fascinating balance to their outer, confident charm . . .

She broke me out of my momentary self-analysis. 'Well, he smokes, anyway; a terrible chain-smoker, so that would stop me wanting to get involved.'

I peered at the screen and screwed up my nose in mock disgust. 'Yuck.'

She nodded. 'Well, it'd only be for that one night, so I suppose I'd put up with him smelling a bit.'

I laughed. 'I guess. But if I was going to fuck him, he'd better spend some serious time licking me, to make up for it.'

She giggled too and then resumed what she was doing.

'Ouch!' I held my breath and tried to control the pain.

'Sorry.' She rubbed my labia where she had ripped off the wax and smiled at me. 'Almost finished.'

I focused back on the TV, hoping it would take my mind

off the fact that a complete stranger was tearing away the top layer of skin from my pussy.

'So do you like men to be in their twenties like you?' she asked, presumably attempting to distract me from the pain.

I shook my head. 'I'm not in my twenties,' I replied, blushing slightly. 'And younger men bore me. I like a guy to be a bit more experienced and worldly – in his mid-thirties, preferably.'

'Oh, I thought you were in your twenties like me?' she said, confused.

I shook my head. 'Nope.'

She continued to spread the wax over me. 'Oh, well, if you don't like younger blokes, what do you think of older men, then?'

'Not much,' I replied. 'I prefer men my own age; give me a man in his thirties any day.'

'How about an older man like Rod Stewart? He's still got it.'

I gritted my teeth, mostly from the pain, but also at the vomit-inducing thought of seeing Rod Stewart naked. 'No thanks. Not my cup of tea at all.'

'Really?' she asked. 'I think he's sexy. I would, definitely. I've had a crush on him for years.'

I stayed silent. She continued ripping off my skin. 'Come on, there must be one older man who you'd shag . . .'

'Hmm. OK then, if I had to: David Lynch.'

'Who?'

'The film director.'

She shrugged.

'*Lost Highway, Blue Velvet, The Elephant Man* . . .'

She looked at me like I was talking nonsense, and in my

head I imagined slapping her hard with the palm of my hand to punish her for her ignorance.

'The TV series *Twin Peaks* . . .'

She stared at me, still confused. I continued. 'Well, anyway, I'd do him – but only because he's so bloody intelligent and I love his work. He's an amazing guy, actually – really interesting to talk to.' I added, 'And he gave me a hug once.'

She seemed unimpressed by my bragging and I gave up, attempting to ignore the fact that she was now pulling my clitoral hood to one side and spreading hot wax in my most sensitive of regions.

As she tugged away, I tried to focus away from the impending agony soon to be felt between my legs. Then she ripped off the wax, and on the verge of tears, I continued the conversation. 'There is one other older guy I'd shag, actually. I know he's ancient enough to be my father, but get David Bowie in a catsuit and I'd jump him.'

'He's quite nice,' she agreed. She pulled my clit to the other side and spread some more wax above it. I bit my lip waiting for the pain, and flinched hard as she tugged away the wax.

'All done!' she said a moment later, somewhat too eagerly, I thought.

I smiled at her, rejoicing that it was all over and I could finally take my poor throbbing pussy home. I was also relieved that I didn't divulge that one of my wank-fodder favourites – the thought of Ziggy Stardust being sucked off by Iggy Pop – was currently running through my mind.

Some things you just don't share, particularly when it's a fantasy about the glam-rock era and the person you are talking to wasn't even born then. Plus, I've learned it's best not to let my imagination run away with me when a complete stranger happens to have their hands in my privates: it can only lead to embarrassment. Or accidents with hot wax.

// posted by thegirl @ 6:53:00 PM

Dear Men,

Yes, you. All of you. We need to talk.

Allow me to bring something to your attention, if I may. That being the problem of how you sit. Wherever you are, you always seem to sit in the same way: with your legs spread widely apart; whether on the tube, in an office, or in that coffee shop in Soho last week, where you distracted me from my writing.

Here's the thing: unless we are going to have sex, I really must ask that you keep your legs together – it would be hugely appreciated if you could. Don't get me wrong: I quite like seeing a man with his legs splayed when he is sitting down, but that, you see, is where problems arise (possibly literally, but we'll come to that later).

I like to think I am aware of the reasons why men might recline in this manner; if I had a penis I would probably sit that way too, so as to allow my crotch some space to breathe (and protect the future of the next generation by keeping my sperm virile). I imagine, being a bloke, it is quite comfortable spreading one's legs apart: it certainly lowers the risk of getting one's dinkle stuck in an awkward position; and we've all heard the stories about penis fractures. (I've actually met one: it had broken at a right-angle – ouch. I am relieved to say it still worked. Very well, in fact.)

According to many body-language experts, sitting like this also serves the function of marking one's territory: spread-out legs take

*up space – which shows other men potential dominance of the
physical surroundings. (Much like being a tomcat, but without the
bad smell. Hopefully.) Perhaps this highlighting of the groin area
is an evolutionary trait to show potential mates what's on offer:
allowing one to 'check the goods' prior to purchase. As if a big
arrow was pointing downwards, a man sitting with his legs apart
seems to be saying, 'Look at me. Here I am. This is my penis. Isn't
it great?!' I can certainly see the advantage in that, but herein lies
the problem: with men's groins so blatantly on show, a woman
like me doesn't know where to look.*

*Let's be honest here: I like to look at men's crotches. This is no
secret. It's not that I am interested in seeing how big or small their
penis might be – far from it – rather, it's just nice to see what's
there. In a sort of knowing-which-side-it-might-be-lying type of
way, or even I-wonder-what-it-would-look-like-hard-underneath-
his-trousers kind of thing. Normal stuff, basically. So when faced
with a Cock Bulge On Display Because A Man Is Sitting There
With His Legs Wide Apart, where else is a woman supposed to fix
her eyes? Yes, I've tried to look at a bloke's face, or his hands, or
even his feet, but with such a prominent visual display of genitalia,
I find it hard to rest my gaze anywhere else but there.*

*My male friends tell me they have a problem with women
who wear low-cut tops; that with any cleavage in view, their
eyes are drawn to it – even if they don't find the woman attractive, or worse, she's a friend. I know this isn't just a heterosexual
thing: a gay mate of mine admitted to me he was captivated by
my boobs and spent much of an evening peering down my top
(with my blessing, I should add: it's just the staring without permission that annoys me). So, likewise, men's crotches.*

I find this situation most unsettling, because whilst I may be checking out a guy's groin, I am not necessarily doing so because I want to shag him, and I would hate for him to think that I did, just because he spotted me cock-gazing. It's just that it's there . . . to be looked at. And I do; I can't help it.

So, in order to avoid being caught staring at your crotches, it would help me if all of you men stopped sitting like that, and instead pressed your legs together in a dignified manner, thus hiding your packages from view. It would be better for all that way, I think.

Thanking you in advance,

Yours sincerely, in dark glasses to hide her eyes,

Girl x

// posted by thegirl @ 11:22:00 PM

Wednesday 12th July

One of the worst things about working on a film full-time is that you have almost zero free time: doing 60–100 hour weeks means 'spare time' doesn't exist. Any time off is spent asleep, from exhaustion, so there are certain things I miss when I'm working:

1) Being fucked hard from behind and getting my arse spanked.
2) Sucking a cock and rubbing it between my tits.
3) Having my legs around a guy's shoulders as he pummels me over and over again.

Obviously, I wouldn't say no to any of the above, and it's wonderful I now have some spare time in my schedule to have sex, but there is also another gap – besides the one between my legs – that needs filling.

And that gap is food: I miss cooking. I love to cook. It's one of my favourite pastimes. Give me some fresh ingredients and some heat, and I'll get cooking.

There's something seductive about food for me: it's all linked to sex, I reckon; eating good food is like having a miniature orgasm in your mouth. And I love the fact that food – like sex – involves all the senses.

It even involves similar preparation:

- Pick the best ingredients that catch your eye
- Have a quick feel, to make sure they are ripe
- Handle delicately
- Put them on a slow heat
- Add spice
- Inhale their aroma
- Lift gently to ensure no breakage
- Display with care to ensure best presentation
- Place delicately in mouth and savour the flavour
- Devour enthusiastically

Is it any wonder that when people enjoy food, they groan with orgasmic delight?

I remember cooking for Kathy and her boyfriend David a few months ago. I had done a full-on meal: asparagus tips with chilli and lime butter; roast organic leg of lamb with rosemary and garlic; roasted vegetables with thyme and sea salt; white chocolate cheesecake with a raspberry centre.

To say we were all stuffed afterwards was an understatement. We sat there, barely able to move, but nicely tipsy from all the Rioja.

Eventually David got up to go to the loo and Kathy and I reminisced about our childhoods. We talked for ages, the conversation moving on to gossip in Kathy's music industry workplace, and I suddenly realized that David was still absent. Kathy was a bit drunk, so I went to see if he was ok.

Instead of being in the loo, he was – red-facedly – picking at the joint of meat left over in the kitchen.

'Oh god!' he said, groaning, his hands and mouth full of flesh. 'I'm so sorry; it's just that . . . fuck . . . this is SO good.' He carried on chewing and grinned at me, sheepishly.

I laughed and handed him a carving knife and told him to help himself. As he attacked the meat some more and I walked back to Kathy, I momentarily beamed with pride: I loved that he wanted more of my food.

I really miss having someone special who is eager to eat my food – and who enjoys it. It is such a compliment: it's almost as good as being told I give the best blow-jobs (it might be a lie, but every woman wants to hear it). I just adore cooking for others; I get off on their pleasure – just as I do during sex. Making a guy groan with delight by putting something in his mouth gives me satisfaction; it gets me off.

Show me a man who makes happy sex noises when he eats my food; and who then makes happy food noises when he eats my sex, and I'll be a happy woman.

Especially if – after rogering me good and proper – he then wanted to clean the dishes.

// posted by thegirl @ 12:14:00 AM

115

The Girl's Guide to Summer Delights

BBQs	*Dating*
Weather	

There's no guarantee of what lies ahead. Things could turn out to be fine. But at any minute they could also become rather unsettled and morbidly grey, so you end up wishing you had just stayed in and had a wank instead.

People Invited

They must make for intelligent company, sustain your interest all night, and/or make you want to fuck them. Otherwise, what's the point?

Alcohol Consumed	
A bin full of cold beers, some bottles of Pimms and plenty of sparkling wine says a good night is on the horizon.	**a)** A cocktail and a glass of wine with the meal says, 'Perhaps we'll have another date.'
	b) Two bottles of wine with the meal says, 'I sincerely hope we snog at the end of this evening.'
	c) Five beers followed by two bottles of wine says, 'God you look sexy . . . let's go back to yours, unsuccessfully attempt penetration, clumsily fumble about for a bit, and then wake up the next day trying to remember each other's names.'

Foods to Avoid	
Cheap meat, because it makes you look like a tight-wad. Plus, it's a challenge to offer round a factory farmed, hormone-injected, mass-produced, mechanically recovered 'meat product' and successfully pass it off as once belonging to part of an animal.	**a)** Soups (small risk of slurpage – sounds emitted from any body orifice during a date are a no-no).
	b) Spaghetti (high risk of chin-spillage – which is never a good look).

Marinading/Cooking	
Stage one: Prepare sauce and mix in herbs; add meat and leave to soak in a cool place.	**Stage one:** Anticipation of the event: 'Will s/he or won't s/he call me?'; 'Is s/he interested in me?'; 'I'm already wanking twice a day thinking about her/him: that must be a good sign.'

Marinading/Cooking (cont'd)

Stage two: Turn meat so all parts get covered in sauce; replace in fridge.	**Stage two: a)** Don't respond too eagerly when you receive a text or phone call because if s/he is one of those 'playing it cool' types, you could find yourself without a date. **b)** Don't play it too cool, because if s/he is one of those 'can't be bothered to play games because it's fucking childish' types, then you could find yourself without a date. **c)** Don't admit they have provided you with wank-fodder for the last three days (even if it is true). The time to share this is when your date has their tongue in your mouth. Or their hand in your crotch. It can wait, basically.
Stage three: Place meat over coals. Ensure it is being cooked through heat and not fire – burned flesh is horrid, especially if it's not fully cooked underneath the charred exterior. Timing is thus very important: too long over the heat and the meat is overdone; too short and it'll still be raw. No one likes food poisoning – not even masochists.	**Stage three: a)** If during the date, snogging has been plentiful, then progress to some gentle bodily groping. A slight hand on your date's lower back is good; grabbing their arse is not. They might like it, but the restaurateur may have some words to say about it. **b)** If things are progressing nicely, then placing a hand on an upper thigh and squeezing firmly is always appreciated – as long as you are prepared to follow through with the damp heat/erection that you have caused, that is. No one likes a tease when there's no guarantee of a climax. **c)** If you're hoping to eat out/suck off your date later on, it's always nice to ask whether this dish might be on offer – preferably when you're nibbling their neck, whispering in their ear and have your hand on their upper thigh. You'd be surprised what can be on the menu when i) you approach your date in a polite and respectful way, ii) you've made your date extremely horny.

Sating Appetites

The key to successful barbeques and dates is slow timing and preparation: get it wrong and people tend to vomit; get it just right and everyone has a smile on his or her face – especially with the bonus of an orgasm at the end of the night.

Thursday 13th July

Speaking of food, I was at the supermarket tonight, stocking up on supplies, when I got into an odd conversation at the checkout.

'You're very well organized,' a silver-haired gentleman in his late sixties said, grinning at me. 'Your shopping: it's very neat.' He pointed at the food I had placed on the conveyor belt and he beamed at me again.

I felt myself blush. 'Well, yes, I like to keep things in order: it's easier to pack that way. See, here's all the larder stuff; over there is all the cold produce; and at the back are the things I stock up on, like coffee and tea. Separating them out helps me pack it properly with everything in its place, and ensures that unpacking is made easier when I get home. I hate to have raw meat next to salad stuff – ugh!'

'Well, you don't need to justify it to me: it seems like a great system you have there.' His grin grew even larger.

Embarrassed by my noticeable obsessive shopping organization, I tried to look occupied by absentmindedly rearranging the tins of (organic) chick peas and (non-organic) red kidney beans.

'You're a good stacker,' he continued, gesturing the tins.

I smiled and turned back to the conveyor belt.

'One could say you're well stacked,' he sniggered.

I wasn't too sure I had heard him correctly, so gave him a half-smile and pretended something else needed neatening amongst my shopping.

'I said, "You're very well stacked,"' he repeated, and

dropped his gaze so his eyes were level with my T-shirt-clad breasts. He then beamed at me again, and continued feasting his eyes on my boobs. 'Like I said, "well stacked": you've got a great rack!' he said loudly, almost proud of himself for saying something so hilariously funny.

In another situation – with a man my own age – I would have pulled him up on these comments. I would have pointed out that this type of innuendo does not flatter me; that I find such remarks sexist and objectionable; that I would prefer it if my breasts were not stared at and commented upon. Flirting or not, this man's approach was inappropriate: no man has the right to comment on my body. (Unless I have asked him to. Or we are in bed together and his remark about my boobs being large/attractive is related to the fact that he is busy sucking on them.)

But because this man was older than my own father, I felt I should give him a little leeway and be polite to him; age should bring respect from younger people, I think. So I only scolded him gently:

'Let's leave it there, then,' I suggested, aware that his eyes were glued to my nipples. I pulled my jacket over my boobs the best I could to try to cover myself.

He seemed to take the hint and removed his gaze from my chest area, returning to continue stacking his own food on the conveyor belt. Grateful for the pause in sexual innuendo, I began to pack my shopping away whilst the cashier ran the items through the till.

When I had finished paying, I looked over at him, smiled gently, and said goodbye. With a glint in his eye and a mischievous grin, he leaned towards me.

'Keep that rack highly stacked!' he exclaimed, with a hearty giggle.

I smiled awkwardly and made my way to the exit, privately laughing to myself that a man of his age would certainly know a thing or two about droopage.

// posted by thegirl @ 10.22:00 PM

Saturday 22nd July

Craigslist Guy called me last night and invited me over today. I didn't hesitate in saying yes to his invitation. Well, what girl would turn down a ready-meal shag?

So I went there prepared. You know, accidentally missing my underwear; it's all the better for having a quickie, I find.

When I arrived at his place, Craigslist Guy waltzed me into his lounge, sat down on his couch and pulled me up over him. Lifting my dress, he immediately discovered I wasn't wearing any knickers, which made him beam at me, and pulling me closer, he pressed his erection firmly against my groin.

Pleased at the result, I made a mental note to forget to wear pants more frequently – I do rather like to feel a breeze in between my legs, it must be said. Plus, of course, I would save a fortune in lingerie costs.

We ground our hips together and kissed, and I wondered if he would think me rude/greedy/demanding if I asked to grab a condom now, and immediately sit on his cock without any foreplay. As I pondered this – hoping that it would be soon, because I was fucking soaked and probably dripping onto him – he kissed my neck gently and ran his fingers through my hair.

'God, I've missed you so much,' he said and smiled at me as he outlined my mouth with his fingertips. 'It's so good to see you again.'

Like a rabbit paralysed in the headlights, I was in shock, too stunned to speak.

He missed me.

He has met me on only four occasions.

He missed me.

He doesn't know me, we're not friends, and we're certainly not dating.

He missed me.

I sat with my pussy pressed up against his hard cock and felt my slickness dry up almost instantly. There I was, ready to fuck, and he went and dropped that on me: great.

He carried on kissing me and I felt annoyed, violated somehow. He had broken the rules, he had crossed the casual sex boundary: how could I relax and enjoy the sex now that he had brought missing me into the equation?

The answer to that, of course, is that a few minutes later, a little bit of selfishness, combined with a good dose of concentration and a very dirty mind, resulted in my climaxing all over his hand – which seemed to please him as much as it did me. We continued to have more sex after that too: I got spanked, fucked hard from behind and had my pussy licked for half an hour. And I gave him a combined blow-job/hand-job/bum-tickle that'll give him something to wank over for some time, given how hard he shot all over the place.

But all the while, I kept thinking of how my suspicions

about him were right: he seemed to want more out of what we were doing than I did. He wasn't being truthful about what he wanted and I guess neither was I, given I knew he wanted more but continued to have sex with him. Living up to my sexblogger moniker, I guess.

Casual sex, though shallow, can be fantastic, laid-back and lots of fun, but when one party needs more from the other person and it's not reciprocated, someone's feelings inevitably get hurt. This is why I am so completely honest and upfront with the people I sleep with: I don't want them or me to feel shitty about any aspect of our relationship or dalliance at any point.

It's ironic that many people seem to assume that it's just women who go along with casual sex in the hope of it developing into something longer and that men are the ones who want sex and nothing else; in my experience – and certainly from feedback I get from the women who read my blog – the opposite is frequently true. More than once I've been told that a guy really has no interest in more than just an occasional shag, but then he's demanded to see me four times a week and calls me five times a day 'just to talk' – that's not what I would call 'casual'.

Of course, it's a compliment if a guy is that into me, but if we've agreed that the situation is purely casual, having him try to push the intimacy is not only annoying, but can also put a strain on the sex: a one-sided emotional shag is never fulfilling – for either party.

Perhaps this makes me sound brutal or as though I don't want a man to fall for me: that's not true; of course I do. I'd love to meet a special man who finds me intelligent and funny and sexy, and who would be willing to put up with all my neuroses and bossiness and late-night demands for penetration. It would be wonderful to meet a man who sparked my mind, nurtured my soul and set my heart racing and pussy pounding: I hope he's out there. And when we do meet, I'll probably be on my period, looking my worst, tripping up on my big feet and spilling wine down my top – but he'll still think I'm the bee's knees. Fantastic – when it happens, I am ready for it.

But Craigslist Guy is not that man. It's just a shag: casual sex. Nothing meaningful, nothing more. With him expressing an emotional want – small though it was – it was enough for me to accept that I shouldn't see him again.

I will admit that I did – for a brief moment, when he was giving me yet another orgasm – wonder if he and I could, or should, ever be more than fuck-buddies, but I realized I could never date a man who omitted the use of capitals and punctuation in his emails and texts, and who always used smiley-face emoticons at the end of his sentences. I may be a mere sexblogger, but I have some standards.

Guess I'm going to have to break it to him now.

// posted by thegirl @ 12:22:00 AM

Sunday 23rd July

Thankfully, Craigslist Guy seemed to take it well last night. Well, besides trying to convince me to stay longer at his place with the offer of yet another orgasm, that is. You know, as much as I love sex – and god, I do – I wasn't at all tempted to stay, after what he said to me. Maybe I am seeking something more with someone, I don't know; what I do know is that Craigslist Guy and I would never be a couple, and to continue seeing him would have been selfish on my part, and possibly caused us both some hurt.

I really don't need this aggravation in my life, especially with the impending publication of my book, the email press interviews I'm doing about it, and all my worries about trying to maintain my anonymity. I think it's best that I called it a day – even if I will miss the sex.

Monday 24th July

I'm glad I stopped things with Craigslist Guy before things became entangled, but it's made me face up to some things: there are lots of drawbacks to being single.

The loneliness of returning from work and entering an empty flat is horrible. As is not being able to cuddle someone and have them make you forget what a shit day you had, whilst they kiss your forehead and tell you that everything will be OK. And let's not forget making love; your body intertwined with theirs as you shudder simultaneously in your climaxes and smile at each other – knowing that this moment is about the two of you, the love, the mutual passion.

But the thing I am missing most right now about not having a partner is this:

Being able to fuck someone without speaking – and still know that they love you.

I long for the brusqueness of a quick, rampant fuck; the

furiousness of a horny moment where spontaneity rules, but where there is still intimacy and emotion.

- Where my partner opens the door and pulls me inside, pushing me forcefully against the wall, kicking the door shut with his foot as he kisses me intently.
- Where he turns me around and places my hands on the wall; grabbing my hips so I can feel his erection pressed against my arse.
- Where I hear him unzip himself, and then pull my skirt up.
- Where he tugs my pants to one side and slides his cock between my legs.
- Where he pushes himself into me and grabs my arse with his hands.
- Where he pummels me until I can't control it any longer and I frantically try to maintain my balance as my orgasms take over.
- Where I hear him groan and feel him throb as he too lets go.
- Where we then turn to face each other, smile and say 'hello' as we kiss slowly.

There is nothing like the roughness of a hard fuck, blended with the love of a relationship; it is a wonderful and exciting combination. No hard shag with a casual fuck-buddy can ever come close to it. I miss having that intimacy with someone – a lot.

Of course, there are other drawbacks to being single, besides being unable to have a silent, rampant quickie, but somehow, the fact I haven't yet been able to model for a partner my new 'fuck-me' black leather peep-toe five-inch stilettos doesn't really compare. (Even though they are the sexiest shoes I have ever owned and they have been sitting – unworn – in my cupboard for the last few months.)

So I guess my dalliance with Craigslist Guy has made me realize that perhaps I do want more. There's not really much hope for me meeting a guy at the moment, though: my book's due out on the shelves in a few days and I really don't have time or mental space to look after anyone's needs but my own. Plus, I've got to maintain my low profile, so I'll have to continue to play it cool with all my friends and family, and keep up my pretence.

Secretly, though, I am very excited about it. From being a little notepad for my unfiltered thoughts online, to having millions of readers visiting the blog, I never expected the tales of my sex life to one day be up on the shelves at Waterstone's. That makes me very proud, but, more than that, it makes me happy that even more women will read what I've written and relate to it. One thing I've learned, writing about my erotic escapades, is that I'm not the only Girl with a One Track Mind; I'm not alone in having a hearty sexual appetite or in my refusal to accept being labelled as some kind of 'slut' because I do.

I'm a bit worried about how the press are going to take my openness about sex, though, but I guess there's not much I can do about that. At least I have my anonymity as a shield to protect me if they say anything mean about me. Sticks and stones, right?

// posted by thegirl @ 10.53:00 PM

Tuesday 25th July

God, I'm knackered. You'd think I would have recovered from the sex I had with Craigslist Guy, but it would appear that even a brief shag takes a lot out of me these days . . . Not so much that I can't go to a Maxïmo Park gig, though: I bought tickets for Tim and me months ago, so there was no way I was going to miss tonight's gig, shagged out or not.

We stopped off at a bar prior to the show, and I decided to grill Tim to find out if he'd seen First Date Lady again.

'So, how's your love life? Did First Date turn into Second Date?!'

Tim took a deep swig of his beer and shook his head. 'No, sadly, she ended up going back to her ex and cancelled on me. But there was this other woman . . .'

'Ooh, do tell!' I reached for my martini and took a large gulp. 'How did you meet?'

'She knew one of the guys at work and came out with us for drinks one evening. She seemed nice, quite pretty, a good smile, a great arse.'

I laughed. 'You and arses . . . And?'

'And that night she gave me her number and suggested we meet for a drink.'

'Did you?'

'Yep – the next day. She was really keen – totally up for it.'

'So you shagged her?'

'No. She wanted to, but I just didn't go for it.'

'Why not?'

'No chemistry; she didn't stoke my interest at all. No semi – nothing.'

'Sorry to hear that.'

'It's fine, apart from her getting hold of my email address from a colleague the next day, and then sending me a message asking to see me again.'

'Oh dear.'

'Yeah, well I think she's got the message now.'

'Did she take it badly?'

'I don't think so.'

'Well, how did she respond when you told her you weren't interested?'

Tim paused, a guilty expression on his face.

I groaned. 'Please tell me you told her, Tim.'

He looked down at his feet.

'You didn't tell her?' I exclaimed. 'What, you just thought she could read your mind?'

'No. But she got the message that I wasn't interested.'

I stared at him. 'So you sent her a text, then.'

Tim shook his head. 'Look, she knows that I don't want to see her again, OK?'

'Because you didn't contact her at all, right?'

Tim nodded.

'For fuck's sake, Tim, you're such a typical fucking man, do you know that?!'

'What?' he said, grinning at me sheepishly.

'Do you have any fucking idea how horrible it is – how insulting – to have a bloke do that to you?'

He shrugged and avoided my glare.

'Look, let me tell you something about women. When you didn't reply to her email, she didn't get the message.'

He looked up at me, a mild expression of confusion appearing on his face.

'No. For the first three days after she emailed you and had no reply, she would have been worried.'

'Worried?'

'Yes, worried. Worried that she had made a mistake showing interest; that she had acted too keen and should have played it cooler.'

'Well, that's not a big deal.'

'Whatever. Anyway, when she didn't hear from you for another three days, she would have been hurt, wondering why you weren't replying to her email.'

Tim looked indifferent and I felt my temperature rising.

I continued. 'And after feeling hurt, she would begin to feel offended, wondering why it was so hard for you to just email her back. Three more days after that and she would be infuriated and resentful and have angrily deleted your email address.'

Tim shrugged nonchalantly and I was tempted to slap him. 'Look, I don't see what the big deal is,' he said. 'She got the message, that's all that matters.'

'No. What message she got is that you're just like all the other arseholes out there; that you have so little regard for women that you don't even have the decency to be honest with them.'

Tim stayed silent.

'Do you wonder why women end up so pissed off with men?' I asked him. 'Does it not cross your mind that perhaps if men treated us a little better, we would have more respect for you? Do you not realize that when women get drunk together and bitch about how fucking crap men are, it's because of shit like this? You're thirty-five, not thirteen – why can't you just be a grown-up and say what you really think?'

Tim continued his silence, knowing me well enough to understand that it was best for him to do so until I had finished my rant.

'Tim,' I said, exasperated, 'what's wrong with being honest? How difficult would it have been to quickly email her and say, "Thanks for last night; you were good company and I had fun. However, I am not interested in getting into anything more, but thank you anyway"?'

He shrugged again.

'It's just a simple matter of honesty and respect,' I pleaded. 'Common courtesy, that's all. If more men were able to be truthful and stop all this rude "if I ignore them, they'll go away" bullshit, there would be a lot more trust between us and lead to better communication all round.'

'I suppose that's a fair point,' Tim said.

I nodded. 'If we could all just be honest with each other, surely that would make relations between us better in the long run?'

'I guess, yeah. Presumably, the shagging would be better too,' he said, and we both laughed, relieved that the tense atmosphere was broken.

I reached for my martini and swigged its final dregs.

Tim took a deep gulp of his beer. 'So, how's your love life, then?'

'I don't want to talk about it.'

// posted by thegirl @ 11:59:00 PM

Men As Seen By Women's Magazines

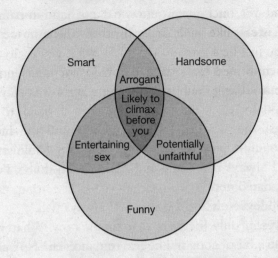

Wednesday 26th July

My conversation with Tim last night has got me all nostalgic. Where did those innocent times go? When kisses meant nothing, and being dumped over email wasn't a concept we could even imagine? I miss those times: nowadays it seems so much weight and importance surrounds dating and sex; maybe it's just the age I'm at?

I remember my first ever boyfriend – if you could call him that – it was love at first sight, for us. After him hurtling towards me with a wide-open toothy mouth during a game of kiss-chase in the playground, we were inseparable.

We were only ten years old but that didn't matter: I adored him. As he did me; he used to send me notes in class.

'I love you,' he would write, in painstakingly methodical

joined-up writing. 'Will you be my girlfriend?'

I said yes, of course, and we'd go hand-in-hand down to P.E., stealing a smile at each other whenever we got the chance.

Somehow he'd even manage to hide love notes in my pencil case, sneaking them into my bag when I was playing netball (Goal Attack position: even then I liked to score). Amongst the Wonder Woman stickers and the Incredible Hulk fountain pen (having progressive-lefty-feminist parents meant I always had Sindy and Action Man dolls), I'd find a new, updated note:

'I still love you,' he'd confirm. 'I always will.'

Ah yes, if only life were that simple now. Whatever happened to a bit of good old honest romance, eh? Nowadays it's all flirty IMs, brief innuendo-filled SMS texts, or teasing tweets; I think a quick handwritten note from a man stating his smitten feelings is far more impressive. And in my case, would guarantee a shag . . .

Anyway, we were in love, which meant

a) I got to boss him around, and – more importantly –
b) I got to kiss him.

Now, we were just kids, so there was no funny business, but even at that age we investigated the use of tongues whilst practising the lip-lock. Most likely our curiosity was due to watching people snog in movies (though really I don't recall that much hot action occurring in *E.T.*, *Star Trek II* or *Tron*) but however we learned of it, it was obviously something we wanted to try out, because we spent a few lunch breaks attempting to suck each other's faces.

He must have been a good kisser, because not only did I kiss him, but so did all my friends. But he wasn't cheating on me behind my back: one day, for some odd reason, I made him stand outside the boiler room and, holding him against the wall, I lined up my friends and made him snog them one by one.

I'm not quite sure what I was hoping to achieve: perhaps I wanted to show him off to them; or maybe I just wanted a second (and third, and fourth . . .) opinion on his kissing skills. Whichever it was, it was done under coercion, and when I was older and a bit more insightful, I felt bad about violating him in this way.

Until, that is, I bumped into him a few years ago. I apologized profusely for what I thought was a terrible, exploitative deed. But he had no memory of the event, and told me not to worry about it. I'm not sure whether I was more troubled by the fact that I had felt unnecessarily guilty about it for almost twenty years and shouldn't have, or instead that the occasion – and therefore me – hadn't made an impression on him at all. Whichever it was, at least I had absolved my guilt – and made him laugh, when I informed him I had kept all his notes. (I still have them, old romantic that I am.)

Hopefully, I make a bit more of an impression on a guy now. Well, at least I no longer have to push a bloke against a wall in order to test out his kissing skills, so I guess that's some progress.

// posted by thegirl @ 10:32:00 PM

Sunday 30th July

I've come to a conclusion: I love my mouth. For starters, I like how it looks. Even in my less narcissistic moments, I enjoy gazing at my mouth. I love the shape, the texture and the deep coral-like colour of my lips; this combination seems so seductive. The thought of covering up these elegant lines and the smooth, silky softness with a thick sticky mess like lipstick seems illogical. Far better to leave my lips as nature intended, freeing me up to indulge in a little bit of occasional thumb-in-mouth action á la Jean-Paul Belmondo in *À bout de souffle*.

I'm not sure whether my affection for my mouth is just down to my liking its appearance, though. I think it's also about the fact that it ticks all my 'pleasure' boxes. For example: eating. Is there anything as delectable as enjoying an explosion of flavour inside your mouth? Let's face it, having food pass your lips is not just about sating hunger; it's more to do with satisfying all those demanding, yet excitable, taste buds, which are just waiting to be titillated by a plethora of juicy mouth-watering morsels. At least, it is in my case: I do love rolling some sexy titbits around my mouth before I swallow.

Obviously, mouths aren't solely for food; with all their nerve-endings, their part in kissing is pretty damn fun too. I adore the glorious sensuality of kissing; I enjoy the gratification that tasting food can bring; I love the sexiness of how my lips look and feel. What else could possibly add to my oral fixation? Well, I suppose there's one other thing that gives me a lot of pleasure . . . When I'm not admiring my lips, putting something between them, or attaching them to another person, I do rather enjoy what comes out of them: speech.

With my large gob, I'm the first to admit I am, quite literally, a loudmouth. I've tried to be that quiet person sitting in the corner: it just isn't me. Given the chance to use my mouth, I do, but that isn't solely because I like the sound of my own voice. Rather, it's just down to the simple fact that I enjoy the feel of words dancing around my tongue and over my lips: it's my version of hedonism.

I do try to bite my lip when in company to offer up a break in my miniature talk-orgy; but usually I just end up with overly nibbled flesh and a sense of frustration. Still, if keeping my smackers shut allows me to indulge in a bit of self-absorbed lip-pouting, I guess that's worth remaining quiet for. Temporarily, anyway.

// posted by thegirl @ 11:39:00 PM

AUGUST

Thursday 3rd August

Something very weird just happened and now I'm really worried.

I was having an afternoon nap when my doorbell rang; it couldn't have been the postman, as he delivered the mail this morning. When I answered the intercom, the person on the other end said they were a courier with a package for my address, so I grabbed an old T-shirt and pulled on a pair of jeans and wandered downstairs in my bare feet to answer the door.

It was a delivery of flowers, which surprised me: who would send them to me? It's not like I'm dating anyone special right now.

The courier asked me to sign for the bouquet, but held the delivery note in such an awkward position that I had to lean all the way out of the door frame to pen my name on his pad. Most odd.

It was only when I had taken the flowers and closed the door behind me that I read the note attached to the bouquet.

'Congratulations on the book, Zoe. Best wishes, Mark' it said.

My heart pounded in my chest and my throat felt so tight that I suddenly found it hard to breathe.

Someone knows about the book. Someone must know that I am Girl with a One Track Mind.

◎

I ran upstairs, into my flat, and slammed the door behind me. Who sent me the flowers? Who could it be that knows?

My first instinct was that maybe someone at my publishers made an error when they were asked to send me a congratulatory bunch of flowers and somehow came across my name in my kept-under-lock-and-key-only-seen-by-lawyers book contract. I might be currently keeping a low profile, but today is, after all, the day my book is published, so I guess it would make sense that my publisher might send me some flowers; I thought I'd call my editor to check.

No dice. After asking around, she confirmed that no one in the department had sent me flowers and that there was no one in the building called Mark. Not even she had seen my contract and neither had anyone else: everyone still knew me only as Abby, not by any other name.

My second instinct was that perhaps Blog Boy was playing a joke on me. He is one of the very few people who know about the book as well as knowing me offline, so perhaps the flowers were a cheeky gift?

'They're not from me,' he said, trying to reassure me on the phone. 'If they were, I would have told you before sending them, so as not to worry you. And I certainly wouldn't have signed using a fake name.'

'Really?' I asked. 'Do you promise me? I'm really freaked out right now . . .'

'I know you are,' he replied. 'I promise you: it wasn't me that sent them to you.'

'Well, someone knows who I am. Someone's trying to let me know that they know.'

'Maybe a fan of your blog has figured it out,' Blog Boy said, cautiously. 'I know some of those guys can be a bit persistent: maybe somehow one of the more creepy ones knows?'

He could be right: with the announcement of the book's publication, the abusive emails I regularly receive had increased ten-fold. Maybe one of the more vitriolic readers who resented me and who disliked what I wrote about was trying to scare me?

'It's possible,' I replied, 'but I doubt it: how would they have found out who I am? I've been so careful not to divulge any clues about me. I mean, not even my agent knows my real name. And it can't be anyone from work: most of them don't even know what a blog is.' I paused in thought for a moment. 'No, I've got a horrible suspicion it's something worse than an over-eager blog reader.'

'What's that?' Blog Boy asked.

'I think the flowers may have been from a newspaper, and – fuck, I can't believe I am saying this – I think they may have taken a secret photograph of me whilst I was signing for the bouquet. Something about the whole thing was just odd.'

'Please don't take this the wrong way, Zoe, but why would a newspaper be interested in you? It's not like you're a celebrity!'

'I know. And I honestly have no idea. Call it my media

instinct: my gut tells me something's very wrong and I just have a horrid feeling a newspaper's involved and that I might be about to get outed.'

'I really hope that doesn't happen; I'm sure it won't, though. There's no story in it; I doubt a newspaper would want to run something on you.'

'I agree. But god, I am worried.'

'I guess all you can do is see if anything surfaces tonight and wait to ride it out.'

'Yeah, I guess so.'

'And if you need anything, just call, OK?'

'Thanks.'

It was good to talk to Blog Boy – I'm so glad we're still friends – but I don't feel very reassured after speaking to him. At the bottom of my stomach is a horrid nagging feeling that my world is about to be thrown upside down and that there's nothing I can do to stop that happening.

Friday 4th August

I'm still worried about the delivery of flowers that I had yesterday, but I've heard nothing since. Surely I'd have received an email or comment left on my blog by now if anything was going to happen? Newspapers act fast, don't they?

Fuck it, I need to get out of my flat, I've got to go outside some time. I think I'll pop down the road and pick up some fruit and veg. Bit of late summery fresh air will do me good.

☺

I just returned from the greengrocer's. I'm now in shock; I'm shaking as I write this.

As I arrived home, someone was leaving a message for me on my home answering machine. 'This is a message for Zoe Margolis,' the woman's voice said. 'My name is Anna Mikhailova, I'm a reporter for the *Sunday Times* and we're running a story on your being Abby Lee, the author of the anonymous sex blog and book *Girl with a One Track Mind*.'

I stopped in my tracks, unable to believe what I was hearing.

The voice continued: 'We've got photographs of you, taken on your doorstep yesterday, but they're not very complimentary and don't give the right image for your persona, Abby Lee. If you agree to do an interview with us, we'll take some more photos at a professional photoshoot . . .'

I didn't hear anything else: I felt vomit make its way up from my abdomen and I ran to the bathroom to throw up.

When I came back into my living room, I stood staring at my answering machine. Now quiet, its only sign of life was the intermittent flashing of the red 'message' button. I could barely move, barely believe what I had just heard.

I must have stood there for three or four minutes, just looking at the blinking electronic device, and running over and over in my mind what the message had said.

They know who I am.

They know about the blog.

They're going to 'out' me.

I was right, in my conversation last night with Blog Boy; I can't believe it.

My heart raced and I racked my brain to try to think what I should do. My first instinct was to go online: maybe I'd find some answers there? I'm not sure what I was looking for, though.

There were four emails from the same journalist in my inbox, each one confirming that the news story was definitely going to be run. In one of the latter emails some photographs were attached: they had indeed taken secret shots of me from my garden; they had used the delivery of flowers as a ploy to get me to my front door. What was this, a 'Cherie Blair moment'? Bastards.

Suddenly, my phone rang once more. I watched and waited for my answering machine to kick in; it was the journalist again, repeating the same message as before, and adding: they were going to print the story, whether I did an interview with them or not.

Feeling my nausea come on again, I ran to my bathroom, with only one thought in my head: what should I do?

☉

I'm freaking out right now. So I turned to Bobby, thinking he might have some advice.

Bobby is a well-known radio personality and, given that I work in media too, we share many acquaintances. Because of this, I immediately trusted him, so even though he had got in touch with me via the blog earlier this year – and I wouldn't usually meet with a reader – we had attempted to go on a date (unsuccessfully, due to our clashing schedules) and had spent some months emailing, texting and chatting on the phone.

So I knew that I would feel safe sharing with him, and given his high profile, he would be able to offer me support and guidance about the press – which I desperately need. More importantly, perhaps, his 'celebrity' status means he understands and respects my need for secrecy. I sent him a blunt text.

> I'm about to get outed. My life, as I know it, is over.

He phoned me immediately. 'Fucking hell! You sound like you need some company – and a drink. Want to meet for a pint?'

'Fuck, yes,' I replied. 'But I'm really scared right now – could I just jump in a cab to yours?'

He agreed and gave me his address; I quickly showered, grabbed a bottle of wine from my fridge and made the decision to hail a taxi: at least I could just jump straight from my front door into the vehicle and travel to Bobby's flat without worrying about navigating London – or any more evil journalists lying in wait.

As the cab made its way through the metropolis I thought about the absurdity of the situation. Here was I, potentially about to have the walls crashing down on my privacy, my anonymity lost forever in a newspaper exposé, the world about to learn all the details of my sex life, and I was off to spend time with a man I'd never met in person, and who knows me only as Abby Lee.

When I hopped out of the cab and we finally did meet in the flesh, you could say it was under very unusual circumstances. I'm there, totally anxious that my personal life is about to be thrust into the limelight; Bobby is in the middle of a major work tsunami; I guess we both appeared a bit stressed when we greeted each other. In addition, though, I still refused to tell him my real name – just in case the newspaper decided not to go ahead with the exposé – and it felt odd to have him call me 'Abby'. I suppose it was no surprise that there was a little awkwardness between us upon meeting.

I wasn't expecting to shag him, though. Even though I'm quite obviously a Girl with a One Track Mind and we were sitting on his sofa, cosily chatting, drinking wine and eating a takeaway, I didn't for one minute think that later on we would be getting naked with each other.

This might have had something to do with his spending more than an hour detailing every girlfriend of his over the last ten years, and how he was currently worrying about the level of romantic interest that another girl had for him. Whilst I was a little bored by him going into such detail about his love-life fuck-ups, I was still enjoying his company: he's a sharp guy, brilliantly witty, very intelligent and pretty handsome, so I actually found it refreshing that he was even more narcissistic and self-absorbed than me.

And his private monologue was, I suppose, a momentary distraction, given my own, current, personal distress. To his credit, he did at one point display some emotional insight, remarking, 'I guess this seems a little trivial, given your present situation.' Well, yes, exactly: my entire private life is about to be thrown into disarray, with god knows what sort of media circus ahead of me, and here is a thirty-five-year-old man fretting over whether a twenty-four-year-old ignoring his text messages 'meant anything'. And I thought I was neurotic . . .

But he was also supportive and offered me some advice, suggesting I ignore what the press say and that I shouldn't be ashamed of what I have written and the life I have led. We continued chatting and I relaxed with him, which is exactly what I needed. After some hours had passed, we both realized it was very late. I had planned on leaving his place by cab, but Bobby suggested I stay:

'It's late, and I think we could both do with a snuggle,' he offered. 'And maybe a little snog.'

He had a point. It would be nice to cuddle someone: I was stressed; he was, well, anxious in his own way. But it was odd to imagine cuddling up to him in bed; there seemed to be zero sexual chemistry between us: at no point in the evening had either of us touched each other in a flirtatious way, let alone kissed. Even with the wine we had drunk, to suddenly share a bed would feel weird. Especially if snuggles led to other things . . .

I broached the subject as best I could:

'Snuggles would be nice,' I agreed. 'But don't you think it'd be a bit strange? We don't know each other, and it's not like we've been gagging to shag each other all evening; I certainly wasn't planning on having sex with you. Not that you're unattractive – it's just, well, my head is all over the place, and if we were going to do it, I don't think tonight would be the best time.'

He nodded in agreement. 'We could have a limit on what we do,' he suggested. 'Maybe just cuddle and kiss; no more.'

I nodded back at him.

'And,' he continued, 'I'd feel a bit shit if we did shag, because I've been going on all night about that other girl; it'd be a bit rude if I then fucked you.'

Well, precisely. So we agreed that sex was out, but cuddles were in, and we made our way to his bedroom.

We sat on the bed, fully clothed, and I suddenly felt embarrassed. It was the weirdest thing: I don't particularly have an issue with my body – but here I was, with all my clothes on, and I felt exposed.

'This is really odd,' I said. 'I don't think I've ever been in this situation before: getting into someone's bed to cuddle them, without, at least, having some prior minor flirtation. How should we do this? Clothed? In underwear? I'm tempted to ask you for a T-shirt for me to wear . . .'

'You're welcome to one,' he said, 'but I always sleep naked.'

'So do I,' I replied, truthfully.

We agreed to remove our clothes simultaneously, jumping into bed as we did so.

'You've got a great body,' he remarked, as he snuggled up against me.

'Thanks,' I replied, feeling his erection pressing against my thigh, the familiar throbbing between my legs begin, and I wondered how long it would be before our cuddling became more intimate.

Not long, evidently: he began to rhythmically push himself against me, and as we kissed, he pulled my leg up over his, so his thigh was pressed up against my wet groin – this was no longer an 'innocent' cuddle. I decided to respond to his movements, and rubbed myself against his thigh; his cock sliding against my lower belly as I did so.

'We're not doing very well on the snuggling,' he teased, and ran his hands all over my body, ending up on my nipples, coaxing them into hard peaks.

'That might have something to do with the fact that you're grinding your cock against me,' I joked, as my fingers discovered his chest hair, his solid back, his curvaceous arse.

'Mm,' he replied, and kissed me some more. We resumed our embrace and my earlier thoughts – that I wasn't that attracted to him; that we had no particular sexual chemistry; that I didn't really want to sleep with him – were banished from my mind as his fingers skilfully entered me, and a moment later I climaxed hard, all over his hand.

So much for my rule about not shagging celebrities.

Later, after I'd given him an explosive blow-job/hand-job combo and we were both lying back in a post-orgasmic haze, he asked me if our not having intercourse could still be described as us having 'sex'. I laughed, and reminded him that regardless of penile penetration, any orgasms occurring count as sex. (Especially the three intense orgasms I had had . . .)

Soon after, he fell asleep. I, however, lay awake all night, thoughts of losing my anonymity running through my head; my heart racing in panic as I considered all the ways in which my life might change as a result. I began to realize that the sex with Bobby had offered me some freedom; a momentary, but much needed, escape from my reality and the worry I was feeling. I wanted the gratification on offer. And he too had his own reasons for needing my company and sexual release.

In the morning, I curled up behind him and gently caressed

AUGUST

him all over his body. It wasn't long before I had his firm cock throbbing in my hand, as I stroked him lightly.

'What are you trying to do?' he murmured sleepily, and turned to face me.

'Wake you up,' I lied, when what I meant was: 'Get you horny and hard, so that I can fuck you.'

We moved together for a while, stroking each other. I noticed that he was avoiding eye contact with me; I put it down to his tiredness, but my gut feeling was that he was dissociating for a reason. I was right: suddenly, with no warning, he pushed me away and jumped out of bed.

Ignoring the internal analysis beginning to surface in my head, I focused on the throbbing between my legs instead: I didn't want to think, I needed to feel something.

'Got time for a quickie?' I said coyly, giving him my most seductive look.

'No,' he replied bluntly. 'I've got a very busy day ahead.' He stood there shifting uncomfortably, still avoiding my gaze.

'It wouldn't take long,' I persisted, pushing the duvet away to reveal my hand sliding between my legs. 'I am soaking wet,' I added huskily, hoping that might convince him into jumping on top of me.

'I'm sure you are,' he said coldly, and turned away from me before exiting the room.

The one-night stand was finished; my instincts were right – I've had enough casual fucks to know when a guy is done. And Bobby's behaviour was clear: he wanted me out; he had no interest in pursuing any more intimacy.

I lay there for a moment with my thoughts; it'd been a while since I'd experienced such outright sexual rejection,

147

and it took me a minute to comprehend my feelings about it. Bar getting neurotic (if a guy doesn't like my sexual appetite, well, fuck him, I say), I felt hurt by the way he behaved, rather than the rejection itself: I'm an adult – I can take someone turning me down.

Bobby may have been tired and have had a busy day ahead; he may have not felt up to shagging; he may have been turned off by my horniness; he may have wished I was the other girl who was in his thoughts; he may even have – in the light of day – realized that he actually wasn't attracted to me and wanted some immediate distance; but with a little tact, some politeness and, perhaps, a little honesty on his part, he could have ensured that things were left between us in a respectful and amicable way. One-night stands don't have to result in coldness between the participants, but this one did. As a result, whatever friendship we might have had is unlikely to develop further, which, given our chats over the last few months, saddens me.

With Bobby's brusque rejection ringing in my ears, I lay on his bed, a little hurt, horny as hell and wondering what to do. Given the situation, I ended up doing what any normal woman would: I slid my hands between my legs, had a quick, silent wank and then a decent, but brief, orgasm.

And then I wiped my wet fingers off on his bed sheets.

Shortly afterwards, when he came back into the room with a coffee in his hand, I was already in my bra and pants and he was none the wiser.

I departed his flat a few minutes later, waving him goodbye, with not so much as a peck on the cheek from him.

Hopping into a passing cab, I then phoned my mum:

'I know it's early in the morning, but there's something important I need to tell you,' I said. 'I'm on my way over now.'

I spent the rest of the cab journey crying.

Saturday 5th August

Thirty minutes later, I arrived at my parents' house. They were still in their dressing gowns, and offered me breakfast, which I gratefully accepted. Over tea, toast and Marmite, they asked me what was wrong, and I sat there, trying to explain what was happening.

The thing is, my parents are not what you'd call old-fashioned or narrow-minded. They are open, honest people, and have always been upfront with me about sex: there was no shame about the topic in my household when I was growing up. Nevertheless, of all the difficult discussions one might have with one's parents, divulging to them that I have a book out featuring my most intimate sexual experiences and thoughts pretty much comes top of that list. My parents wouldn't chastise me for what I've done, but do they really need to read about how often I masturbate? No. So confessing about the book was going to be a challenge: on the one hand trying to emphasize the positive – 'But my book's doing really well on Amazon!' – contrasted with: 'My identity is about to be revealed, and you might be embarrassed by people reading the book because it is, er, very explicit.'

It wasn't easy telling them. My mum, certainly no prude, asked me straight up if it was pornographic. My writing was explicit, I told her, not pornographic: I never wrote with the objective of titillating, and amongst the graphic depictions of sex, my blog was filled with thoughts, feelings and debates about sex: a very, very personal diary.

We talked for some while, me trying to explain why I had not told them the truth prior to this; why I had divulged intimate details of my sex life by writing about it on the Internet; that it had been read by millions and become so popular that I obtained a book deal; and that a newspaper had somehow found out it was me behind it all and was going to reveal my identity in an article. They listened intently and their expressions were focused and serious. I guess I was scared they would judge me, or be upset with me, but I underestimated my parents: when I had finished my difficult explanation, they both looked at each other, then at me, and told me, almost in perfect unison, that they loved me.

I broke down into tears: I am so lucky to have them.

☙

After the third pot of tea, my dad suggested I check my email.

'Just in case,' he said. 'Perhaps they won't be running the story?'

I nodded in agreement, and we all trudged upstairs to my mum's office and I logged in to my email on her computer; I tried to remain hopeful.

But this is what I found in my inbox:

Aug 5, 2006 11:08 AM

Dear Miss Margolis,

We intend to publish a prominent news story in this weekend's paper, revealing your identity as the author of the book, *Girl with a One Track Mind*.

We have matched up the dates of films you have worked on – *Harry Potter and the Order of the Phoenix*, *Batman Begins* and *Lara Croft Tomb Raider* – and it is clear that they correlate to your blog. We have obtained your birth certificate, and details about where you went to school and college.

We propose to publish the fact that you are 33 and live in [my address] – London, and that your mother, [her name], is a [her profession] – based [her address]. The article includes extracts from your book and blog, relevant to your career in the film industry. We also have a picture of you, taken outside your flat.

Unfortunately, the picture is not particularly flattering and might undermine the image that has been built up around your persona as Abby Lee. I think it would be helpful to both sides if you agreed to a photo shoot today so that we can publish a more attractive image.

We are proposing to assign you our senior portrait photographer, [his name], and would arrange everything to your convenience, including a car to pick you up. We would expect you to provide your own clothes and make up. As the story will be on a colour page, we would prefer the outfit to be one of colourful eveningwear.

We did put this proposal to you yesterday, but heard nothing back. Clearly this is now a matter of urgency, and I would appreciate you contacting me as soon as possible. To avoid any doubt we will, of course, publish the story as it is if we do not hear from you.

Yours sincerely,
Nicholas Hellen
Acting News Editor
Sunday Times

As soon as I read it, I began to cry. I turned away from the computer and faced my parents, who were stood behind me. Barely able to compose myself, I pointed at the screen.

'Look,' I said, my voice stammering. 'You both need to look at it.'

It was one thing to expose me in a newspaper and throw my life into upheaval; but it was another thing altogether to violate my mother's privacy too.

I waited for my mum and dad to finish reading the email and was unable to prevent myself sobbing out loud whilst they did so. I was so worried about the effect the article would have on my mum's job and her private life: how could they bring her into it?

Maybe I should just cave in to the newspaper's demands? If it meant they left my mum out of it, then it would be worth it. When my mother finished reading the email, I told her I would do whatever the newspaper wanted – participate in their fucking photoshoot, or give them the interview they had been demanding – if it meant they excluded information about her. I was ready to comply, cave in and submit to their threats: it was worth it to protect my mum and my family.

You know what my mother said?

'Fuck them.'

She told me not to dignify the email with a response and that I should continue to ignore their phone calls and emails.

'Let's take what they throw at us,' she said. 'We're with you all the way.'

As the tears streamed down my face in gratitude and relief, my mum hugged me and told me that whatever happened, she and my dad would be behind me and back me up. I am so grateful for their unconditional love and support; I am very lucky to have it.

And now I wait for my private life to be thrown to the wolves. I feel like vomiting. Again.

⊚

It's Saturday night and I am waiting for all hell to break loose tomorrow when the newspaper article comes out. I am hoping, of course, that they decide not to run the piece, and that it will all be forgotten about, but the *Sunday Times*' last email to me makes me think I should prepare for the worst. I need to ensure that if people find out that I have a book coming out with explicit details about my sex life, then they should hear it from me, not in any scummy news story – who knows what rubbish it will say about me?

I decided to telephone a few people, starting with my grandmother.

'I need you to know something,' I began, unsure of how to approach the subject. How does one tell one's ninety-year-old grandparent that they've written thousands of words about their sex life; that they have a predilection for blow-jobs; that they dream of being sandwiched between two men, one hand on each cock; and that all these things are known by the millions of people who have read their sex blog?

I guess the answer is: you don't. My grandma is of a different generation: one for whom 'crap' is an offensive word. I imagine she wouldn't think much of me were she to know how often I use the word 'fuck' . . .

'What's wrong?' she asked, gently. 'Are you OK?'

'Not really,' I said, stifling my tears. 'Something's about to happen that is going to have a big impact on me and my life, and potentially on you as well, and I just wanted you to hear it from me, first, rather than be faced with other people's lies.'

I explained that I hadn't been truthful with her: that I wasn't just a runner on a film set, but that I also spent my time writing, which had led to a book about my sex and dating life being published. And, I continued, it is very explicit, but I had written it all anonymously, because it was very truthful and honest, and now a newspaper was about to name me in an exposé, so I was very upset.

There was silence at the other end of the line, and the panic set in for a moment: maybe she would be ashamed of me? I counted the seconds until she spoke and my heart raced.

'Zoe,' my grandma eventually said. 'Did writing this book make you happy?'

'Yes,' I answered truthfully, it had.

'Then I am proud of you,' she said.

My heart skipped a beat. 'Really?'

'Yes,' she replied. 'If you're happy with it, then I am happy for you.'

'Oh, thank goodness,' I exclaimed. 'I was so worried you would be ashamed of me.'

'Ashamed? You're my granddaughter: I love you.'

I started to weep as her words sank in, partly from relief and partly from the overwhelming love I felt from – and for – my grandma.

'It's not going to be nice, all of this,' I warned her. 'I think the article will be horrible and make me out to be a bad person.'

'Well, we all know that's not true,' she said, reassuringly. 'And you know that whatever happens, I love you. You just call me if you need anything.'

With that, we said goodbye, and I breathed out a massive sigh of relief. I guess if my grandma was OK with it, then maybe other people in my life would be too?

Now was the time to confess to Tim and Kathy and Fiona. Each of them asked me, when I rang them, why I felt I had to lie to them all this time: surely I would want to share my good news about the book? I tried to explain that I just didn't want them – my closest friends – knowing all of my sexual activities and reading about my innermost neurotic thoughts. So in order to keep my anonymity protected, I hid it all from them. They voiced understanding, support and sympathy, but I could sense they felt a bit betrayed by me; understandable, really. I asked each of them to promise not to read the book or blog, and, to my relief, they all agreed.

I'm not sure I can ask everyone to promise this, though. I'm dreading my colleagues finding out: I'll never be taken seriously on the film-set floor again.

Sunday 6th August

I didn't sleep last night, through worrying about it all. At 6 a.m. this morning, my dad went to the newsagent's and picked up a copy of the paper. The story was in there, page three of the news section. Page three! How could revealing my identity be considered such worthy news? Not only that, it was illustrated with the secret photograph they snapped of me in my front garden. Thank god they pixellated out my face: it was a dreadful picture.

It was awful seeing my real name in print, and being described in the article as 'shameless', 'sordid' and 'seedy'. Granted, I am not ashamed of the sex I have had, and granted, I've graphically described some pretty explicit experiencees, but why attack me for those things? What's wrong with having a healthy attitude to sex? I bet if I was a bloke they would have called me a 'stud' instead.

Worst of all, perhaps, was the headline the newspaper plastered over the piece: 'By Day She Worked On Harry Potter, But By Night . . .'. I had no idea what response my bosses on the movie would have upon reading this, but I knew one thing: it wouldn't be good. I felt utterly sick to my stomach just thinking about it.

At 9 a.m., things went ballistic. My phones – both my 'Abby' phone and my private mobile – began ringing off the hook.

I think I need to post something on my blog about the newspaper exposé and set the record straight about what has happened. If I don't, the online world will just gossip, and it's better for them to hear it from the horse's mouth than believe any rumours.

I'm in no mood to write – I'm feeling far from cheerful – but I've got to pull it together. Otherwise they'll have won; they'll have shut me up.

☺

Dear blog readers,

Just days after the publication of my book, my true identity has now been publicized in a national newspaper exposé.

I guess I was lulled into a false sense of security regarding my anonymity because my identity has been hidden for a number of years, and I know of other sexbloggers who have been hounded by the press, yet still managed to keep their identities private. Whilst I may have a high-traffic blog, and now a book in the shops which details my sexual adventures, I've not done anything illegal, or written about shagging a politician, or led a secret life as a prostitute so why, I figured, would anyone really be interested in who I am?

For the last few days, a journalist from the *Sunday Times* newspaper has been pursuing me. They have invaded my privacy, violated my boundaries and subjected me to constant harassment on my personal ex-directory home telephone. They have also accosted me on my own doorstep in order to take a secret photograph of me; the photographer hid in my front garden in order to get the shot.

157

I have no wish to give this newspaper extra publicity, but I do want to state for the record that I had nothing to do with this article, and that none of the information in it came from me. I also want to ask the people who have read it not to take it at face value: it's just a 'story', and one in which I had no input. And the outcome of it is that my life is no longer a private matter.

Knowing that the news has broken today – regardless of my wishing to remain anonymous – has meant I have been forced to tell my family my situation. They now know about the blog and book and are aware of the explicit content of each; to my immense relief, they've all been wonderfully supportive.

With my real identity now thrust into the spotlight, I don't think I will be able to post on the blog in the way I once did. I do hope to be able to continue to voice my thoughts – in whatever way I can – somehow, though.

Thanks for your understanding and support,
Abby

// posted by thegirl @ 1:32:00 PM

Monday 7th August

It's the following morning and my dad just called me into the living room. Peering out into the street from behind the closed curtain, he gestured that I should come over. I looked through the tiny gap in the curtain and saw what he was looking at: four paparazzi photographers were camped out in the street outside my parents' house, their foot-long lenses pointed in the direction of the windows and front door.

Oh god, what have I got my parents involved in?

❧

The paps keep ringing the doorbell and trying to poke their camera lenses through the letterbox. My dad's tried to stick a sheet of paper against it, to prevent them doing so, to no avail. I feel trapped, with nowhere to go, hiding at the back of the house. I keep shaking all the time; I guess it's nerves. I can barely eat anything I'm so anxious.

My upstairs neighbour telephoned me earlier, to say there were photographers outside our flats too, and that she had told the journalist from the *Daily Mail*, who was asking questions about me, to fuck off. I thanked her and apologized profusely: who else is going to be affected by this?

❧

This never seems to end. My phone has not stopped ringing. Newspapers, radio stations and television news stations: all wanting to interview me. Where did they get my telephone number from? I even got a phone call from *The Richard and Judy Show*: how can they possibly expect me to appear on television when all I want to do is hide? I'm not used to this attention, I have no idea how to deal with it: I've rejected all approaches. I just want to disappear.

If it's not the media pursuing me, it's my work colleagues bombarding me with phone calls; or friends and acquaintances

I've not spoken to in years – all of them hearing about the blog and book via yesterday's newspaper article, and wanting more gossip about it, no doubt.

Can you believe an old friend from a decade ago, Ronan, phoned me earlier and said he'd been offered money by a tabloid to 'spill some beans' about me. I'm no celebrity; why would anyone be interested in me? Why won't they leave me alone?

After Ronan telephoned (and promised he would say 'no comment' to the paper) I decided not to answer any more calls. I just can't cope with any more of this.

☾

My mobile just rang again. This time the number of one of my line managers appeared on its screen; I couldn't avoid this call.

'You're the only thing people are talking about on set, you know,' he informed me.

Yes, that's what I keep hearing: I've had dozens of calls from members of the film crew telling me that everyone's talking about me and that they've printed out bits of the blog and are reading it on set, trying to find out who I've written about. Every time my phone rang, I felt more and more anxious, waiting for the inevitable call. And here it was; I could hardly breathe on the phone.

'The producers called an emergency meeting about it,' he continued. 'It took most of the morning: everyone was panicking.'

'A meeting? I . . .'

'The press,' he interrupted. 'They've been all over us: kids' movie and sex, you know how it is. We had to get a plan of action in place to deal with them.'

I felt my stomach tightening up into a tiny ball.

'Anyway, I think the worst is over now. But you've caused quite a storm here, you should know that.'

'I'm so sorry,' I said, my voice beginning to stutter from the tears I was holding back. 'I had no idea this would happen, it was all out of my control. Please, I want to assure you, I will not disclose anything about the production. I'm not going to talk about the film to anyone, I promise.'

My stomach was now a tight knot.

'Good. Anyway, I just wanted to see how you were, and to say well done: looks like you're quite the notorious author now.'

'Well, I guess . . .'

'I'm sure you're going to be a huge success.'

'I don't know about that . . .'

There was a pause. 'You do realize that the bridge has been permanently burned now?' he added.

This was what I was waiting for: the final outcome. How could they take me back under their wing now? No film producer would touch me: they'd never hire someone who had brought bad press to their door. In the freelance film world where your reputation precedes each job you are hired for, my career, inevitably, is finished.

I remained silent on the phone. What could I say? I was sorry, but it wasn't my fault: I didn't write the headline, I never named the films I was on; I never identified any of the people I worked with. I knew losing my anonymity would be bad, but I guess I hadn't grasped that in one brief moment the career I had spent ten years working towards would suddenly be removed from my grasp. It hurt.

'Anyway,' he continued. 'I wish you all the best. I hope your career as a writer goes from strength to strength.'

I feel too sick in my stomach to agree with him, but there's a small part of me that very much hopes he is right. What else have I got?

Wednesday 9th August

So many people are spreading vicious rumours about me right now. Not only am I trying to contend with the damage this article has done to my personal and work life, but the response on the Internet has been overwhelming. Reading the accusations that my 'outing' is part of some publicity campaign to increase book sales is so unbelievably hurtful. Here I am, watching my life fall apart in front of my eyes, and they're suggesting I signed up for this? That I wanted this to happen? If they could see how much I'm crying right now, how I've been unable to eat for the last week, how I cannot sleep for all my anxiety, then they'd change their tune.

Maybe I need to counteract their lies and accusations by challenging them on the blog. I guess this is what they call 'Damage Limitation', right?

Thursday 10th August

These past few days have been hell. It's like I am living in some alternate dimension where nothing seems real, and I am stuck in a kind of nightmare.

I have had to deal with my entire family knowing that I write an explicit personal sex diary, the contents of this publicly thrust into their faces; all my friends are now aware of the most intimate details of my sex life; I am the primary gossip on the film set and am receiving dozens of phone calls from work colleagues.

I have been in hiding for the last seven days, scared to go out, because photographers have been camped outside my flat, and also my parents' home. I don't want to be confronted by the journalists pursuing me or have more 'paparazzi' shots taken.

Journalists have also been contacting people from my past – even the vaguest acquaintances of mine – and offering them money to talk about me, or provide photographs of me. They've approached my neighbours too, who are fed up of seeing men with long-lens cameras standing in our front garden.

My phones have not stopped ringing: somehow the press has got hold of both my 'Abby' phone and my personal number and they are driving me mad with their requests for interviews. To begin with I just turned everything down; now I'm just letting voicemail pick up instead.

I have not known how to deal with any of this new, odd, unwanted 'celebrity'-type interest in my life: I've had no guidance to assist me. All I've felt I can do is apologize to everyone potentially affected – my family, friends, neighbours, colleagues, acquaintances, lovers – for any intrusion into their lives. Needless to say, I've not been sleeping very well the last few days.

I am still completely stunned that anyone would find me or my life remotely interesting, and I had hoped that things would have settled by now, and that I could continue my life without any more invasions of my and others' privacy, but sadly this is not the case.

Because of this media focus, I have decided to deal with the situation face on: it's just not possible for me to sit indoors hidden away for ever. So I have agreed to do an interview with the *Guardian* newspaper, published tomorrow. I am hoping, perhaps naively, that this might counteract potentially derogatory tabloid pieces, or, at least, that these papers might get bored of harassing me, and move on to 'proper' news, say perhaps the Middle East, Iraq or the UK government's foreign policy. Well, I can but hope.

// posted by thegirl @ 12:32:00 PM

Saturday 12th August

My dad came into the kitchen just now, a glum look on his face. Immediately I worried: what now?

'You know how the press are camped outside?' my dad said, somewhat hesitantly.

'Yes?'

'Well, I kept seeing them go in and out of their vans, and I'm sick of it, sick of the way they are harassing you – harassing us.'

'I'm so sorry, I wish I could make them go away.'

My dad nodded. 'Anyway, I got fed up, and so when I went to buy the paper just now I thought I'd have a word with one of them – tell them to get lost.'

'You approached them?!' My anxiety shot up again. What did he say to them?

'Sort of . . .' My dad looked over at my mum, who was sitting there with a half-formed smile on her face. Was this some kind of joke?

'And?'

'And I went up to one of the vans, peered in the darkened windows, and expected some photographer to be sat in there with a long lens on his camera.'

'Was there?'

'No. It was empty.'

I exhaled quietly.

'But as I was peeking into the van, this guy comes up to me.'

'Oh? The pap?'

'No. Worse.'

My mum giggled softly.

I was confused. 'Who, then?'

'This bloke comes up, says, "Oi! You! What the fark are you farking doing looking into me farking van, eh?"'

'I still don't get it! Who was the guy?'

My dad grinned. 'Some builder – livid because he thought I was trying to nick his tools.'

'Hah!'

'And it took every bit of negotiating skill I have to try to convince him not to punch me!'

'Bloody hell.'

'Yep.' My dad got up to put the kettle on. 'I think the paps have gone now, thank god: I didn't see any when I went out.'

I breathed a sigh of relief. Maybe, just maybe, the worst is over now.

Monday 14th August

I am pleased to say that photographers are no longer camped out in my, or my parents' front garden, thank goodness. But the 'naming' of me last week has had some longer lasting drawbacks: ones which I am still trying to comprehend and cope with.

I feel I need to explain myself here. One of the reasons I wanted to remain anonymous was not because I am in any way ashamed of my lifestyle, interests or beliefs – the opposite, in fact – but because I was worried that the people whom I've been intimate with might recognize themselves in my writing.

There's no way I could have expounded on my thoughts if I knew a guy would be reading what I had written about him; I'm far too insecure to want a bloke to know, in such fine detail, what's going on in my head. Unless, of course, he thinks it's really cute that I always spill wine down my top; or he finds it adorable that I'm really clumsy; or he's seen me first thing in the morning with my stupidly frizzy hair, and still wants to shag me rotten. But divulge my most intimate thoughts and feelings before then? Not a chance.

Hence my writing the blog – and book – anonymously: doing so gave me the freedom to write about all my obsessions, worries and neuroses, and explore them in relation to my own, personal sex life; I could talk about people and situations and try to make sense of my feelings; I could be open about events. That is, until now. Now I've got a large chunk of my life – the most intimate part – available for all to see. Now all the people I've written about, albeit disguised, also have their lives and their sex lives available for all to see.

I've got to admit, when I was 'outed' last week, I was tempted to delete the entire blog immediately; it was my first instinct to protect the people I had written about, as well as myself. But if I had, it would suggest that I was ashamed or embarrassed by my writing or my life – I'm not. And I can't delete an entire book.

So when a number of ex-lovers contacted me these past few days, it was with some relief on my part that the majority congratulated me – before asking, 'Who'll play me in the movie?!' – rather than stating, 'I'm really upset by what you said.' I've never been purposely derogatory or bitchy about the people I've slept with; it was the invasion of their privacy I was worried they'd be hurt by. Which is why I disguised so many of their personal details: I wanted to protect them from any embarrassment or distress.

Even though I have had photographers hounding me, and journalists poring through my entire blog archives and book, door-stepping my friends, looking for 'seedy' stuff to print about me; even though my family, friends, colleagues

167

and ex-lovers have been reading all about my private life; even though I have had to field hundreds of enquiring calls and emails, I have decided to leave my blog as it is, take a deep breath and deal with things head-on, come what may.

I'm scared, but I can't hide away forever.

// posted by thegirl @ 3:56:00 PM

Friday 18th August

I've got to admit something: I need a man.

With all that's happened and my life being held up to public scrutiny, spending the evening in the company of a fine gentleman would make me feel a whole lot better right now. I'd like nothing more than to curl up in a guy's arms and cuddle him all night. Not to mention get fucked hard too. But – and the irony of my being a sex diarist does not escape me – even this is not very likely for me.

For a quick shag, there's always the possibility I could call up a trusted ex-fuck-buddy for some emergency sex. Broaching the possibility of shagging them strikes me as somewhat difficult, though, given their knowledge of my present circumstances:

Me (after the small-talk): So, do you fancy having some fun?
Them: [Silence.]
Me: I promise not to write about it.

Them: On page 42 you said the guy 'shagged like a rab-
bit'. Was that me?
Me: [Silence.]
Them: [Silence.]
Me: Sorry . . .
Them: [The sound of a telephone hanging up.]

I could contact Craigslist Guy for a quick one-on-one, and he
would certainly fuck me well, but I don't think that would be
fair; I'm really not the sort of person who could just use him
like that, given I know he wants more with me.

I suppose I could go out and meet a new guy at a bar, or a
party, but I don't really fancy jumping into bed with a complete stranger; right now, I need more familiarity and intimacy than that – I'm feeling a bit fragile.

Besides, given how much I have written about other people's bedroom habits, if I shagged someone who knew about
my blog, or book, there's always the possibility that they
might report what I was like in bed; it's only fair, after all.

'You've got no worries about that,' Blog Boy reassured me
a few days ago, when I was anxious and tearful about it on
the phone. 'No one, I repeat no one, could ever say you were
a bad lover.'

It was nice of him to say, and it boosted me to hear it, but
it wasn't enough to assuage my fears: I'm barely taking phone
calls right now, let alone feeling confident enough to start up
anything with someone new.

At the moment it seems I am fucked whatever I do. But just
not in the way I'd like, sadly.

Saturday 19th August

I've been getting so many 'unknown' phone calls recently and such a multitude of text messages that my nerves are on edge; I feel like I don't know who to trust – people are coming out of the woodwork all over the place.

Because of that, I've been a bit oversensitive, I think. This resulted in my sending the following message, after receiving a series of anonymous texts from an unfamiliar mobile phone number:

> If you're going to send anonymous texts, at least ensure you use the correct grammar and capitalize your words. In sending me this childish crap, you have only highlighted your immense stupidity, and that's made me even more sure that I have no interest in meeting up for a drink – let alone the fact that I don't know who you are.

Do not do this, even if you are stressed out and think you are a smart-arse intellectual snob like me. Because, inevitably, the texts will be from an old boyfriend of more than a decade ago, Chris, who, after being insulted about his poor grasp of the Queen's English, will then phone up and angrily demand an apology, whilst accusing you of being unsympathetic to the fact that he left school at fifteen and never had a formal education.

My feet might be big at size eight-and-a-half, but evidently I am more than able to get them both into my mouth at the same time.

Sunday 20th August

Yesterday's text fiasco – I had to spend a good five minutes apologizing to Chris – has reminded me of something that I really value in a guy: word play. Words excite me, they really do. Chris was wonderful in many ways, but he just didn't have the vocabulary with which to impress me: show me a man who has a way with words and, in typical Girl with a One Track Mind style, you'll find me with very wet pants. It's the best aphrodisiac in my opinion; forget good looks or a trim physique – find me a wordsmith any day and I'll be a happy woman.

I don't refer to a man's ability to be talkative, though: that is something completely different. Rather, someone who knows how to be a linguist; who can use his tongue for more than just licking pussy.

Perhaps I've always been turned on by men who can do this because it shows a certain dexterity of their minds: an ability to analyse; a propensity to deconstruct; a questioning of ideology; a cogitation on ideas. Or, in other words, think far beyond their cocks.

Too often I have met and conversed with men who are unable to move past the fact that they have a stiffy in their pants; their communication seems solely limited to their being horny – and it shows. 'Mmm, baby!' a guy might holler, as you wait to be served by the bartender. 'You're damn fine! What's your name?' You turn and spot them copping an eyeful of your tits, arse, or, if you're very unlucky, your crotch. If they were a cartoon character, their tongue would be on the floor with drool appearing out the corner of their mouths. Not very attractive, by any means.

There is nothing wrong with expressing one's horniness and desire to fuck the other person, but when that is the only way a guy can relate to a woman, it does get rather tiresome.

Men who aren't able to stimulate my mind bore me, and men that are boring turn me off; without a mental challenge, I make my excuses and leave, even if it means forgoing an orgasm. Admittedly, I have fucked a few dull, non-conversational men, but I've rarely gone back for seconds afterwards. With no decent conversation the orgasms become rather mundane, in my opinion, and rarely worth the effort. Faced with such a man, I might as well wank: at least I'd be done quicker. And wouldn't have to wax my nether regions either.

Selfish this might sound, it's true. But being with a man who has a way with words makes my heart race with excitement: I'll be picking out what dress to wear a week in advance of a date with him; consuming as much literature, current affairs and media as I can, to be able to converse with him in an equally intellectually stimulating way. And of course wanking furiously before meeting up with him too, so that I ensure the connection between us is cerebral, rather than purely clitoral.

If only more guys realized this, they could avoid using tired chat-up lines; in my case they'd be far more likely to get into my pants if they showed off their brains, rather than their ever-hard cocks.

Although I'd also be quite partial to one of those right now, it has to be said. But I really don't feel like I can say that on my blog. Not with so many people I know reading it.

The Girl's Guide To:
Flirty emailing

1. If you're going to flirt, try to be original. Copying and pasting someone else's quips will get you busted eventually.
2. Avoid puns at all times. Don't ask why, just believe me: puns are never sexy.
3. Spellcheck. There is no excuse for bad spelling or grammar. Laziness is not a get-out here.
4. Likewise, make sure you capitalize properly: you may think you're being post-modern writing in all lowercase; but the recipient will just think you're illiterate. Never a good opening for potential nookie.
5. Don't write in txt spk:
   a) this is the wrong medium for shortened words
   b) people who write in txt spk are lazy, ergo: crap in bed.
6. Step away from the emoticons. Do not pass GO. Do not collect £200.
7. Wordplay can be fun, but make sure you check your thesaurus first: it's not impressive if even you don't understand the words you're using.
8. Be succinct. No one wants to read a book-length email. Get to the point; use ironic bullet points if necessary.
9. Warmth and wit are useful tools; arrogance and self-absorption aren't. In other words, ask the recipient of your emails questions; don't just talk about yourself.
10. By all means use innuendo and double entendres. But you're taking your life into your own hands if you attempt to flirt whilst alluding to sexual activity with an ex. Trust me on this.

Monday 21st August

Hey Zoe, how's it going? Wat u up to?

Another text message from a number I don't recognize. I hit reply:

Who is this? I don't have your number in my phone book . . .

He texted straight back.

It's Dan. Long time . . . How u bin?

A blast from the past: someone I used to work with many years ago. I've been getting a lot of those recently: hearing from people I haven't spoken with for years; people I haven't seen since I was at school. None of them randomly contacting me; all of them know about the book and blog one way or another.

With so many strangers calling me, my modus operandi now is to ignore a call if I don't recognize the number on my phone, so that I can then prepare a suitable response after listening to my voicemail – it's a good self-protective mode. Tim recently recommended I also add the letters 'DNA' – Do Not Answer – in my phonebook to the numbers of people I don't wish to speak with. Ordinarily I would have teased him for suggesting such a thing, given his childishness at dealing with dumping women, but right now I think his idea is a good one.

Really, though, there are only very few people that this would apply to: Dan is one of them. This was, after all, the man who, when his orgasm was achieved, would stand up, put his clothes on and tell me he had to leave. When I pointed out that I was pre-orgasmic and needed some relief, he responded with,

'I'm sure you can sort yourself out.'

Well, yes, of course I can, but that's not the fucking point, is it? I spent many a night frustrated – in every sense – when Dan and I were seeing each other. I have no idea why I fucked him so many times when it was always so unsatisfying; possibly because I was at a low point in my life and thus behaving somewhat masochistically – I still haven't figured it out.

It was too late for regret. I berated myself for having deleted Dan's number some time ago; I would have to reply to him now. But I paused before sending the text: Did he know? I dreaded finding out. I waited a few minutes, decided on an appropriate response and then texted back.

Hi Dan. Long time no speak. Things are good – very busy, but all
is well. How are you?

My phone beeped instantly: he wasn't wasting any time.

Good. What have u been busy doin?

Besides retching from txt spk, you mean? Cautiously I replied:

Working; was on a film, then writing, it's all good. You?

Wat u writing?

Gulp.

Just stuff; this and that, nothing special.

We should meet 4 a drink!

Why? It's not like there is much we can talk about if we did meet – it wasn't exactly an intellectual connection which brought us together. It's not like we would chat about the waste of resources in the movie industry, or the repression of women's rights, or even whether fashion models should make political statements against forced labour in textile work-shops. (Answer: yes, they bloody well should.)

No, what we have in common – the only thing – was that we both liked to fuck. And fuck we did. All night long. But it wasn't even that good: I certainly don't want to go back for more. And if he does know about the book, I really don't want to be grilled about it or whether he is in it: I am getting that on a daily basis already . . .

I sent him a polite text back declining his offer and he left it at that, much to my relief. But, such is the way my brain works, almost immediately I couldn't help but think about his beautiful cock, and I was very tempted to use that image for some quick, short-lived 'material'.

Then I remembered how selfish he was, and went off to make a cup of tea instead, knowing that I would enjoy it far more than any of the sex we ever had.

Tuesday 22nd August

I'm still at my parents' place: I feel safe here. I'm so grate-ful to my parents for all they've done for me, and their unconditional support these last couple of weeks; I'm also thankful that they both promised not to read any of the book or blog. There are some things a parent doesn't need to know, and I'd list 'how my daughter sucks cock' as top of the list.

This morning, though, I was caught off-guard by my mum, as we sat eating toast and drinking tea.

'The blog,' my mum began, hesitantly. 'Um, we have read a little of it.'

My mouth dropped open in horror.

'We couldn't help it!' she blurted out. 'We just had to know what it was that you were writing. Everyone else knows.'

I shifted nervously in my seat, preparing for the worst, a slow, sinking feeling pulling me in the pit of my stomach.

'And,' she continued, 'it's very well written. You've quite the touch for emotive storytelling.'

Well, she's my mum: of course she's going to say that. Still, I thanked her, but wondered what exactly it was she had read. Part of me didn't want to know; another part of me needed to know.

'You appeared to be very sad in that blog post,' she added, 'but that man you were with that you wrote about seemed really nice.'

'What man?'

'The one who cuddled you while you were upset and was

177

supportive to you even when you left him in the midst of everything.'

I was confused. She continued: 'The American man. He was a regular lover of yours, yes?'

Karl: my long-time midwestern American fuck-buddy, whom I last saw many months ago. The concluding chapter of our dalliance came when I was in tears during orgasm because I was still upset about it not working out with Blog Boy; and being intimate with Karl whilst I was in that state had kind of fucked with my head. I had ended up running from his apartment as soon as the sun rose, and in doing so, risked my friendship with him. That aspect of the night I didn't mind my mum reading about. What was more of a concern, though, was the fact that I had described, in explicit detail, all the cunnilingus Karl had been performing on me, and suddenly it hit: my mum and dad had read all of that too.

Ugh. It was not a nice moment. I shrank back into the chair in my parents' kitchen and wished the floor would open and swallow me up.

The thing is, my parents are very open and honest people and I have an upfront relationship with them. In my house, when I was growing up, sex was never a taboo subject. It was seen as something good, to be cherished and enjoyed. My parents always gave me advice about relationships and guidance on safe sex; they provided me with condoms when I was a teenager and ensured I knew that no matter if I turned out straight or gay, that they would love me regardless.

Because of this, I was kind of OK with my parents knowing about my tales of 'shagging' or 'casual sex' or 'fuck-buddies'. But to have them read about some man's tongue licking me out for hours on end? No: god, no. Cunnilingus is too personal, it's too intimate: it's graphic detail that you don't want your parents to be able to picture, even if everyone else can. Of all the posts on my blog or chapters in my book, my parents had to read the one where I described how I sat on Karl's face most of the evening. Ugh, again.

'When we saw how personal that post was, we stopped reading,' my mum admitted. 'It was like reading your diary – and no parent should read their child's diary. We both felt really uncomfortable about it, so we shut the web page down and we haven't looked at it since.'

And I believe her: she's too upfront and honest to lie to me like that. I thanked her profusely, grateful for them respecting me and my need for privacy. I know they won't look at it again: they have too much regard for my wishes and I trust them to respect that.

I just wish it were the same for everyone else in my life.

SEPTEMBER

Friday 1st September

Tonight I realized just how affected I am by being outed: no longer do I have any confidence in chatting up men.

Until recently, approaching a bloke wasn't really an issue for me. Sure, I had nerves about doing it, just like the next woman, but over the years I've learned to channel my nervous energy into being talkative, rather than letting the anxiety eat me up. Instead of worrying, I would flirt, crack a joke or tease a guy in a friendly way in order to break the ice.

But things have changed for me now. I feel tongue-tied; my old inner confidence is non-existent. Unfamiliar self-consciousness now fuels my anxiety; self-doubt lays the tracks for my feeling vulnerable. Where once I felt strong and self-assured, I now feel exposed and even a little paranoid. I worry that I am transparent: that my motives behind talking to a guy – e.g. that I fancy him – are obvious.

Earlier this evening I decided to take the bull by the horns and get out there again. And by 'out there' I mean 'outside the house': I've become such a nervous – even paranoid – hermit recently with everything that's happened. But I can't carry on like this: I've got to live. So I went to my local gym, and whilst I was there encountered a sexy man.

Gym Guy had given me eye contact when we were both

standing in the shallow end in the pool. With this non-verbal communication, the old me – the anonymous me – would have immediately chatted to him. The new me went and sat in the steam room – alone. He joined me a couple of minutes later, causing me simultaneous delight and terror in equal measure. Instead of talking to him, though, I sat there quietly; legs pressed up against my boobs, my arms around me in self-protective mode.

Did he notice how frizzy my hair was? Could he see I had tried to hide my belly behind my thighs? Was he thinking, 'Oh god, I'm stuck here alone with a girl and she's going to try to chat me up'?

I think that was the crux of the matter: that my motives, no matter how lacking in crudity, would seem transparent somehow. How ironic, and what a role reversal: usually it's men who suffer harsh indictments when they approach women, the expectation being that they're only pursuing sex. What a limited, sexist perspective.

Anyway, I was filled with self-doubt: lots of it. There was a paranoid voice in my head that I rarely, if ever, hear; especially one that is so self-deprecating. And rather than relax in the steam room, as I previously would have done, now I was hoping that the steam was hiding my imperfections – and my anxiety – instead.

Then he cracked a joke; I practically wept with happiness and relief at his breaking the silence. Nervously, I counteracted with something ironic in response; thankfully we both laughed. We kept up the banter for a few minutes; but all the time I was worrying that I was talking nonsense. Then he told me he was heading off to the sauna.

'I'll join you in a minute!' I replied, jovially, as he walked out the door.

And then I spent the next five minutes berating myself.

How dumb I must have sounded: a complete stranger telling someone that they will 'join' them. How obvious it must have been to him that I fancied him – how stupid of me to make it so blatant.

But then, I was attracted to him. He was handsome; his hairy chest was very sexy; the fact that his feet were definitely bigger than my own size eight-and-a-halfs did fill me with inner joy. But I worried that he might, by some tiny chance, know about the blog and book – and therefore judge me.

The thing is, I'm receiving an incredible amount of emails from guys now that I've been outed, and most of them comment about my appearance and whether or not they find me fuckable. Whilst I don't seek validation about my appearance from others, it's complimentary that some men express that they do find me attractive, but on the other hand it's painful to receive and read the nasty remarks they make when they don't.

Right now it seems that it's a free-for-all: just because I've written about my enjoyment of sex, I somehow deserve to have my sexual attractiveness judged, as if that's the fundamental component of assessing my worth as a person. Well, being a woman, I guess that's to be expected, and being thrust under a media spotlight just highlights the sexist double standard: would I be judged in the same way had I been a man? I doubt it.

Privately, this has made me distraught: why do people feel the need to be so cruel? I've been hurt by some of the things said about me, what I've written about and how I look. The hateful attacks have wounded me in other ways, affecting my confidence and leaving me feeling open, exposed and vulnerable.

I now feel I no longer have any secrets; nothing new to discover about me; no shield of privacy for my protection. So regardless of the slim possibility of a bloke knowing about 'Abby', being outed has left me – emotionally – feeling sucker-punched: my personal life – and how I live it – will never be the same again.

So when I finally plucked up the courage to follow this guy into the sauna, it was with much trepidation. He smiled at me as I entered and – with no one else there – I chose to sit on the bench next to him, with enough distance between us so he didn't feel I was sitting on his lap (though I would have liked to, for sure).

He broke the ice again, which I was thankful for; I was barely able to speak. We cracked a few more jokes and I relaxed a little. But I still felt tongue-tied. The old me would have asked him questions, tried to find out what he was like. I couldn't.

Too late: he stood up and exited, saying the sauna was too hot for him. Gutted, I sat there and berated myself for not being more talkative: with my old courage I would have made far more progress by now. A few minutes passed and I left too; the heat was making me tired, so I lounged on a chair by the pool. Then I spotted him swimming. And again he was looking at me.

Previously, this would have been enough confirmation for me to advance things with him: eye contact + following me into the steam room + conversation x two + further eye contact = enough interest to pursue the situation. As he got out of the pool, the old familiar voice inside my head shouted, 'Ask him his name!!!', but with my new nervous exterior, all I could do was lie there, hoping I was looking pretty and intelligent enough for him to want to talk to me again.

When he walked past me, he grinned and said, 'See you, then.' There was a brief moment – like a snapshot in time where you can feel the tension in the air – and I knew it was up to me to speak, given he had initiated the dialogue. But instead, I smiled sheepishly back, mumbling, 'See you,' in response, and when he then walked slowly away towards the changing room I knew I had missed my chance.

It seems I need to find a way to regain my confidence with men; it's going to take me a while, I think: I still feel very fragile. Until then, I guess I'll just have to go to the gym as often as I can: besides getting me fitter, hopefully I'll see this guy again – and talk to him properly next time. Worth getting some sore muscles over, I reckon.

// posted by thegirl @ 11.22:00 PM

Saturday 2nd September

I decided today that I need to get away from it all and have a break; I am exhausted, in every sense of the word. In addition, Harry, my oldest friend in the world, arrives in town shortly from New York, and I've been worrying about how he – and his wife – will react to the knowledge that I wrote about his and my teenage sexual experimenting. So I booked a day at a spa in Hertfordshire that Fiona recommended, and hopped on a train up there this morning.

It was just what I needed, very relaxing: lots of swimming, steam rooms and quick hops into the sauna. I also treated myself to a Thai massage, to help me de-stress, but it had an altogether different effect on me.

When the time came for my session, I walked into the massage room and was greeted by a small, slender young woman, dressed in white overalls. The room had softly dimmed light, candles and soft music, but before I had a chance to take it all in, the masseuse demanded I remove all my clothes.

'All of them?' I asked, unsure if I had misheard her.

She nodded. Well, it did say 'Full Body Massage' on the info page of the website when I booked it: I guess that meant nude. Fine: I proceeded to slip off my jeans and top and then she quickly gestured toward my bra and pants. I self-consciously removed them too, feeling awkward in my nakedness as I stood before her. How odd, I thought, that I should now be so uncomfortable with my nudity in this situation; how ironic that the opposite would be true if it was a guy I was having sex with.

She flattened the sheet on the massage bed and told me to lie down on my front. The clean, crisp white cotton felt cool on my skin as I positioned myself on the padded bed; it smelt of lavender and geranium – lovely. She moved swiftly around me, her hands dancing on my back, circling my curves, her oiled fingers rhythmically flexing against my skin. It was lovely, so relaxing, so . . . hold on a minute: those are my breasts, what the hell . . . ?

My breasts might be big and when I'm lying on my front I know they are liable to, er, spill out a bit at the sides, and I'm aware that if one runs their hands up from my hips to my armpits, they will inevitably meet my boobs on the way, but there was no denying it: this woman was purposefully stroking my tits.

Because I've never had a professional massage before, and wanted to have something that fully relaxed me, I had assumed that a 'Full Body Massage' would mean that my legs and arms were rubbed down as well as my back. I didn't for a minute think that some woman's oiled-up hands would be gently manipulating my mammaries.

I lay there, her slippery fingers circling the curves of my breasts, and tried to think. Surely this was out of bounds? Shouldn't she be focusing on my back and shoulders, rather than letting her hands slide down my sides and under my tits? Didn't she realize that doing such a thing was inappropriate? Or maybe that was the point? Perhaps I had inadvertently stumbled across a masseuse who was getting a kick out of the fact that I was prostrate and therefore in a compromising position and she was, god forbid, taking advantage of me?

Clearly, my neurosis was getting the better of me. She was a masseuse for fuck's sake, not some randy bugger who was trying to have a quick grope. I was paying her to massage me, and massage me she was. Then it struck me. Maybe this was all part of the package; perhaps she was actually focusing on my breasts on purpose in order to elicit a response? OK, so this wasn't a Soho massage parlour, but maybe in my naivety I had somehow stumbled upon a masseuse who would, as they say, see me through to 'completion'?

I became aware of her hands slowly sliding down my back, smoothing my buttocks tightly and then spreading the cheeks apart. Then she ran her hands slickly over my hips and up towards my armpits, slipping her fingers quickly beneath my breasts and pulling on them lightly, before making her way back down to my arse.

Oh god, she is clearly trying to turn me on. Fuck. What am I supposed to do here? Should I speak up?

'Look here,' I could say, in my poshest London accent. 'That's really uncalled for. I think you should stick to the neutral areas and stay well clear of my erogenous zones.'

But I didn't. The problem was, you see, that I was enjoying it. I could feel my body respond to her touch; between my legs it was no longer a pulse, more a rampant throb. Thank god my arousal was hidden, or as hidden as it could be, being turned on and soaking wet; I thanked my lucky stars that I wasn't a bloke – I can only imagine the equivalent erection a guy would have had from that level of stimulation . . .

No matter how uncomfortable, or embarrassed, how prudish I felt, the fact is that part of me also wanted her hands to somehow 'accidentally' slip between my legs: I longed for her fingers to glide as delicately there as they were doing over the rest of my body. I needed it: it's been a while since someone's been intimate with me, and god, after the last few weeks I need some sexual release; if this masseuse was the one offering, maybe I should take it.

Just as I was debating spreading my legs apart and hoping that she might take the hint, she told me to turn over onto my back. I was half relieved and half gutted: nothing would happen now. I laughed to myself as she laid the sheet over the front of my body. How stupid I was to think that the massage involved any 'extras'; this was in a legitimate well-known spa, for fuck's sake! No naughty freebies there. She laid a scented blindfold on my eyes and I relaxed back into the moment, chastising myself for being such a twat and for getting myself worked up.

Then she removed the sheet, poured warm oil onto my tits and began rubbing them with her hands. What the fuck?

Under the blindfold, my brain felt ready to explode. I have a strange woman caressing my breasts! She isn't doing it accidentally! Oh my god, what do I do? I lay there, immobile, and tried to think.

a) She might be some kind of pervert and I am being violated. Perhaps there is a camera filming this and afterwards all the masseuses will watch the footage and laugh at the stupid Londoner who laid back and let herself get felt up with no struggle.

b) This might just be part of the massage and I am being neurotic: why should breasts miss out on being rubbed? Men get their chests massaged; just because my female mammaries have been sexualized and objectified in society, it shouldn't mean that they aren't treated the same as their male counterparts. They are just another body part, after all; my worry about their being touched says more about my hang-up than the act itself.

c) Feeling my breasts might not be part of the massage but she reckons I look like the sort of woman who'd be up for a little 'extra' on the side and perhaps she'll frig me off if I give her a good tip.

I'm not ashamed to say I ended up hoping it was the latter. Fuck it, I thought, she must know how much she is turning me on: my breasts are very sensitive, and with her deft touch, my nipples were like bullets in her fingers. Combined with my fast breathing, and minor body-wriggling, it was obvious, to my mind, that she had got me horny as hell.

So, blindfold still on my eyes, and breasts in her capable oily hands, I lay back and hoped for the best. Sadly the tit massage continued for only a short while; she then moved on to my stomach, legs and arms, in fact, gave me a 'Full Body Massage' as advertised. Gutted.

Still, she did miss out one part – in the obvious place. Maybe I should have asked for a refund, stating I didn't receive the full service they offered. I doubt they would have included that in the price, though. Even if I was providing my own oil.

Sunday 3rd September

I've been thinking that maybe it's time I took up one of the generous offers of sex I have received since the newspaper article. Like, for example, this latest email I just found in my inbox:

Email: tom[redacted]@yahoo.com
Subject: i want no strings fun
Message: hi zoe im tom i want no strings fun with you i seen your

pic in the news im 30 with brown hair want a SHAG OK MY
NUMBA IS 07 [redacted] TXT IF CAN N WILL RING U BK WEN
DA WIFES NOT AROUND I WOULD LOVE URE TITS IN MY FACE
WITH U ON TOP OF ME I LIVE IN [redacted] BUT CAN TRAVEL
2 LONDON 4 SEX OK YOUR LOOKS R WELL WORTH THE
JOURNEY BABE NO STRINGS THOUGH YA

'Tom', don't hold your breath: I won't be making contact.
Not now, or ever. Besides the obvious reasons (I never asked
to be your 'friend' on MySpace*, fucker), it's safe to say I
have a preference for men who don't cheat on their partners
and who also never use txt spk: they're the two quickest ways
to dry a woman up, I guarantee it. (A lack of personal
hygiene in the cock area is the third way – but then everyone
knows that.)

Seriously, though, when I'm approached with an opportunity to shag a philandering, ignoramus dickhead, how could
I possibly refuse? What a catch!!!

I'm losing hope.

// posted by thegirl @ 7.56:00 PM

Monday 4th September

Finally met up with Harry, who's been busy the last couple of
days seeing relatives. He chose a central London café – one of
his favourites – for lunch; it took a whole hour before I was

---

* Anyone who has 247 million Internet 'friends' is no friend of mine.

able to ask Harry the question that had been burning in my mind, when, finally, his wife left the table to use the bathroom.

'Was she OK with it all?'

He nodded. 'Yeah, she's fine.'

'Seriously?'

'She thought it was sweet, actually . . .'

'She read it?'

'She read it before I did.'

With unintentional dramatic flourish, I put my head in my hands. After a brief moment of silent groaning, I cautiously raised my head. 'Oh fuck, really?'

'Yeah, she read it, then passed it to me, saying, "It's lovely, but it might make you cry."'

'You're kidding.'

He shook his head. 'No. And she wasn't wrong: it was lovely, really touching.'

My heart stopped pounding for a moment. 'Thank god. I was so worried . . .'

'Worried?'

Of course I was worried. Harry's my oldest friend, we've known each other since we were children; our ending up in bed together was the result of youthful experimentation, but at its source was the genuine love we each felt for the other. And I had written about all that, in detail, in my blog and book for millions of people to read.

I bit my lip. 'Well, yeah. I thought . . . I was nervous . . . I just worried that . . . you know, that it might affect things, and I was so scared that it might . . . that I might cause some problems between you . . . I never wanted that to happen; I had no control over all this . . .'

He interrupted me. 'We're fine; everything's fine. You have no need to worry: it was a long time ago – and she thinks the things you said were really sweet . . . And we're both very proud of you: this is a massive accomplishment.'

I blushed, recalling the explicitness of what I had written, but feeling a surge of pride too. To have him say this, to know how they both felt, was a massive relief. And I really needed to hear it because I was worried that as a result of everything that has happened, I might have lost their love and support. Or worse, lost him.

Harry leaned in and took a sip from his coffee. I followed suit, and in my inimitable clumsy way, I proceeded to knock the table with my knee, spilling my coffee everywhere as I did so. He laughed, and as I looked up at him sheepishly and shrugged – it's in my nature to be a klutz – we shared a smile, and I knew that everything was going to be OK between us.

☙

I had a little bit of a row with my mum tonight. I was over there for dinner and my mum and I were sitting around the kitchen table drinking coffee afterwards when she suddenly dropped the bombshell. I'm not sure what sparked it; perhaps it was an article about me in a newspaper that she and my dad had been reading earlier.

'How do you think I feel?' my mum said. 'When everyone else in the world – my friends included – are able to read your blog and book, and yet I cannot? Do you not realize how hard that is for me? People keep asking me what I thought of a particular chapter in your book, or how I feel about the way you've portrayed your dad or me in it, and I don't know what they're referring to. They have knowledge of you that I don't. It's hard for me, Zoe. It's hard for both of us.'

Until she said that, I really hadn't grasped how difficult it might be for my parents. I mean, sure, they've dealt with the fact that their daughter's sex life has been read about by millions of people. And, sure, they've accepted that I've got up to a few things that they may find embarrassing having others know about. But what's harder is that they're pretty much the only people in their social network who haven't read the book – so many of their friends and members of my extended family have (to my dismay) – and for them to be excluded from that common knowledge must be tough.

Indeed, even at a family funeral I attended this week, a woman in her sixties who I'd never met came up to me and asked, 'You're Zoe, aren't you? You write that sex blog: I love it! All my friends read it now; we talk about it a lot. I can't say I agree with or relate to your experiences but it's certainly an education!' I thanked her for her kind words, but felt awkward on two counts: firstly, just moments before, I had been shovelling earth onto my relative's coffin, whilst I wept for my loss. And secondly, in front of my mum, it was rubbed in, yet again, about others reading my book and her not being able to.

After my mum expressed her frustrations to me, I offered my sympathies and tried to come to some sort of understanding with her – or a compromise, at least.

Seeing as I've been lucky enough to write a few newspaper articles recently, I'm going to send her and my dad links to them and that way my parents can read my work, but not be subjected to anything explicit. I, for one, will be relieved by that. I'm sure my parents, however, will read it and do what parents do best: criticize.

'I think you could have argued that a bit better,' my mum will most likely state. 'The conclusion was a bit weak.'

'Nice,' my dad will probably offer, 'but it was a bit long.'

I don't mind what they say, because, like in all other aspects of my life, I take on board the feedback they give me and hope I'll be a better person and a more informed individual as a result.

My parents know and understand that in the blog and the book, I set out to show that it was OK for a woman to express her desire, rather than attempt to be the object of desire, and they've supported me in everything that's happened since I was outed.

So I know that even though I still get hate mail, and horrid comments, and newspapers can be very unkind about me, it doesn't matter what bullshit others might say to, or about, me: the only thing that matters is what my parents think. I want them to continue to be as proud to say I am their daughter as I am to call them my parents.

Tuesday 5th September

I was on the phone to my mother earlier when I heard my mobile beep with a text message. With my landline phone pressed against one ear, I glanced over at the other phone. When I saw who the text message was from, I froze.

'Mum, I'm going to have to call you back.'

'Why?'

'Something's come up.'

I put down the handset and looked at the still-lit screen, my heart pounding. Perhaps if I just delete the text, then I could ignore it. I pushed the phone to one side and paused. Then I looked at the screen again. The letters seemed to glare at me, and with butterflies in my stomach, I read it once more.

> I just heard. So pleased for your success. Guess I need to read your book now.

It was inevitable: he would find out sooner or later. For a moment I wondered how he learned about it; who might have told him. Then I gave up – it didn't matter either way. What mattered was that he knew. My ex, Steven, knew.

Of all the men I have written about, there are three whose response I feared. Not because I had necessarily bad-mouthed them, but because they had gotten to me: to my heart, to my vulnerability. They had access to the recesses of my being that few others have had; they had known another, more fragile, part of me, and thus had the ability to hurt me.

Two of these men – Blog Boy and Harry – know everything: they have both read the book, and are fine with it; I feel blessed that they have been so supportive and understanding about it all. Steven, though, did not know – until now. Because he has not been in my life for some time, I had hoped that he would never know that I had divulged intimate details about him – about us. Whilst I was still anonymous, this seemed like a possibility; I could carry on – perhaps naively –

believing that that he would live his life, separate to mine, and that the sadness I once felt about him would be hidden from his discovery. Until now, that is.

I looked at the phone again.

Delete delete delete.

It would be so easy. My lack of response would say so much; that I didn't want to speak with him; that I didn't care enough to reply; that what was in the past should stay that way. But as I held the phone in my hand, I physically shook; my nerves were on edge. Why should I feel so worried now, so long after everything? Why was my heart thumping so fast I could barely breathe? How much did he know?

I had to reply: better he heard it from me than believe any of the gossip or lies that have surfaced. I began to type back: polite, friendly. He replied straightaway and we began a brief text dialogue; each message getting closer to the inevitable question. Finally, it came:

I must ask: if I am in the book, were you discreet?

Delete delete delete.

Too late to delete. Too far gone to alter what I'd written. Too much said to deny it now. I cannot delete the past.

I imagined him with his phone in his hand, waiting for my reply; aware that each passing silent moment spoke truths that no words could express. How could I deny I had written about him? Saying that would mean my life was not affected by him – but of course it was. He had awoken in me something I hadn't felt for a long time; he had made me realize that I wasn't strange or unusual because I loved sex; he had helped me embrace my being a strong, self-assured person, alongside being fragile too.

Delete.

Memories flashed through my mind as I sat there, phone in hand, and debated what to do. Our waltzing together in his living room; him laughing at my clumsy feet. My wrists handcuffed above my head as he teased me, making me beg for his cock. Watching him shave, as we bathed together; me tickling him with my toes. Him kissing my ankles as he entered me; my feet wrapped around his neck. Eating face to face in candlelight; me dropping crumbs in my cleavage. My straddling him, watching him smile at me whilst he whispered my name, over and over, as we climaxed together. Glimpses of another time; of other people. We are not who we were. And we weren't meant to be.

I typed a message back, telling him I had written about him (though heavily disguising his identity), and that I was sorry he was finding out this way. Live by your word, I told myself; live by your honesty. Until this point, I've had the protection of anonymity to shield me. He may not like what I have said, but the truth is what it is. Whatever will be, will be. He didn't reply to my text – nor did I expect him to. He knows, and that is all.

Of course, I worry what he might think if he reads it; how he might feel. I have no wish to hurt him – we had closure a long time ago, and I'm not interested in stirring up the past. But my words, my thoughts, my feelings, live and breathe beyond me; I cannot delete what's happened as if it were some text on my computer screen. Perhaps, more importantly, now I realize: nor do I want to. I need to accept what's happened and move on.

// posted by thegirl @ 9:14:00 PM

The texts from Steven have made me slightly emotional. I guess I miss being close to someone, the way I was with him. But it's also made me miss the sex we had: god, it was great. We fucked everywhere, even on the patio table in his gorgeous garden: I adore a man with green fingers.

I love a guy who can look after plants; it makes me go all quivery inside when faced with a man who knows the difference between a dracena and a cordyline, rather than just the labia minora and majora.

I think it all started some years ago when I had a fling with a guy, Joe, who loved plants. The first time we went back to my flat, I deposited him in my lounge while I went to fix drinks, and returned to find him caressing my schefflera.

'Ohh,' he said, stroking the leaves gently, 'that's a fine-looking plant there, how old is it?'

'About five years, I think,' I replied, watching him fingering its fronds.

'It's done well,' he said. 'You've clearly taken care of it for it to have grown so big.'

I felt a surge of pride and a throb between my legs as I watched him touch the leaves of my plant as if he were caressing me. His fingers seemed so light and so careful; it made me think they would feel just as gentle inside of me. And later, when I got him into my bed, I discovered I wasn't wrong.

But it wasn't just how he touched the plants that stirred my depths. When we went back to his place a week later, I saw that it was completely filled with plants; each one brimming with life and good health and it made me realize that a man who could look after plants so well would have to be a caring, sensitive person. To take so much care and attention over a living thing showed an ability to think outside of his own needs. Ergo, he wasn't selfish. Thus he would be good in bed (and possibly be Potential Boyfriend Material© too).

He was lovely – my green-fingered, good-at-fingering man. Discovering his love of plants helped make me view them – and men – very differently: I came to understand that to nurture something so carefully was a skill to be improved on, constantly developed over time, and that humans, like plants, need the tender touch.

So when I first visited Steven's house a few years ago, I was very excited to find he had a whole garden of beautifully maintained plants, each one lovingly placed in the ground by him. My theory about him being caring and sensitive because of his plant-love was spot on. Especially when it came to giving me orgasms with those same deft green fingers.

But, after some wonderful months together, it didn't work out. Ironically, it was after I bought him a new house plant that I suspected things were going badly. A couple of weeks after giving it to him, it was completely dead: he hadn't looked after it at all.

At the time, I remember feeling sorry for the plant, that his neglect had made it suffer. It was only some months later – when my eyes were sore from continually crying about our break-up – that I realized how meaningful it was that he had left it to die, and that it was an apt analogy for the state of our relationship.

So I don't necessarily think that having green fingers means a guaranteed ability to be good in bed or to have a meaningful relationship, but I would bet that it is a good measure to judge the former by.

And given the amount of men I have fucked, who are – quite clearly – only interested in their own climax, I would suggest that taking some time to be a bit more sensual and learning to enjoy the process, rather than just the result it brings, would be beneficial to all.

So to those who worry about their skills in bed, my advice would be to go and fondle a houseplant – it might just make you a better lover.

Best go water my plants, I guess: I think am getting out of practice.

// posted by thegirl @ 8:14:00 PM

Wednesday 6th September

Yesterday I did something I said I would never do.

No, I didn't fuck a married man. This girl does have some principles, you know. (And, as Groucho Marx said, if you don't like them, I have others.)

Nor did I have a frig in a public place. (Being fingered by someone else doesn't count. Right?)

Instead, I lowered myself to such a desperate level of patheticness, it was as if I have no shame at all: for the first time since its release, I moseyed on down to my local Waterstone's in the hope that I might spot my own book.

I know, it's shallow of me, and buying from a chain doesn't exactly support my neighbourhood independent bookshop;

but I just had to see if they were stocking my book – since that's where most people would be buying it from – so I swallowed my anti-corporate ethics for a brief hypocritical moment, and hopped on the bus down to the shops.

I didn't expect to encounter my book in my local shop's window display; I was chuffed to see five of them, right in the centre of it, alongside Zadie Smith and Sam Bourne. A little glimmer of excitement began in my belly (OK, and between my legs slightly too; my happy and pleasure buttons seem to be connected) and I entered the store.

To my complete joy, my book was slap bang on the centre of the first table at the front of the shop, in the '3 for 2' offers. Blimey. Twelve copies on display; pushing up against Lionel Shriver and Ali Smith. Fuck me.

Though my paranoia-alert button was set on low for the first time in weeks, I still tried to look inconspicuous, just in case, well, someone in there had read the interview I did with the *Guardian* and might know what I looked like. Not that anyone cares, of course; I just didn't want to get caught looking at my own book.

So, with a sophisticated trouser suit on, my hair pulled back into a ponytail, and dark glasses in place, I pretended I was just a normal customer and not a pathetic author inwardly rejoicing about their book being on display. After spotting it, I quickly moved away from the table to continue book shopping.

Some time later, with a pile of books in my arms, I returned to the table. How sad would I be, I thought, if I were to pick up the book, take it to the counter, and ask the cashier pointed questions about it? I concluded that I would be very sad indeed and that only completely narcissistic, self-absorbed and egomaniacal people would do such a thing. Which, of course, I am, so I immediately grabbed the book, placed it under the heap I was carrying, and made my way to the cash register.

When the cashier got to the last book of the pile – my own book – I stopped her scanning it in.

'Do you know anything about that?' I asked, trying to look mildly, but not overly, interested.

'I haven't read it,' she admitted, 'but it's supposed to be great.'

'Oh, really?' I said, as if I wasn't bothered either way. 'What's it about?'

'It's a personal diary,' she replied.

'Oh, I see,' I said, as casually as I could, praising a god that doesn't exist, for my having taken some acting classes many years ago, and thus being able to put on a decent poker face.

'We've been getting really good feedback,' she volunteered. 'It's been selling very well.'

Oh my fucking god, I wanted to say, leaping for joy and leaning over the desk to kiss her. But I kept my composure by remembering that she was a saleswoman: it was in her interest to make me think the book was worth buying.

'Is that so?' I said.

'Yes, it's been flying out recently, women really seem to like it.' She began tapping into the computer keyboard. 'Twenty-four copies in the last week,' she said, somewhat triumphantly, I noted. 'It's very popular.'

I bit my lip and tried not to appear overjoyed.

'So, would you like it, then?'

I shook my head. 'Nah, I think I've got enough for today; I'll have a think about it and maybe buy it next time.'

I quickly paid for my books and slipped out of the store, and for the first time in over a month, I had a massive smile on my face.

☺

I've just received a really weird email. No, not one of the usual 'You're such a fucking slut!' ones. It's from a TV presenter, quite a well known one, in fact. Well, I know of him, anyway: he's cute, in his early twenties, and a bit of a cheeky chappie. I'll call him Billy. (He sort of reminds me of a goat-herding boy.)

It turns out Billy's a fan of my blog – he heard of it after I was outed and has now caught up with lots of the archives. I'm quite shocked to hear that: I guess you don't expect to learn of someone in the public eye being a fan of your own work. Or, for that matter, reading the intimate and explicit details of your sex life. Part of me is mortified by that, but, admittedly, part of me is also chuffed to bits that he likes my blog. I was somewhat impressed – and touched – by him quoting entire extracts from various years, and referring to passages he had particularly enjoyed; my ego is fully stroked.

He's asked me if I want to meet up for a drink with him. I guess, like many of the other approaches I'm now getting, Billy's read the blog and is only interested in me because of the sexual content of what I've written; I doubt someone like him would ever chat me up otherwise. Would it be really shallow of me to meet him just because he's 'off the telly' and rather handsome? Would it be egotistical to meet him just because he's a fan of my writing? Am I being a total hypocrite about what I've previously said about celebrities?

I don't know. What I do know, though, is that I need a shag, and if his overly flirtatious email is anything to go by, I might be in with some serious luck in that department.

And at least I know he wouldn't run to the tabloids afterwards.

Not unless he wanted me to spill the beans on him too, that is.

Thursday 7th September

I can't believe it. First Billy off the telly, now I've been invited to appear on Sharon Osbourne's talk show. Not that they're connected, of course, but I'm still slightly thrown by the fact that people from the media keep approaching me.

I've decided to accept the invite to go on the show. Partly because I want to set the record straight and counteract the stuff the tabloids said about me, but partly because I also believe it's important to show that I am not ashamed of what I've written about. So many women have contacted me thanking me for speaking out and challenging stereotypes and I guess I feel that to stay quiet now would be doing them, as well as myself, a disservice. Hiding away isn't an option any more.

I'm scared as hell, though. I'm even getting nervous about the fact I don't have a TV-ready outfit. Best go sort that out, I suppose.

I tightened the belt around my waist, and turned so I could see my pencil-skirt-wrapped arse in the mirror. I was pleased by how tightly the material clung to my bum, whilst accentuating my hips. I shifted my weight and undid the top buttons of the blouse, admiring my cleavage. Then my brief moment of narcissism was interrupted by the sales assistant reappearing at the curtain.

'Any good?' she asked.

I shrugged. 'It's a nice combo – and it looks great – but it's not really what I'm looking for right now.'

'What's wrong with it?'

'Think "Sexy Secretary" and you've got it.'

She laughed. 'You don't like that?'

'I'm looking for something a little more sophisticated, and only subtly sexy; not something that will scream, "Bend me over the desk and take me hard" – that's not the image I want to project.'

'I see,' she replied, and waited for me to hand her the skirt, blouse and belt, before she wandered off.

I put my Not Really Giving A Shit Because All My Clothes Are In The Washing Machine trousers back on and slipped my shirt above my head. As I was looping the buttons over my bust, the sales assistant returned, poking her head around the curtain once again.

'Um, you know that book you said you'd written? Does it have tips in it and stuff?'

I blushed. 'Tips?'

'You know, sex tips . . .'

'Well,' I replied, carefully, 'I'm no expert, and it's mostly about my own personal sex life, but yeah, I suppose there are a few pointers in it. They are very graphic, though . . .'

Now it was her turn to blush. 'I'm a grown-up: I can cope with graphic. Would you give me some advice?'

'That depends: what do you want to know?'

She turned an even deeper shade of red. 'Well . . . um . . . it's just . . . my boyfriend, he likes to talk dirty and that, and I'm not really into it; I feel embarrassed.'

'I know what you mean,' I reassured her, whilst thinking that when in bed, I regularly whisper to a lover just how much I want their 'hard cock inside me', and how I need them to 'fuck me now, please, oh god please, I need it'. Somehow I didn't think she was of the same mindset, so I changed my tack:

'Well, what do you like to do?' I asked her, gently.

Her face remained crimson. 'I like the loving stuff: cuddling, kissing, him stroking me. I don't like doing "doggy": god, I hate that!'

'Why's that?' I said, soft as I could.

'It's so impersonal, ugh!' she exclaimed.

I nodded and tried to connect with her discomfort. 'Yes, it's difficult when they're behind you and you don't get to see their face as you have sex.'

'Exactly!' She smiled at me, relaxing a little.

I smiled back at her and remembered how at her age – early twenties – I disliked 'doggy' too: it made me feel so distanced from a lover, so remote from what was going on. It took me years to realize how I could enjoy the position: that instead of disconnecting, it could actually make the bond with a lover stronger; that with his fingers between my legs and a firm grip on my hips, penetration would be the link that joined us. Plus of course, upon discovering that my G-spot would get continually rubbed by a guy fucking me from behind, it was then only natural that I would come (quite literally) to enjoy the position.

I looked at her and, nervous embarrassment aside, wondered how much detail I should go into, and, also, whether I wanted to divulge to a complete stranger – face to face – the sexual awakenings I had in my twenties. I decided to be as subtle as I could:

'It can be hard getting the balance right between what one person and another prefer in sex,' I stated, trying to sound like I knew what I was talking about. 'Personally, I have always found that to get what I want in bed, timing is everything.'

'Timing?'

'Yes. One tip I could recommend is that if you want to make suggestions about sex to your lover, you do it at the same time as you're pleasuring him.' I lowered my voice a touch. 'Do you mind if I am explicit here?'

She nodded. 'Go ahead.'

'You could, for example, be sucking his cock. Whilst he's in the throes of pleasure, look up at him and then tell him that there's something you really want to do, and that doing it would really turn you on.'

'Like?'

'Well, like the intimate stuff you said you prefer. When you've got his cock in your mouth and he's enjoying it, he's going to be far more receptive to trying out other things –

even if he doesn't normally enjoy them. This is because he'll associate the idea you're putting forward with the pleasure he's receiving, and with that connection, he'll then be more willing to try it out.'

'Really?'

'Yup. And, in return, you could suggest to him that if there's something he would really like to do, you'd be willing to try that out too. If you take the initiative and talk to him about what you want in bed, whilst you're in bed, I'll bet that he'll respond positively.'

She grinned at me. 'So I should ask him to do more sensual things, like massaging me and stuff, whilst I am giving him a blow-job . . .'

I smiled back at her. 'Exactly. It's always worked for me. Go for it.'

'I will! That's a really good idea, thank you.'

I picked up my handbag and we made our way to the front of the shop. As I approached the exit, she called out to me:

'I want to buy your book! What's it called?'

It was my turn to blush. 'Um, *Girl with a One Track Mind*.' I felt self-conscious suddenly, and tried to leave the shop.

'Hey!' she hollered, preventing my escape. 'Don't forget to come back!'

I turned to face her. 'Oh, I don't think I'll be buying that outfit, but thank you.'

'No, I didn't mean that! I want you to come back so that you can sign my book!'

'Oh, of course . . . Um, OK then.'

She waved at me as I stepped out the door and I disappeared into the throng of shoppers filling the high street, pondering as I did so how surreal my life has become: I never thought I'd be suggesting sex tips to complete strangers – especially face to face.

Friday 8th September

'Where would you like me to come on you?'

'What?'

'Where would you like me to come on you? How about your face?'

Billy broke out into a grin and I raised my eyebrow at him, pausing for thought. We weren't in bed together; in fact we weren't naked, or even alone for that matter. Instead, we were sat in a crowded pub, having agreed late last night over IM to meet for a drink or five this evening.

But whilst our conversation had turned decidedly risqué – which I was very pleased about – it had not, to my mind, progressed to the point where discussing the placement of his sperm could be done in a blasé fashion.

Call me selfish (do: it'd be accurate), but sex for me is not solely about focusing on the man's orgasm. In my case, I confess, it is usually about mine: there is nothing better than having a climax and I am a fucking horrible bitch to be around if I don't orgasm during sex.

So sex, for me, does not end when a guy climaxes; it is just a temporary blip (so to speak) before continuing with other sensual activities. And I try to avoid porn-film clichés and fantasy representations of sex in my own sex life: that immediately excludes a 'money shot' (and faked orgasms). I can quite clearly state that at no point will there be any likelihood of my having an orgasm purely because a man has squirted his seed somewhere onto my body. Sure, it can feel nice, in the way that heated massage oil feels nice. Sure, it can be erotic, because I enjoy men coming: I get off on their pleasure. But in and of itself, a guy spunking on me is not going to do it for me: my skin is just not that sensitive. Exactly how is my clit or pussy going to be stimulated solely through a guy shooting his wad onto my face? Fair play to those who enjoy having spunk all over their faces; I am not one of those women (or men). Anyway, if Billy wanted to impress me with promises of the sexual pleasure awaiting me, he was going the wrong way about it: suggesting the primary focus – for us both – should be his orgasm pissed me right off.

But back to now: he was cute, we were drunk, and finally my mojo seemed to have returned, alongside some confidence. (I guess there's nothing like a sexy celeb to boost one's ego . . .) I needed to turn this conversation round. I shot him a bemused look and, placing my hand on his knee, squeezed it and said, in a whisky-fuelled, flirtatiously sarcastic retort, 'Darling, surely we should be discussing where it is on you that I shall be coming.'

He stared at me with a bewildered expression, looking as if he half expected me to whip out a penis of my own there and then and spurt all over him. Trying to deflect the unease I saw growing on his face, I flashed him a smile and he visibly relaxed. He looked sexy when he wasn't trying to be so macho; given his twenty-something age I guess that his attempt at bravado was only to be expected. As he looked

sheepishly at me, I softened towards him. I also deliber-
ated how and in what way I should explain my thoughts
on the location of his ejaculation deposit. And I wondered
how long it would be before I got him naked with me on
top of his cock, because all this spunk talk was an unneces-
sary delay to our having some fun. I decided to be tactful,
yet direct.

'Well, how about you come with a condom on, deep inside
me? I'd like that.'

He looked confused. 'No, I meant where on you . . . Your
thighs, your tits, your face . . . That's what I want to do.' His
eyes lit up at this point and I saw where this was headed: not
in a direction I was happy with.

'Look, tits would be fine, thighs, whatever,' I said dismis-
sively. 'The face, however, is out of bounds.'

'Why?' His hand was resting on my inner thigh at this
point, squeezing me gently. I was well aware of the heat eman-
ating from between my legs, but that was connected to the
fact that his delicious chest hair was poking over the top of
his shirt and I was imagining running my fingers though it
whilst fucking him. (I am shallow like that.) I tried to focus,
keep a clear head.

'That's not something I like. At all. There is no way I'd do
that.'

'Why not? It's fun.'

'I just don't like it. And the only way I would do it is if it
was with someone I loved and he really, really wanted me to.'

He grinned at me. 'I really, really want you to.'

I squinted at him and debated the level of tact I would be
capable of in relation to how much whisky I had ingested,

and also the level of annoyance I felt about the current conversation.

'Look, this, us, this is just casual, right? I'm not going to do something like that on a one-night stand.'

He looked disappointed. 'Really? Oh.'

I grasped his hand that was still placed on my inner thigh. 'No. Definitely not. But I can think of a few things we can do that will be much more fun.'

A mischievous smirk appeared on his face and not long after we ended up in a local hotel bed, devouring each other impatiently.

Finally, I got the release I had been waiting for. God, it felt good: all the stress and pressure easing away the moment I climaxed and for a brief while I forgot about the whole 'outing' thing.

In the early morning, after we'd snoozed a little, sex appeared to be on the cards again: hurrah. After nudging me awake, Billy got on top of me, straddling my chest and pinning down my arms with his thighs. He seemed to be pleased with his positioning and he began to stroke himself, occasionally dipping his cock into my mouth for good measure. I watched his face as his thrusting increased in intensity and I knew it wouldn't be long before he climaxed. I also knew that if he didn't shift I would have his come all over my face. Amidst my tired, somewhat horny haze, I felt myself flush with anger.

'Don't spunk on my face,' I said gently, but firmly. 'Do it on my tits.'

He gave me a cheeky smile and continued stroking himself, thrusting his cock closer to my face.

'Seriously,' I said, more direct this time. 'Don't.'

'Oh yeah, what are you going to do?' he replied in a fuck-you voice, his thrusting even faster.

Before I could think, I heard myself speaking; the words exited my mouth as if they belonged to someone else. Weeks of fury and stress building up to this one moment: the anger in my voice was evident.

'Oh yeah, well you see this?' I lifted my hand from under his thigh and clenched it into a tight fist. Then I pushed my knuckles deeply and firmly into his balls and twisted my hand so he could be sure of its delicate placement. 'I would punch you very hard, right here, if you came on my face. So don't even think about it.'

I smiled at him, sweetly, but with seriousness. Billy immediately let go of his cock and seemed scared to continue stroking himself.

Though I would never have carried through my threat, I disliked his coercive approach to sex: being pushy like that is no way to treat women. I might be confident enough to state my needs, and express my limits, but there are plenty of other women who cannot, and men like Billy need to know that they have to respect others' boundaries.

I motioned that he should shift down my body, so his cock was no longer near my face, and I indicated that he should continue rubbing himself; he then gripped his cock like a man demented and a few minutes later his spunk landed all over my belly. When his cock had gone soft, and he had caught his breath, I insisted his hand and tongue pleasured me again a few more times; he dutifully accepted my demands. The final tally (if one must count these things) was probably about six or seven orgasms for me, to his one, which obviously pleased me immensely.

I think I made an impression on him, though perhaps not because of my multiple orgasms: I reckon I scared him so much he will never try to coerce another woman into doing something she didn't want to do. Plus, of course, I don't have to wash his come out of my hair. Result.

⊚

After chastising Billy thoroughly for his in-bed pushiness, I waited for him to return from the bathroom so I could wash all his spunk off my stomach. Fuck, that man produces a torrent.

He'd left the door open, though, and I could hear the sound of splashing water. A moment later, he began talking to himself:

'Yeah, looking good. Even I would fuck me.'

Oh my god, I've just had sex with a narcissist.

Billy exited the bathroom and his hair was freshly groomed, slicked down with water into a pretentious Hoxton style.

Oh Christ, not only a narcissist, but a fucking hipster too. Jesus.

On the verge of snorting out loud, I excused myself into the bathroom too, but rather than fixing my hair, I spent a few minutes wiping myself down with a flannel to get all his come off me and then switched my phone on to see if there were any important messages.

Priorities, see. Sod the hair.

A few minutes later, I exited the bathroom – hair still frizzy – and Billy was lying on the bed looking at me with a quizzical expression on his face.

'What took you so long?'

'I was checking my email on my phone.'

'On a Saturday morning?!'

I felt my face begin to blush. 'Yeah . . . If I don't check it frequently, it tends to stack up and get a little overwhelming.' I put my phone down on the chair. He shifted over on the bed, and I lay down on it.

'Many to deal with, then?' he asked, sliding his arm across my back and stroking my neck. Regardless of him being a Nathan Barley wannabe, I felt a familiar throb begin between my legs, so I snuggled closer to him, laying my hand on his chest.

'Nah. Just four: not urgent. I'll deal with them when I get home.'

He nodded and pulled me close. We lay there in silence for a minute and I wondered if we had enough time for a quick shag. I lazily ran my fingers over his torso, delicately grazing his nipples through his shirt as I did so; I hoped it might lead to something more.

'When you were next door, I noticed you had left your knickers on the table,' he remarked, casually.

'Oh, right,' I replied, still working on the gentle nipple action.

'Yeah, I saw them lying there, so I picked them up and smelled them.'

'What?' Surprised, I pulled away from him and frowned.

'Your pants: I smelled them.'

I cringed. 'Why would you do that?'

'There's nothing wrong; I just wanted to smell them.'

'But why?'

He shrugged. 'I dunno. I just did.'

I groaned and felt myself flush with embarrassment. Reaching for the pillow behind me, I smothered it over my face to hide my red cheeks.

'Come on,' he said, in a reassuring voice. 'Why are you embarrassed? It's nothing to be embarrassed about.'

'I can't believe you smelled my pants!' I moaned, through the pillow.

'I can't believe you – of all people – are embarrassed,' he joked, nudging me. 'You're the infamous sexblogger!'

'I know,' I whimpered, my voice still muffled. 'But I am embarrassed; I don't know why.'

And I didn't. It wasn't that I was ashamed about my body or that I have issues with hygiene, or my own personal 'aroma', or what he might have thought about it. It's not like it would be the first time a man had lifted my underwear to his nose and breathed in my scent. In the past I have found it both captivating and arousing when I've watched a man inhale my desire and then his cock has stiffened in response; knowing it had turned him on was a huge turn-on for me.

But when a man I barely know – except, perhaps, through watching him on the telly, which somehow makes it worse – smells my underwear without my being there to witness it, it just felt wrong. I might have been fine with him having his tongue between my legs just hours before, but I felt more exposed, vulnerable and naked now than during the cunnilingus; I almost felt violated.

'It's not because I'm weird or anything,' he volunteered apologetically, reading my mind. 'I don't go around secretly smelling women's knickers – honest! I just wanted to smell you.' He reached over and removed the pillow, which was still clamped down on my face. 'Come on, stop hiding!'

I lay there, now pillow-less, trying to compose myself, and put my hands over my face to cover my continued blushing.

'Anyway,' he continued, 'after you told me in the pub last night that you were so wet you had to blot your pants with toilet toll, I just had to smell that for myself.' He chuckled.

I smiled inwardly, remembering how highly aroused I had been. How my attraction to him had taken me by surprise; I hadn't expected to fuck him and I certainly hadn't expected to want to fuck him so very much. Especially given my 'no-fuck' rule for celebrities. But his description of all the things he was going to do to me, directed into my ear via a soft whisper, combined with a firm hand on my thigh, had made me yearn for him to be inside me. Sod the rules.

Somehow, after hours of non-sexual conversation, the dynamic had radically changed. Before I could analyse how, or why it had, his lips were on mine; my hands were traversing the brief expanse of naked skin between his shirt and his jeans; and his fingertips were drawing small circles along the back of my neck. We both sat there, wanting, and it was no longer a question of if we would get naked, but when. I wondered if all this was imprinted into my underwear like some kind of invisible scent marker: my transparent excitement; my undeniable desire; each moment of the arousal he induced in me; all captured in the lacy material of my thong.

But it wasn't until I returned home later today that I was

able to discover the evidence of this for myself. I immediately pulled my knickers out of my handbag and inhaled them deeply. The musky aroma of my arousal from the previous night was faintly perceptible; but I was almost disappointed by how slight the smell seemed, given how turned on I had been.

As I filled the sink with water, ready to hand-wash my underwear, it suddenly occurred to me that maybe I should have offered Billy the delicate G-string to keep. He might have appreciated the gesture, I suppose; perhaps he would have enjoyed the olfactory memento of our time together. But that would have just boosted his ego, I expect, and given his in-bed attitude, the only thing I wanted to inflate was his cock, for my pleasure, not his arrogance.

Anyway, the string I was wearing is one of my favourite pairs of pants, so there's no way I would permanently hand it over to a man I am certain I'm not going to see again: there can only be one narcissist in my bed and it had better be me.

Saturday 9th September

I'm still a bit pissed off about Billy's behaviour last night. Perhaps I overreacted slightly, but I do think he was pushing things. Had I been ten years younger, and a little less worldly, I probably I would have caved in and allowed him to get his way by ejaculating on my face – even though I didn't want him to. But back then, I was too naive and too insecure to assert myself in bed with a guy. So much has changed since then . . .

You know, I've nothing against people wishing to express

their sexual desires, or fetishes, or fantasies, but these things should be openly discussed and debated and full consent obtained from both parties. Billy demanding he come on my face – especially after I had explicitly stated in the pub that I didn't want to partake in that – was too forceful for my liking; I don't like men who pressurize women in that way.

Anyway, I'm done with Billy; can't say I'm that bothered, really. It might have been nice to have my pathetic shallow ego boosted by a little D-list celeb attention – with what's gone on, god knows I need that right now – and it certainly raised my mood having him fuck me all night, but apart from loving himself so much, Billy's just too immature and cocky for me. Young men like him have their advantages, sure, but spending just one night with him has reminded me of what they're lacking: a bit of experience, worldly maturity and a brain. No ever-ready hard cock can make up for a lack of decent, stimulating conversation, and you know what? I really miss that. I wish I could just curl up with someone – a person I really trust and care about – and be able to talk all night, laugh at the world and share how I am truly feeling, instead of just writing about it secretly.

☾

After much pressurizing from her, I finally agreed to go out with Fiona this evening. I think I had been hesitant about it for a few reasons:

1) I had lied to her, my good friend, about the blog and book.

2) I didn't reach out for help when I needed it.
3) I wrote about her in the book.

With all of that, I guess I was anxious about how she might react. Tim, I know, is fine: he had a go at me on the phone, called me stupid for not telling him and then offered his sympathies and asked when we were next meeting up for a beer. He's relaxed like that, and I know he doesn't have an issue with anything I've written about him. Kathy was a bit upset that I had excluded her from what was happening in my life, but then she informed me that she had bought the book last week. I must have audibly groaned on the phone because she immediately said,

'Oh, don't worry, I'm not going to read it! I just wanted you to get your royalties and to make it get to the top of the Amazon charts.'

Bless her.

Fiona, though, has been colder with me when we've spoken. I sensed she was upset from the quietness in her voice when we last talked; I guess she felt hurt that I had not felt I could trust her, even though we talk very openly about things. I can't blame her; I'd probably feel the same.

When we met this evening, I planned to launch into a huge apology and explain everything, especially that what I was uncomfortable about were my friends reading the emotional and personal aspects of my innermost thoughts, rather than all the bits about wanking. Although, if I am honest, that makes me uncomfortable too: my neighbour phoned me again and said that she'd begun to peruse my blog, but that she'd been put off by the amount of masturbation I described.

'I just don't need to know that about you,' she said.

Well, quite.

So I geared myself up for a big talk with Fiona, and you know what happened? She was sitting in a bar in Angel, waiting with a large dirty martini – my favourite drink – and a huge grin on her face, and suddenly all my worries melted away. We immediately hugged and I cried a bit and everything was fine: no huge apology was needed. I can't express how relieved I am. It's good to know my friends are OK with all that's happened. Maybe that was my worry: that with recent events, my friends would judge me, and that my friendships would be at risk. It's not happened: at least, not yet. My nearest and dearest are sticking close by: without them I'd be a mess, I just know it.

Drunk Chart

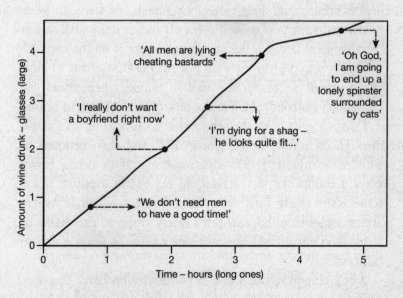

Sunday 10th September

Never phone someone when you're drunk, they say. This is because, invariably, you'll say something you'll regret.

Like, for example, that the receiver of the call is your best friend ever and that even though, when sober, you could take or leave their acquaintance, at 3 a.m., when inebriated, they're suddenly the best thing in your life. Or, possibly, you feel compelled to grovel at your ex's feet and beg them to take you back, even though you know in your heart of hearts that you could never be with a man who picks his feet whilst watching TV (and leaves his skin-droppings on the couch). Or, worse, because you've got the booze-horn, you dial a fuck-buddy and try to convince them that it is in their best interests to give you a good seeing-to, even though their breath stinks and their three-inch pubes got stuck in your throat last time you sucked them off (amazingly, such things seem forgivable when the possibility of sex is on the cards).

This is why I absolutely do not (to the best of my ability) allow myself access to my mobile phone when under the influence of alcohol; I leave my phone in my bag and ignore it. I do not give in to the temptation to pick it up and scroll through its phone book, press 'dial' and then proceed to embarrass myself. I can embarrass myself in other, better ways, I think, like, say, having an orgasm in a public place. (One particularly fun night, three years ago, on D'Arblay Street comes to mind . . .) But I rarely stoop to the shame of a drunken phone call: the outcome of that is never going to be good.

Not giving in to the drunken-phone-devil is hard, I have to

admit, but not impossible to control: it just takes some practice. And a mantra-like chant that you repeat to yourself
when inebriated – 'Don't fucking call him. Don't fucking call
him –' usually works.

What I do have difficulty with, however, is Drunken
Internet Behaviour (DIB©). Many a time I have come home
from a night out and, upon entering my flat, I somehow manage to immediately stagger over to my laptop and then start
typing out some bollocks that, when read the next day, makes
me groan with mortified embarrassment.

You know the type of thing: it's either writing a drunken
post on my blog – 'Oh, woe is me, I want a boyfriend/I need
a fuck/I wish I had some painkillers for my PMS' – or, even
worse, leaving drunken comments on others' blogs: 'I need a
shag, hahahahaha!!!' Pathetic, really; I have had to apologize
to some other bloggers for this in the past: not behaviour I am
particularly proud of.

What's even worse, though, are drunken emails. Yes, I
know, we all do it, but I am particularly susceptible to the
practice. Combine this with certain drunken ideas of
grandeur that I am Ms Witty Queen of the Year, and the
resulting mix is a cringeworthy blend of stupidity and desperation topped off with a dash of self-deprecating cheesy
humour: not funny in the slightest.

Generally, I just try to ban myself from accessing my laptop when stumbling in a bit drunk; it's the easiest way I've
found to avoid potential sobered-up regret. Overall, because
I am a control freak – I like to know that I can stay on top of
events (and men, clearly) – this method works. But it's not
always dependable: which is why, this morning, I found

myself reading something I had sent last night to a guy I slept with a while back, and then had to hold my hands up to the sky and ask myself, 'Why???'

I reckon the email had started off reasonably well:

'I am quite a bit pissed,' I had stated in the opening sentence. 'This is a disclaimer, should I wish to disown this email at some point in the future.'

Good approach; two points for honesty, at least. Then things got a bit worse:

'I wanted to say thank you for the night I came over, and sorry about things,' I offered, feeling the weight of the world on my shoulders. 'I may seem to be sitting on some moralistic high-and-mighty horse about what happened, but really I'm not.'

Er, actually, yes I am. He behaved like a twat, not me. But evidently, three martinis were now making me think differently. I lowered myself even more:

'You're a pretty good bloke I reckon,' I gushed, absent-mindedly forgetting how self-centred he was. 'It seemed like we connected quite well, so if you're up for the occasional beer and chat that would be fine by me. If not, that's fine too.'

I should really be a professional mediator with my optimism; always seeing the positive in people – no matter how much of an arsehole they might be. This guy hasn't even contacted me over the last few weeks to see how I'm doing, and I know he knows about my being 'outed'.

Things got worse. I grovelled some more and put the icing on the cake:

'I just wanted to clear the air and make sure that if we ever bump into each other, we'll do so with a smile – and no unease.'

Ah yes, the 'let's be friends' thing: good in theory, not in practice. Whilst I am on good relations with the majority of men I have slept with or dated, there are sadly a minority with whom friendship is impossible.

But being drunk, and thus in a forgiving mood, I imagined that things could be smoothed out with him; that it was worth my effort to work at a friendship. Our paths will undoubtedly cross once again, so it would make sense to be friends, or at least friendly, right?

Of course, when I sobered up I knew it wouldn't happen: we can't be friends. And whilst it was sent drunkenly, his total lack of response to my email confirms that: friendship, no matter how minor, is a two-way thing.

Where does this leave me now? Well, back to banning myself from accessing the Internet when pissed, of course. Still, it now may be a bit more difficult to prevent this behaviour, given that I have recently purchased a new 3G phone with broadband Internet access (in order to free me from being tied to my laptop to do email, plus, I love new gadgets, and this is the sexiest thing I have ever owned).

Guess I'll just have to find a lock to put on my bag, to prevent myself from touching my phone when drunk and avoid succumbing to such twattish communication. Or, instead, perhaps just find something else more fun with which to occupy my hands . . . I know which I'd enjoy more, and somehow I don't think the latter would leave me with regrets in the morning.

// posted by thegirl @ 11:48:00 PM

Monday 11th September

I've had quite a bit of time to think about things recently. There's been plenty to keep me occupied, as you might imagine. Besides trying to reassemble some form of private life, I've also had a particular thought developing in my mind: Men who wank too hard can experience difficulty having penetrative sex with women.

I'd like to challenge the media-supported myth that only women experience difficulty in climaxing: some men cannot obtain an orgasm through penetration either, no matter how much they thrust and grind.

(Disclaimer: this theory is based solely on my own experience, not scientifically accurate in any way, and most likely incorrect, due to massive generalizations I make, but I think it has some validity all the same.)

Now, I don't mean to say that all men who enthusiastically embrace their cocks have problems with intercourse – far from it: I'm all for men who enjoy self-love with a passion. What I am talking about is men who attack masturbation with such gusto that anything else pales in comparison: vaginal penetration, for them, means a loss of friction and sensation, decreased pleasure, and thus difficulty climaxing inside a woman.

Why have I come up with this conclusion? Because I believe that aggressive, rampant, intense wanking desensitizes men's cocks, making intercourse a disappointing experience for them (and their partners) and I think this is a tragic shame.

Only familiar with a firm grip producing their climax, the

delicacies of intercourse pass these men by. They are not able to sense the subtlety of a vagina pulsing and clenching; they cannot focus on how wet and slick a pussy might be; they might not notice the fluctuations in heat, tightness and softness; they cannot feel the contractions of a female orgasm occur, the billowing of the internal vaginal walls softly caressing their cock head. They miss out on all this, I believe, because they have desensitized their cock's ability to feel.

I'm not going to say I have the tightest pussy in the world, and that the men who have had difficulties climaxing with me are weird somehow for not exploding deep within me. But I will vouch for my pretty decent intramuscular vaginal ability, given fifteen years of doing Kegel exercises, and I think I've picked up some respectable sexual skills from the lovers I have had, so when faced with a guy for whom my pussy seems to do nothing, I will admit it has surprised me a little.

However, I'm only mildly, momentarily insulted by their lack of appreciation for my internal cock-grip; sex is, after all, about more than just how nice my pussy feels (surprising, I know). I'm always keen to do other things; to experiment and play in order to obtain mutual pleasure. So besides dropping to my knees for a wet blow-job/hand-job/cleavage combo, I'll also quite happily give a guy a seductive look and ask him to play with himself for me. This achieves two things:

1. It shows me what method of penis stimulation he enjoys, and how best I might help him achieve orgasm.
2. It turns me on to watch him wank.

(The second point, of course, goes without saying.)

So, watching a man wank – getting some insight into his personal, private self-loving activity – is the thing that I ask almost every lover I have had, to do. I am not a mind-reader or an expert in bed: I too need guidance in order to pleasure someone. Watching a man masturbate gives a few minutes of insight into his individual sexual preferences, and, I have found, offers clues as to his enjoyment (or not) of penetrative sex.

I have noticed major differences between men. There are some men who touched their cocks so lightly, you'd be surprised at the rigidity of their erections; their penis being so sensitive, even their finger gliding along the shaft induced a strong throb and large drop of pre-come. There are men who just squeezed the tip with their fingertips and their cock pulsed in response. There are men who could climax just by holding their balls and pressing down on their cock with the palm of their hands. And then, like Billy, there were the men who grabbed, tugged and throttled their penis so fast and so hard that their hand motion was a blur; their cock quite literally taking a bashing. I have watched many men masturbate in front of me and of them all, men who perform the latter action appear to also have had the most difficulty coming whilst inside me.

I don't think this is a coincidence. I really believe that the lovers who were able to come with ease also had the most sensitive cocks. They were, without fail, also the most sensual lovers I have had; they were able to be inside me, not moving, and yet could come just from my pussy clenching around them. The sensitivity in their cocks allowed them to climax in whatever way they chose: slow, fast, deep, shallow, soft, hard – not just having to pump in and out as fast as they could in

228

the hope of them achieving orgasm.

The men who could only tug themselves into oblivion always seemed to be missing out when inside me. Faced with a soft, fluttering pussy, rather than a solid grip, these men found it didn't fulfil their needs, and so couldn't climax – unless they pulled out and frantically tugged themselves off.

Watching – and being with these men – saddened me. It reminds me of awkward teenage sex, where no one really knows what they're doing, or how to have fun. I make this connection because seeing a man who can only climax in this limited way makes me think that he's still somehow at that awkward teenage stage: not quite sure what to do, not experienced in various ways to feel pleasure, but knowing that the end result feels bloody nice, so he might as well do what he's always done, because, well, that works, doesn't it?

I don't think it does. These men are being robbed of their sensitivity – and thus their ability to enjoy sex to the fullest. I think these men need to unlearn their rough, frantic, rampant masturbatory habits; they need to discover new ways to enjoy their desire, maybe even abstaining from masturbation (and especially their exposure to crap porn) to increase their sensitivity; and find out just how pleasurable a really sensitive penis can be. By slowing down, by exploring themselves, softly, gently, they'll discover a whole new way to experience their arousal. And this will help them to really know – perhaps for the first time – just how wonderful being inside a woman can feel.

// posted by thegirl @ 9:47:00 PM

Tuesday 12th September

I'm not sure why, but I was just thinking back to a time about ten years ago, when I decided to go through a period of abstinence from sex. I know, Girl with a One Track Mind, trying to be celibate: ironic, to say the least. But at the time, I was really fed up with men. I was disappointed with my single status and annoyed by the lack of romance in my life. No man I met ever seemed to be interested in developing things beyond the physical with me; I was saddened by the emotional gap that I felt needed filling.

So I made a decision to not have sex for a while and to only sleep with a man if we were involved more deeply than on a casual basis. Doing this, I figured, would help me meet a better class of man: one that wanted me for my mind and soul, as well as my body. And given my bad choices of men at that point in my life, I thought taking sex off my agenda might help me think more clearly too.

I managed eighteen whole months of no sex. Amazing, I know. For me, anyway, given my healthy appetite; but with my quitting cigarettes in previous years, I figured, how hard can it be to quit fucking for a while?

Very hard, as it turned out: I was horny ALL the time. The thing about it being on men's minds every eight seconds? That's nothing: it was on my mind for each of those other seven seconds too. The thought of sex preoccupied me from waking to sleep; there wasn't one moment where I didn't think about it.

Let's just say my hands got to know my nether regions very well.

As I reached the eighteen-month mark, I had an appointment for a gynaecological exam; a sexual health MOT to check all my bits were in working order and to update my cervical smear test.

I don't like internal exams; I don't think any woman does. I can definitely think of far nicer ways to spend my time than having

1. some stranger prodding my insides;
2. a freezing cold metal contraption being inserted into me and then uncomfortably holding my vagina open;
3. swabs and sticks scraped against my cervix.

So I wasn't exactly looking forward to getting a check-up. But, you know, it must be done – making sure my sexual and reproductive health is good is important to me – so along I went to my local clinic.

For some reason – and I'm sure this isn't standard practice – the male doctor who examined me did so without a female nurse present. Nowadays (given my assertiveness) I would complain about this, but back then, I just wanted to get the episode over and done with. So I lay back, put my feet in the stirrups and let him get on with it.

(I should repeat here that I hadn't been touched by a man for eighteen months. It is an important point.)

The doctor pushed gently on my belly, told me to relax and then inserted a finger into me. I looked at his hand pressed up against my vulva and desperately tried not to think of a cock against me. But it was too late: his touch had produced an instant response in my highly sensitive body. As he swivelled his finger, finding my cervix and tracing the outline of my womb, I realized how wet I was. Admittedly he had lubricant on his finger, but with the gentle pressure inside me and his firm hand still placed on my belly, I felt myself fully aroused; as he slipped another finger inside, I felt my body convulse and tremble and I knew that I wouldn't be far off from an orgasm.

'Are you OK?' he said and I felt my cheeks flush with embarrassment as I realized he could surely feel how engorged my private parts had become.

I nodded back at him and tried to focus on something other than the sensation between my legs, in the hope that I could turn myself off. I was terrified that I might climax in front of this man; disgusted with myself that I had become stimulated by the merest touch of another person, and a doctor at that.

Thankfully, he then removed his fingers, telling me that everything was in order, and then swiftly inserted the speculum, scraped my cervix, took some swabs, and then left me to get dressed, red-faced, engorged, aroused and all.

I was so embarrassed about the incident, I didn't go back to the clinic for some time – and when I did, I insisted that only female doctors examined me. Even with my mild Sapphic tendencies, I figured at least I wouldn't be thinking of cock when they had their hands in my insides. (Of course, I took other precautions too, like never again having an examination when I was sexually frustrated or horny.)

And that night, after having my insides explored by a doctor, I also finally had them explored by a rather delicious cock: I dragged my friend out to a bar so I could pull, and then ended up bedding some eager young bloke who was only too happy to fulfill my needs.

This episode in my life made me realize that abstaining from sex is all well and good for some, but it left me unhappy: instead of meeting a decent bloke, I spent eighteen months horny and desperately missing sex, only to then get into an embarrassing situation as a result.

Thankfully, I am now in a different place mentally and emotionally. Whilst I may wish to meet a 'good man', there is no way on earth that I am giving up sex in the meantime.

// posted by thegirl @ 9:19:00 PM

Wednesday 13th September

I can't believe it: I've just appeared on television for the first time, talking about the blog and book with Sharon Osbourne on her chat show on ITV.

I had arrived at the studio (after being picked up in a luxury car by one of the television company's drivers – another first for me) with a little bit of time to spare and I was taken into a private dressing room. So many times at work I'd be the first one in of a morning, making sure the room for the artistes was heated and lit and comfortable. Now it was me relaxing amongst the cushions and being asked if I wanted a cup of tea; very odd.

Shortly after, a runner came to escort me to the make-up room. Memories of early mornings and fleeting gulps of coffee came flooding back as I entered the brightly lit mirror-filled room. But this time I wasn't leading someone else to the chair: I was to sit in it myself.

It was an odd experience having someone applying make-up to my face. I'd watched the process hundreds of times, of course, as I waited for actors to become polished and beautiful, ready for their on-screen close-ups. As the soft brush licked my skin applying a swift cover of foundation I found myself struck by the surreal nature of it all: I never thought I'd be sitting in 'the chair'.

War-paint swiftly applied (three inches thick, at my estimate: I needed it), I made my way back to my dressing room and moments later the sound guy came in to mic me up. I smiled inwardly as he explained how to fit the wires around the nape of my neck and down to the radio pack hanging on my belt behind me: I know broadcast equipment like the back of my hand – I lived and worked with it for over a decade.

After he'd left, I went to the loo: I needed a pee, last-minute bra adjustments were called for and my lips begged more lipstick with their nervous dryness. Ever the assistant director, I had checked my watch when I entered the toilets, estimating I had just enough time before being called on. I was wrong: a minute later the floor manager darted in and told me it was 'time'. We rushed along the corridor and I resisted the temptation to tell her that I used to do a job just like hers; that I also used to have to run into toilets to grab the 'talent'; and that I used to get pissed off when the 'talent' would fart-arse around making last-minute phone calls, or having a quick fag, or finishing off their crosswords. With my boss screaming in the walkie-talkie hooked into my ear, 'Where the fuck are they? We are ready to shoot!', I would have to delicately attempt to convince them that they needed to come to set NOW. I'd often get the blame for their being late, of course. The 'talent' probably never knew that; they certainly rarely apologized for their delays. And here was I, unintentionally pulling the same fucking trick. God, I was embarrassed: I apologized profusely, but I'm not sure if the floor manager believed me.

Approaching the large set, I was shocked to see there were five cameras set up. Sure, I'm used to the movies with their big special effects scenes and nine film cameras rolling at once, but I found it surprising that a talk show would use that many cameras. Realizing there was a huge live studio audience of three to four hundred people only increased my nervousness, and as I stood to the side of set, I felt my legs wobble underneath me.

I knew I would be scared, but I suppose I shouldn't have been surprised how terrified I was, given that I always wanted to remain anonymous, and here was I – as myself – in front of a huge studio audience, surrounded by all those cameras, and about to be interviewed by a celebrity talk-show host.

I suppose it didn't help that as I was about to walk onto the set, two male crew members chatted about me:

'That must be Abby,' the older bloke said, gesturing towards me.

'Who's that?' the younger guy asked.

Both of them eyed me up.

'That's the girl who's shagged loads of blokes and written about it,' the older one replied.

Is that how I'm forever going to be known?

When I finally sat down on the on-screen couch, I discovered

Sharon was very sweet – in fact she was lovely – and she really tried to put me at ease as she asked me questions about the book, my blog and my family. It was nice that she was so kind and supportive to me, and even nicer that the audience gave me a cheer when I talked about refusing to let the 'outing' get me down any more. Before I knew it, it was over, and I was headed back to my dressing room, and off home.

As the car slowly wound its way back through traffic-filled London, I thought how absurd it was that it was me sitting on the couch with her and not some bona fide celebrity. Who would have thought that a lowly runner like me would end up being the focus of attention?

// posted by thegirl @ 11:43:00 PM

OCTOBER

Wednesday 4th October

What's going on? Billy, and now Matt: I'm being pursued by D-list celebs. Better than tabloid journalists, I guess.

Matt, a singer in a well-known band, first emailed me via MySpace some weeks ago.

For the record:

1. I hate MySpace.
2. I hate people who use MySpace.
3. I am only on MySpace to keep up with a few bands I like.

With Twitter and Facebook around, who wants to use the childish, loud, annoying interface of MySpace?

But it was on MySpace that Matt dropped me a line saying hello, and given his band is one whose music I appreciate, I replied.

Well, it's not often you get to speak to the cute lead singer of a cool band, is it? I was viewing his emails in a purely professional context, honest.

Anyway, turns out he's also been reading the blog, bought the book too, and now wants me to autograph his copy; I can't believe it. He's asked me out for a drink this evening;

somehow I doubt it'll purely be a drink, though . . .

I know I'm being shallow, and contradicting everything I said about not shagging fans of my blog. My rule about celebrities has also fallen by the wayside enough times now to be non-existent. I know for sure Matt is not Potential Boyfriend Material©, but would it be so bad if we were to end up in bed together? No one needs to know . . .

Thursday 5th October

I met up with Matt last night. And yes, reader, I shagged him.

We ended up in a little hotel off Bayswater after drinking a few too many cocktails in Ladbroke Grove. The sex? Well, let's just say it was great, beyond great, even: he was an excellent lover and seemed to know all my right spots without my having to show or guide him at all. I actually felt a bit intimidated by his prowess. I know, me, with my supposed reputation, right?

I've been left a little mortified by the whole experience, actually. Not because of the sex, but due to a horrifically embarrassing conversation we had this morning. We were in bed when he informed me that my orgasms were 'incredible'.

'What, because the aftershocks I have can reach 9.5 on the Richter scale?' I joked.

'No,' he replied, quite seriously, 'quite a few women have those. I meant your actual orgasms: they're very, um, intense . . .'

When he made that remark, I thought he was referring to the fact that I ground my teeth together as I came; or that I dug deep scratches in his back with my nails; or how my body went rigid at the height of my climaxes.

I didn't give it much more thought at that exact moment, because I was a bit preoccupied: his fingers were between my legs at the time, and I was headed towards yet another pleasurable seismic event.

But a few minutes later, post-climax, I've realized that he was insinuating something else entirely: when I was pushing down hard with my pelvic floor muscles as I orgasmed, I farted, loudly.

And not from the 'front bottom', neither.

I know it may not be a big deal to others, but right now, as I write this, I am cringing with embarrassment. 'The Farting Sexblogger': I can just see the headlines now. Ugh.

I don't think I'll be seeing Matt again: farting and fantastic sex aside, fucking someone in a band might be fun, but I'm definitely no groupie. The last thing I need right now is more gossip about me and my private life.

Friday 6th October

There is an urban myth that somewhere in the wilderness that is sex, there is a man who is God's gift to women. That this bloke is so good in the sack, to sleep with him is to experience sexual nirvana; nothing and no man can compete with his talents. His absolute devotion to pleasuring a lady is his only want; his own sexual release is secondary to her delight. And because this man has such amazing fuck-skills, a woman should only have him just the once, before passing him on to the next woman.

Let me tell you: this man is no myth. In fact, there isn't just one of these blokes – I personally have met a handful of them, and they all have two things in common:

1. They are amazing in bed.
2. They are not interested in having more than a shag.

It's the natural flip-side to the coin: the zenith of fucking, versus the nadir of relationships – it's an even balance in the scale of life, I think. That's not to say that spending time with these men is bad, as long as a woman is aware of the limitations of such a bloke: he is not meant to be with one woman; he has no taste for commitment.

Such spectacular sex is only ever transitory. This is the problem with fucking such a heavenly creature: we crave his skills again; we long for his hour-long devotion to cunnilingus; the way he prays religiously at the temple of our punani. On those long, dark nights where we need a soft kiss on our lips and a delectable multi-functional cock inside us, we want him back. But we can't; we're not meant to – he is for others to experience. That is the way it should be; that is the law of nature.

Women should fuck him with passion, and when done, he should be passed on for the next woman to experience amazing sex. Call it sisterly solidarity. How could such men ever take on a girlfriend? They are gifted, blessed even; call me a socialist hippie feminist, but I think they should be perpetually single for the good of all womankind.

So any ladies sitting on such a bloke right this minute should pass him on when they're done: somewhere in the world there's a woman due a damn good orgasm, and it's only fair that we all get a go. . .

// posted by thegirl @ 9:19:00 PM

Saturday 7th October

I hate Saturdays.

Why? Well, because it means my local high street is always filled with couples. They are everywhere with their sickly loved-up-ness, holding hands like pathetic teenagers, rather than the thirty-something adults they are. It's disgusting.

There they are at my local fruit and veg stall, sniggering to each other as they push and prod the vegetables; their talk of dinner parties holding up the line. And there they are again, at the newsagent's, smirking at each other as they queue up with the *Guardian*. And there they are once more, sitting at all the cafés, making eyes at each other as they sip their cappuccinos and read the day's news, ignoring the sad singletons who wander forlornly past.

It's sick, I tell you, sick. OK, it's not, but it's annoying: everywhere I look are happy couples in their mid-thirties, an in-my-face reminder that I am single. It forces me to confront the reality that I don't have that same companionship; that I don't get to walk down the street with my man; that I don't have that happy, sunny, loving outlook – and, to be honest, it really fucks me off.

Don't get me wrong: most of the time, I have actually liked being single. I've rather enjoyed the freedom it's afforded me.

It's exciting to have an interchangeable love-life buffet: I've enjoyed the 'serial dating' I've had over the years – meeting lots of new and interesting men ... and their cocks too. Which was always nice.

But recently – and especially on Saturdays – I'm really missing not having a partner. I shuffle past all the couples walking arm in arm on my high street and I find myself wishing I was one of them. I watch as they share a private joke and it makes me long to have that same connection with someone. I see one of them subtly fondle the other's bum as they're walking and it makes me yearn for the same intimacy: it feels like an age since I shared that with someone.

I'm not going to dwell on it, though: whilst I may envy those who are in love, I am not one to wallow in self-pity – love'll happen, at some point; I'm ready for it when it does (I think). But there is one thing that I really yearn for: waking up early on a Saturday morning and reaching behind me to find my partner's cock, sliding it between my wet thighs and then having a long, slow, deep fuck.

I can't think of a better way to start the day than with a half-asleep, intense mutual orgasm. Aside from the obvious intimacy and pleasure derived from this, there's also the fact that it would put me in a good mood for the rest of the weekend.

// posted by thegirl @ 7:47:00 PM

Sunday 8th October

You know what? Sometimes a girl just wants to be made love to.

It's all very well my happily gagging for a hard shag: faced with the right bloke, it's not something I turn down.

But right now, I know this: I want to be fucked slowly, Saturday-style.

I want to be with a guy who takes his time; someone who wants to discover and explore my body and who wants to caress every inch of me until my skin feels electric.

I want a man who will:

slide his fingers through my hair as his lips touch mine
softly stroke my arse, the curve of my back, the nape of my neck
explore my belly, my hips, the inside of my thighs with soft, sweet kisses
lightly touch my breasts, drawing circles around my nipples
see the excitement in my eyes as he lowers himself down my body
hold my hands in his, as his mouth greets my burning desire
pull me gently onto his face as his soft tongue pleasures me
squeeze my hand as the first climax hits me and my body convulses
push his hard cock against my thigh as he moves up my body
kiss me deeply as he presses his body close to mine

laugh, as I try to angle myself so his cock will slide into me
smile as my frustration increases
position himself so only the tip of his cock is inside me
make me so desperate that I beg him to fuck me
lie still and kiss me deeply

And when I cannot stand it any longer, when I am crying out in frustration and desperation, I want him to:

slide into me as far as he can go
refuse to move inside me
make me more frustrated as I lie there, filled, but unful-
    filled
wait until he and I can stand it no longer
finally give me what I am begging for

And then I want him to fuck me:

take me so slowly, the movement is almost imperceptible
push me to the edge of orgasm, so I am on the verge of
    tears
have me on the brink
not let me come, until he is ready to come
on and on, slow, but steady
make my heart race
make me drip
force my nails into his back

And when he gets near; when he finally feels his own surge approach, only then would he pummel me hard, fucking me with all his might, until our orgasms combine to send simultaneous electricity across both our bodies.

And when we'd stopped shaking and had caught our breath, then he would slide his fingers into mine, kiss me deeply, look into my eyes and smile.

It's been a long time since I made love. I miss it.

Tuesday 10th October

'So joor da notorious granddaughter, den?' remarked the nonagenarian as she greeted me at the door in her velvet-toned Hungarian (with a hint of German) voice. 'Vee've heard all arbout ju here.'

'Good things, I hope?' I stammered, hoping that her sight-impediment would prevent her noticing my cheeks flush with embarrassment.

'Of course!' she replied, ushering me into my grandmother's flat. 'Joor de sex-writer, aren't ju? Joor famousse here – everyone vants to read joor book!'

I looked over at my grandma, who was sat on the couch, a smile on her face. I was grateful that she too had poor eyesight, and thus was unable to see the expression of worry that was etched onto my features. 'Oh really, it's nothing, just boring stuff about my life. Anyone for a cup of tea? I'll put the kettle on . . .'

My grandma's friend wasn't going to let it go so easily. 'From vart I heard, it's radda racy – if it vasn't for the fact dat I am blind, I'd have read it myself. Udder people here have und I'd like to know vat I'm missing out on!'

'It's nothing you wouldn't know about already, I'm sure,' I answered, hoping that would nip the conversation in the bud.

'Don't be so sure,' she replied, wagging her finger at me. 'Ju youngsters do und say things vee just don't understand. I'm sure ju could teach me a thing or two.'

'Well,' I said, hesitantly, 'you know what they say: "Young people think they invented sex and that they are the only people to have it" . . .'

'Joor right, of course vee also had sex, but life vas different back den: vee didn't talk about it. So I vish I could read joor book!' She cackled, and my grandma joined her in laughing.

I moved over to the couch and sat down next to my grandma's friend so I could be in her field of limited vision. 'Whilst I wish you still had your sight, I'm also glad you can't read my book, because it's very personal, and I'd really prefer my family and friends not to go through it.'

She reached over to me and took my hand in hers. 'Darlink, you ave narding to be ashamed of. Vee are proud of ju und joor success and vee vant de best for ju, don't vee?' She smiled at me sweetly and my grandma nodded.

Suddenly I was filled with warmth for them: two women in their nineties from a different generation, a different time, even a different country. I wanted to tell her how touched I was by what she said; that her – and my grandma's – acceptance of me and what I might represent to them – youth, modernity, change – was unbelievably honourable. I felt humbled by the respect they had for me; and I felt ashamed at how my generation treats its older people – as if they are worthless, and their lives and history meaningless. Tears quickly made their way to the edges of my eyes and I stood up abruptly to busy myself in the kitchen.

A few minutes, later I heard my name being called and I wandered back into the living room, teapot, cups and saucers in hand.

'She wants to know some modern swear words,' my grandma said, gesturing towards her friend. 'I thought you might be able to suggest something.'

Stifling my laughter and not wanting to offend either of them, I asked what they considered rude. When they stated that 'bloody hell' was very offensive to them, I decided not to recommend any of the terminology I make use of on a regular basis . . . Later, when the tea was finished, they both confessed to 'using the F-word', as my grandma put it, but admitted that was only done privately, or under their breath. Given that, I thought it best not to suggest the usage of 'prick', 'wanker' or 'arsehole' to my grandma's friend.

As I was leaving, she pulled me to one side and made me promise I would teach her how to swear 'properly'. I agreed I would, if only to hear her delectable accent form the words, 'Fark ju, ju vanker!' I won't be recommending she learn 'cocksucker', though: some things are best left to the unsavoury mouths of the young, I think.

Thursday 12th October

A recent conversation with my mum:

My mum (calling out from her office): Guess what? Sup-posedly I can get a bigger penis.

Me (in the next room, updating Twitter on my mobile phone): Oh really?

My mum: Yes. There are these special pills, you see, and it's promised that my penis will grow larger if I take them.

Me: That's amazing!

My mum: Shall I buy some, then?

Me: Definitely: it sounds like an unmissable opportunity.

My mum: Do you think the fact that I don't have actually have a penis is relevant?

Me: You'd better not mention it; they might discriminate.

My mum: Fucking spammers.

I love my mum.

// posted by thegirl @ 8:48:00 PM

Friday 13th October

Whilst at my parents' place yesterday, I had the most awful experience; it was almost worse than their finding out about my writing about my sex life. Almost.

I was showing my mum photographs of my grandma, which I took a few days ago.

'So if you just press that button there, you can scroll through the party pictures,' I said, handing her my digital camera and walking towards the kitchen.

A few minutes later I returned laden with a fresh pot of tea.

'What are you looking at?' I asked, seeing her still scrolling through the pictures on the viewfinder.

'Oh, nothing in particular,' she replied.

I leaned over the table to look at the digital screen, expecting to see the shots I had taken of my grandma. Instead, to my horror, were photographs of my trip to New York, from earlier this year. In an instant I realized that she must have viewed all the other pictures which I had left on the camera between then and now; she would have seen me oiled up, my breasts bursting out of a tight rubber dress, wearing five-inch stilettos on my feet, when I had done some self-portraits for my own amusement. I suddenly felt sick to my stomach.

I grabbed the camera from her hands and switched it off. 'Did you look through them all?!' I squeaked.

She nodded. 'Yes.'

'So you saw . . . everything?'

She blushed. 'Um, yes.'

'All my saucy pics?'

'Yes.'

Inwardly I screamed, loudly. Outwardly I gritted my teeth and went into damage-limitation mode. 'Well, they weren't for your eyes. I said to look at the pictures of Grandma: the other photos are private. You shouldn't have looked at them.'

'Sorry,' she said, quietly.

'Let's not discuss this again.'

'Best not to,' she agreed.

We drank our tea in silence and shortly afterwards I made my way home. It was only when I looked through the camera later that I realized that even though I was embarrassed by her finding those pictures, I had got off lightly: also stored on the memory card were other, more compromising photographs, specifically the ones I snapped of my New York fuck-buddy's erect penis. It's one thing to have your mum see you dressed up in sexy gear, but it's another thing entirely for her to view the material you use to masturbate with. Ugh.

Suffice to say all these photographs have now been deleted from my camera. (But not before being uploaded – and backed up – onto my computer first, that is.)

// posted by thegirl @ 9:27:00 PM

☉

Having my mum see those photos of me scantily clad has got me thinking about something. I reckon that if a woman has had erotic photographs taken of her by a sexual partner, these will, at some point, appear on the Internet – usually without her knowledge.

Like many women, I have, over the years, participated in various forms of online communication with men. Nothing out of the ordinary: just your typical emails, live chatting and heated mutual masturbation via the keyboard. A normal day at the office for some (or so I am led to believe). Anyway, during these 'encounters', there is invariably a point where one person or another requests some pictures. Depending on the circumstance – respectable online dating site; sordid casual-sex chat room – the exchanged pictures will usually consist of a facial shot (read: head and shoulders), (minus any body fluids – bar perspiration), or something below the neck. It is the latter that I am thinking about specifically.

If a man feels compelled to send me a picture of his cock, I expect to see a picture of their cock. Preferably hard.

Definitely in focus. Hopefully surrounded by the owner of said cock's hand, gripping it sexily, to give it some context.

What I don't appreciate is being sent pictures of a guy's cock with a woman also attached to it. You know the type: she's on her knees, sucking him; she's bent over and he's fucking her from behind; she's on her back and he's tugging himself off over her belly. All the women in these pictures are identifiable; not only are their bodies on display – more often than not their faces are too.

Now, I have two issues with this. The first concerns my own selfishness: if I want to wank over a bloke's picture, I want to imagine myself in the scene with him – not be faced with another woman in my place. Personal pictures are different to porn; the context is more intimate, thus it's more difficult to imagine being part of someone else's interaction.

The second issue is of far more concern to me: when I ask who the women in the pictures are, every man has said to me, 'Oh, that's just my ex.' When I have pressed them further, and asked about her consenting to his using the pictures, they then reply, 'Don't worry, she doesn't know.'

And she doesn't. Time and time again, I have received pictures of men having sex with their ex-girlfriends, in some shape or form; my hard drive is filled with images of anonymous women I will never meet; women whose readily identifiable images are freely available to all on the Internet.

I bet none of these women gave their consent for their pictures to be used in this way. I very much doubt that in the heat of passion, when their boyfriend suggested they 'capture the moment', these women thought their partner would at some point be using those same images to chat to/masturbate

with/fuck other women off the Internet. I expect that many –
if not all – of those women would shudder in horror if they
knew that their image was being used in this way.

I guess it's no surprise: we are constantly surrounded by
images of women in various states of undress, selling everything
from magazines to cars; it's almost taken as a given that
women's bodies are sexualized commodities, so why should
men think of getting permission to use intimate photos when it's
acceptable to profit off these same images in mainstream media?

So, what's the answer? I'm afraid there's only one: if
women don't want to run the risk of their erotic pictures
being shared on the Internet, then they can't EVER let any be
taken. Seriously. I know it's hard when he's got his cock in
you, you're fucking turned on, and you're in love and everything is hunky-dory, and when he says, 'Oh god, it'd turn me
on so much to have photographs of this, let me get the camera,' you think, 'Well, we love each other, no one else will see
them, what's the harm?' I know you wouldn't be thinking,
'But what if we ever break up? What'll happen to the pictures?' But that's what you need to remember: if you do ever
break up, then at some point, those pictures will find their
way onto the Internet, in some shape, manner or form, I can
almost guarantee it.

This is why I have never, ever let a partner or lover take
erotic pictures of me (bar one picture which was just of my
arse, in which I cannot be identified). And I'm obviously now
even more relieved that I haven't: it's bad enough that people
have got to know all my intimate thoughts and the details
of my sex life, without them then being able to see visual
evidence of it too.

Of course, there'll be some women who couldn't care less that personal images of them in various states of sexual arousal are freely available to view online, but I expect that many would be uncomfortable with this knowledge.

But for all the women who've had their image exploited in this way, let it be known that I always refuse to fuck that arsehole who used to be your ex – it may not be a huge step for womankind in terms of empowerment and equality, but if it means one less prick gets laid as a result, then that's a step in the right direction, in my opinion.

// posted by thegirl @ 1:14:00 PM

Saturday 14th October

I had the weirdest evening last night. First I had a meeting in town with a film producer, who is keen to take my book to the big screen. This was obviously very exciting – who would have thought that a measly floor runner, who's lost her job in the film industry, would one day be invited to Soho to talk about making a movie of her life? I'm thrilled to bits, and really hope that something happens. It'd be some good karma in my life, I think.

Second, after that meeting, I met up with Tim in Soho for a few beers. I was probably on my third or fourth drink and lining up at the bar for another round when the bartender said something incredible to me.

'I know you,' he announced, as he handed me my credit card receipt.

'What?' I was confused: he didn't seem familiar to me at all.

'Your name,' he said, pointing to the receipt I was now holding in my hands. 'I recognized your name. You're the author of *Girl with a One Track Mind*, aren't you?'

Ah. Right. I get it. I nodded, and bit my lip nervously.

He smiled at me. 'I knew it, I knew it was you as soon as I saw your name. I love your blog!'

I felt myself blush and wasn't sure how to respond. 'Thanks,' I stammered. 'That's very nice of you to say.'

He continued. 'I think it was awful what happened to you, but be proud of what you've written! It's great you've continued on with the blog even though you got outed: it shows you're not ashamed about sex, and it's really important that that message is out there.'

What a nice thing to say; I was speechless with gratitude. He smiled at me, and I relaxed.

'Anyway,' he said, 'I don't want to hold you up, but would you mind giving me your autograph? It'd mean a lot to me.'

I was stunned. My autograph? I almost burst out laughing: he had me mixed up with an actual celebrity! I didn't laugh, though, because he was being absolutely serious and his kind words had touched me. Then I had a sudden idea.

'How about I sign a copy of the book for you? Would that be OK?' From my handbag I pulled out the book I had carried with me to my earlier meeting (but not given to the producer as he had brought his own copy with him) and I opened the front cover. 'Who should I dedicate it to?'

Now it was his turn to blush. 'Um, Clark, please. Wow. Thank you!'

I wrote him a little note and paused before signing it. Whose name should I use, Zoe or Abby? I decided on the latter – it seemed more appropriate. Signing it 'Zoe' would have felt too personal, somehow. As I handed him the book his face broke out into a huge grin.

'Right,' he said, 'this round is on me.' He grabbed some tequila from behind him and filled two huge shot glasses with the liquid, before thrusting them in my hands.

I said thanks and he smiled at me again, and I shuffled back over to where Tim was sat and shared my story with him: he too was dumbfounded.

We're off to some tech party later. Not really my scene – I don't know many in the industry – but if it's filled with cute geeks, I'm more than happy to tag along whilst Tim networks.

Sunday 15th October

You know how you're at a party, drunkenly caning the free whisky like there's no tomorrow and then a sexygeekboy sits down and starts chatting to you, and before you know it your legs are touching and then he's whispering in your ear that he has an early morning flight and 'Do you want to leave now and make a night of it?' and you're grinning and saying, 'Yes,' and then you stumble back to his hotel room and fuck each other furiously, and you're wondering how the hell this dropdead gorgeous man ended up in bed with you, and then he leaves for the airport, and you curl up in his bed with a huge smile on your face, waking a few hours later to check out of the hotel, and then you Google his name and discover that he's not just any sexygeekboy but one that also happens to be famous on the Internet?

Yeah, that.

Must be something in the water.

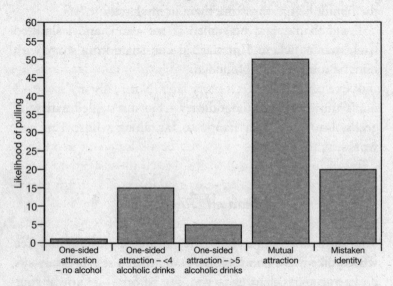

One Night Stands

Saturday 21st October

I went over to Kathy's place today for lunch. It's the first time we've seen each other since I was outed. But instead of feeding me, she held me to ransom with demands that I give her sex tips, or she wouldn't make lunch. Kathy is an excellent cook – and a hard bargainer:

'Please tell me,' she demanded, after pressing me for almost twenty minutes.

With a growling stomach reminding me how hungry I was, I moaned a reply. 'Really, there is nothing I can possibly tell about blow-jobs.'

'You must know something that would help me.'

'Oh, come on, I'm not some fucking sex-expert!'

'You wrote a whole book about your sex life!'

I sighed. 'But it wasn't solely about sex. There was a lot of psychoanalytical and political deconstruction of events and feelings, rather than just descriptions of bodily functions. It's not erotica . . .'

'Yeah, yeah, yeah – but there was lots of shagging in it . . .'

She had me there. 'True . . .'

Kathy looked at me with her best puppy-dog expression. 'Please. Just give me a few tips; I need them. Pretend I am a reader of your blog. You've written loads of stuff for them – why won't you help me out?'

Checkmate. I took another large gulp of wine. 'OK. But don't expect a refund if it doesn't work; it's just my opinion, based on my experience.'

She grinned at me excitedly. 'I'm all ears.'

I swallowed nervously. Writing anonymously about your sex life is easy; talking about it openly with your friends, in explicit detail, is another thing entirely.

'Right, well, obviously my first rule with a blow-job is that it can never be too wet.'

'Wet?'

'Yes. Sucking their cock in the wettest, juiciest, sloppiest way possible. Men seem to love that – the ones I've been with, anyway. So you can't have any qualms or embarrassment about saliva or drool dripping down your chin; it's not about keeping your lipstick pristine – it's about their cock sliding around in your slippery gob, got it?'

She nodded enthusiastically.

'If your mouth is dry, always have a glass of water handy: it'll keep you hydrated as well as ensure your mouth is moist. Plus, it has the added bonus of changing your tongue's temperature slightly, which then increases the sensation they feel on their cock. Win/win.'

'This is good, tell me more. Come on, I need to know!'

'Er, OK, well, that was rule number one. Number two is always use an element of surprise: that never fails to work.'

'What do you mean? Creep up on them and offer them a blow-job out of the blue?'

I laughed. 'Well, yes, spontaneity is always a bonus when it comes to sex, but that isn't quite what I meant. What I'm talking about is your technique: make him try to anticipate your next move, but then surprise him with something he didn't expect instead.'

'Like . . .?'

'Like when he thinks you're about to suck him hard, don't. Instead, tease him by just licking the tip. Or, when you're softly nibbling his shaft, suddenly thrust him deeply into your mouth. Or, just do a variety of things and mix them up so he never knows what comes next: kissing his thighs, sucking his glans, squeezing his nipples, giving him eye contact and smiling at him, stroking his shaft, nuzzling his balls, licking his perineum, rubbing him between your tits – whatever.'

Kathy nodded slowly. 'I get it. Don't stick with just sucking.'

'Exactly: it's boring, for you as well as him. And that is what he'll expect – sucking, I mean. That's the bullshit you see in pornos – suck suck suck, head bobbing up and down like a lunatic: that's not real; that's not what it's about – not for me, anyway. You can't really go far wrong with a good suck, but if you can be more sensual, mix it up a little, and never do what he expects, you'll have him on the brink for a long time. Plus, his whole groin area is filled with nerve endings, so by constantly changing the sensations you are giving him, you'll be firing off so many pleasure neurons in his brain he won't know what hit him. Or, in other words, you'll have given him a stonking hard-on.'

Kathy giggled. 'I like it. But I'm dying to know the next rule! There is another one, right?'

'Yeah. One more; in four stages. But this one is hard to describe. I'll have to show you.'

I looked around for something cock-shaped to demonstrate with. After debating about sticking my mobile phone in my mouth, I decided on two fingers instead, given that they would be slightly more enjoyable to insert, and less likely to fill my gob with radiation.

'Ok, so, you've got the enthusiasm, the wet mouth, lips over teeth, suction in place, etc. . . .'

She nodded.

'Right, so the next move is to add the Tongue-Tickle©.' I licked the underside of my fingers to show her. 'You want to do it around the tip, on his frenulum. The key is to vary the speed, pressure and duration of this; view it like you're tickling him – you want the element of surprise to get the best effect.'

Kathy copied my tongue movements on her own fingers. 'I think I get it.'

'And you can lick it lightly or longingly like a lollipop – either way, it'll feel good.'

She grinned. 'Excellent. What's next?'

'Ok, here is where it gets a little tricky. You've got the sucking and the Tongue-Tickle©, right?

'Right.'

'Now you need to combine them.'

Kathy frowned, her fingers deep in her mouth. 'I can't do it,' she said, removing them. 'It's not possible to do it together.'

'Yes, it is,' I reassured her. 'Slide your fingers back into your mouth. OK, now suck softly. That OK?'

She nodded, slowly.

'And now move your tongue up and down as you suck. Wiggle it around, but don't stop the suction with the rest of your mouth.'

Kathy's eyes lit up and she pulled her fingers out. 'I've got it! I've fucking got it! My god, I bet men love this shit. Jesus, you're a fucking genius knowing all this stuff. I can't wait to try it on David!'

I laughed. 'Steady on, we're not done yet. Ready for the next step?'

She nodded again, this time more enthusiastically.

'Ok, once you've got the mouth and tongue combination, you need to add the vertical action. Like this.' I sucked on my two fingers and bobbed my head up and down, like some kind of demented pigeon trying to find a loose seed in my lap.

Kathy successfully copied me and grinned. 'This is great. What's next?'

'Well, it's a little tricky and you can't sustain it for a long time. But it is worth trying, even just for a minute – he'll love it.'

'Tell me!'

'OK. Now you need to add the horizontal circular movement.'

She stared at me. 'What?'

'The twist. Like this.' I sucked on my fingers, dabbled with my tongue, moved my mouth up and down, and then turned my head from side to side.

'You've got to be fucking kidding me,' she said, despairingly.

'No, really, you must try it. Look, just swivel your neck a little.' I grabbed her head with my hands and tried to turn it to one side. After some coaxing, she managed to twist it without my assistance, and I sat back to watch her in action, whilst rehearsing the movement myself. For a moment I wondered what someone would think if they walked into the room: two grown women with their fingers in their mouths; sucking hard, dabbling with their tongues, ducking their heads up and down, and swivelling their necks simultaneously. If only men knew what effort we put in, to look so stupid – and give good blow-jobs . . .

'Fucking hell,' Kathy said, coming up for air. 'This is great; you've thought of everything – I have got to try this out . . . Where the hell did you learn this technique?'

'Let's just say I've spent some quality time experimenting.'

// posted by thegirl @ 9:29:00 PM

Wednesday 25th October

After receiving a really horrid comment from someone else on my blog today, I find myself asking the question that pre-occupied me a year ago: is there something wrong with me because I love sex so much?

Craigslist Guy even teased me about this one night, calling me a 'sex addict'.

'Have you ever had a partner who was really up for sex?' I asked him. 'Have you been with a girl besides me who was always in the mood; who jumped you at any opportunity; who really loved shagging you?'

'Of course,' he replied.

'Did you think something was wrong with her?'

He paused and then smiled. 'No, it was great, actually; she had a very high sex drive.'

'As do I.'

I guess that's what I need to remind myself. Just because a woman enjoys sex, it seems that she must be seen as pathological in some way; that she must be abnormal, or bad, or – as in my case – some kind of addict. Why can't women just like sex? Why can't we be seen to enjoy it, without being called 'sluts' or 'whores' or 'addicts'? Why must something be wrong with us, just because we openly express our needs, desires and wants?

The comment I received earlier really underlined this.

' . . . before she was outed by the media,' the commenter began, 'I read Zoe's blog, as did my boyfriend. And afterwards we both agreed unanimously that it had to have been written by a man.'

I have had this accusation levelled at me many, many times over the years. It used to make me laugh, but I also got angry: why can't a blog about sex, written in a graphic way, be authored by a woman?

The commenter continues:

'We thought this because in most of the sexual encounters described in her blog, Zoe comes a ridiculous amount. And I do mean ridiculous. Often during the first sexual encounter with a new partner.'

I won't deny this, because it is true. Yes, I climax easily. And? For that I must be male?

'Now unless you are a VERY lucky women,' she continued, 'so lucky in fact that the mere touch of a man sends you on a cascade of orgasms, that just doesnt happen! Its a male fantasy, of the type you find in the story section of a cheap porn mag. We were asked to believe all these (very talented) men knew exactly what to do first time.[sic]'

And this is where this particular reader has got the blog, the book, and me, all wrong. The fact I can orgasm frequently and easily is little to do with how good a lover a man might be and ALL to do with the fact that I know my body well, and I know how to bring myself off, as I've repeatedly said.

Having orgasms hasn't always been easy for me. In fact, I spent years, as many women do, not climaxing at all, and when I finally learned how to, I was still not able to come with a guy like I could on my own. So what changed? Well, I wanked lots, mainly.

I documented all this on the blog and in my book and at no point did I ever state that my ability to climax was purely because the man I was with was some Casanova. I've fucked men who ejaculated after three minutes of thrusting; or who painfully jabbed their fingers in and out of me as fast as possible; or who could not stay hard for more than a minute or two, and you know what? I've climaxed with them all, and each time, my ability to do so was because I knew exactly how I could obtain an orgasm – and I ensured I received (or gave myself) the stimulation necessary to bring me off.

That's not to say I haven't been with some amazing men, who not only taught me how to be a better lover myself, but whose sensuality and sexiness had me dripping wet upon just kissing them. Sometimes the chemistry just clicks and when it does, the sex can be magic. But even given this, without my ability to relax – and I mean both physically and mentally – I would still be struggling to orgasm, like I did throughout my early twenties. So what I've documented is not pretend or fantasy, but my own, real, experience of sex – that's what made it so hard to be outed.

The commenter still had more to add, though: 'What did she do, distribute a manual of the best way to bring her to orgasm to the male population of London?'

She had got it so completely wrong. She was obviously one of those expecting the man to be responsible for her orgasm; or she was lacking the confidence to ask for what she wanted, being someone who was unable to switch off the horrid insecurities that impact on sex ('Does he think I'm fat?'; 'Will he consider me a slut for fucking him on the first date?'; 'Am I shit at hand-jobs?').

You know, when I began writing my blog and book, I felt like I was a freak: as if I was the only woman unafraid to express her appetite for sex. I felt terribly alone in that.

Everywhere I looked it seemed that as a woman, I was either supposed to have difficulty orgasming and be inhibited about sex, or else I was supposed to be donning a thong, shaking my tits at some lads and screaming about how 'empowered' I was. I related to neither, and I was sick of how my sexuality as a woman was restrained by these limited stereotypes. Where were the women who loved sex and refused the 'slut' label? Where were the women who felt OK about their bodies, but weren't interested in making money from them? Where were the women who grasped that sexual liberation doesn't mean the 'freedom' to pose for *Playboy*, but instead means being able to have the sex that they want and still be respected by both their partners and society?

I've learned I am not the only one with these points of view. In fact, the thousands of emails and comments I've received from women who've read the blog prove the opposite: there are many, many women with one track minds. All of our perspectives belong; none of us should feel like freaks.

I might be more enthusiastic than many women with my joyful approach to sex, but that doesn't mean that I am the only woman thinking about it, or doing it – I'm just one who's been prepared to write about it and broadcast it to the world. I never planned on anyone knowing it was me who was saying it, is all.

// posted by thegirl @ 7:48:00 PM

Sunday 29th October

With all the online attacks I receive, perhaps I should just post the following on my blog, set the record straight?

I want to be judged purely on the basis of my appearance.

I love it that men might think me attractive, because, like, that's all that matters to me.

I feel validated if men want to fuck me: the more that do, the merrier.

I think it's great that how I look is more important than what I have achieved.

I want to teach young girls that to get ahead in life, all they need is cosmetic surgery. They have to fight gravity and age; otherwise no man will ever want them!

I hope more women realize that if they'd only make themselves more attractive, then they would be more successful in their jobs. It's all about being desired by men! Anyone that says it isn't is an ugly feminist that needs a good fuck.

I think Jordan is a feminist icon. Making money out of your body? Now that's real empowerment: a modern-day fight for equality. All women should strive for this.

I like denying myself pleasurable things because women should be martyrs.

I ate a cake once, in secret, but I try not to be naughty: skipping pudding means I'll be slimmer and more attractive to men! Anyway, who says obsession with one's weight is boring?

I always hold off from having sex on a date because not 'giving in' to men means I have power over them.

I insist men pay for me on dates because that makes me feel feminine. The fact I earn more than them is irrelevant. Men buy and women put out: that's just the way it is. You can't fight human nature!

I think women should take responsibility for rape, by covering up more. Men, poor things, get worked up by seeing women's bodies and it's not their fault they then can't control themselves. Testosterone is a very powerful thing!

I always fake my orgasms because I want men to think they're expert lovers.

If Belle from *Secret Diary of a Call Girl* can prep her vagina with lube to pretend to her customers that she's sexually aroused, so should all women.

I adore that when people say 'sexy', they mean 'female'.

It pleases me that the default position in how sex is marketed is always male and heterosexist, or female and bisexual. Because women never want to see pictures of naked men: all of us are happier just to look at other women, don't you know?!

I love it that porn is so focused on the male perspective, because as a woman I obviously have no interest in seeing it portrayed through a female gaze.

I don't need to wank because, like, I'm not a man. Also, my lovers might get jealous.

I have no need for orgasms because cuddling is so much
   nicer and women don't have the same sexual urges as
   men, anyway. Also, what's an orgasm?
I like accusing women of being 'sex negative' if they
   reject the mass-market monopolization of their sexuality as a financial commodity.
I want to follow the advice in *How to Make Love Like
   a Porn Star* because my ambition is to be as sexually
   empowered as Jenna Jameson is. Also, I need to perfect my technique in faking orgasms. All women do.

But then, would anyone know I was being sarcastic? Somehow I doubt it.

// posted by thegirl @ 8:43:00 PM

NOVEMBER

Wednesday 1st November

I just got off the 'phone to an Australian radio station. I still haven't got my head around the fact that people take such an interest in me; the requests for interviews are now a daily occurrence. A year ago I was doing sixteen hour days on film sets, now I seem to spend all my time talking to the media or writing articles; I'm even being asked to give public talks. I never expected my life to turn out like this. Given what happened to me, I guess I've made lemonade out of lemons, as the cliché goes: being a writer now gives me something to look forward to in my professional life. Wish I could say the same for my personal life . . .

Thursday 2nd November

The problem with being known as a sex diarist is that your reputation precedes you. Not so much in the 'what a slut, shagging all those blokes' way (although I am still receiving obnoxious emails and comments from people to that effect) but more in the 'I have certain expectations of you and those are pretty fixed' presumptions people make.

So, when I meet guys through my mutual acquaintances

and am introduced as 'Girl with a One Track Mind, the sexblogger', they tend to react to me in one of two ways: either extremely sexual (and often inappropriately so), or extremely cautious. The former is not such an issue for me: since I've been forced to merge my online and offline lives, I have, ironically, also taken a step back from pursuing casual sex. Men might occasionally make advances, online or off-line, and whilst that obviously boosts my ego a bit, I don't take them up on it: they're interested in Girl with a One Track Mind, not the real me.

What I find especially hard is when guys react to me in a hesitant way, as if after shaking their hand I'm then going to attempt to grab their cock; as if I would make a move on them immediately, or otherwise write about them. These men assume that my primary interest in them is for sex and if they're not interested (or even if they might like me) they then relate to me at arm's length. And given I've lost the ability to know whether a guy's chatting to me because he's being friendly, because he's interested in me, or because he wants a Girl tick on his damn scorecard, none of this makes for easy communication, or, sadly, dating. It's certainly affected my confidence in the latter.

In a conversation a week or so back with a man called Jay whom I met last year through Fiona, he made an offhand comment that he hadn't read my book; I then made him promise that he wouldn't. 'Why?' he asked, 'Surely there's nothing to be ashamed of or embarrassed about? We all have sex.' 'Yes,' I replied, 'we do, but I want someone to get to know that side of me, as well as all the other aspects of me, by getting to know me – Zoe – and not by reading it in a

book. And I want to get to know them on an equal basis too.'
He nodded and agreed and promised not to read it, and most
likely didn't take the hint that I was actually referring to my
wanting to get to know him away from all the book stuff. We
continued discussing public vs private lives and the effects of
Internet 'celebrity' and I sat there gazing into his eyes, wondering what it'd be like to kiss him and hoping that he didn't
realize I had a mild crush on him. Pathetic, I know.

And this, for me, is the crux of the matter. I'm not even able
to be me any more. The flirtatious me. The talkative, wanting
to get to know someone because I find them really interesting
me. And definitely not the sexual me. I'm left so insecure by
the guys who think I'm just after sex, that I find talking to
men a serious challenge now: I'm so desperately trying to not
be the Girl that I can't even communicate properly any more.

Picture the scene.

Prior to me being outed:

Me: Hey, let's have dinner sometime!

Him: Dinner?

Me: Yeah, you know, that thing you do where you eat and
talk? (I nudge him with my elbow and smile.) I've heard it
can be fun.

Then either:

a) **Him** (grinning): Heh. OK then. When?
b) **Him** (grimacing): Thanks, but I'm kind of seeing someone.

Then either:

a) **Me** (grinning): Great. Next week?
b) **Me** (sheepish): Well, no harm in a girl asking, right?

The situation now:

Me: Um. Would you like to have dinner sometime?
Him: Dinner? Hahahaha.
Me (making sure my body language remains neutral, for fear that I may be perceived as being sexual): Yes, you know, food. And conversation. Maybe some wine?
Him (frowning): Zoe. You're asking me to dinner. Seriously? Just you and I?
Me (blushing, stuttering and unable to maintain eye contact): Yes. I mean, as friends, obviously, I wouldn't want you to think it was anything else. Although if you liked me too that would be really nice, but god, I don't expect you to, because you probably only go for really beautiful women and I mean, yes, sure, you're a nice guy, um, you're very handsome and everything, but this is just dinner, no pressure, and you really don't need to worry that I would jump you or anything because even though I'd love to, I think you're worth much more than a quick shag, plus I really want to get to know you because I think you're really interesting, and I thought it might be nice to hang out sometime, away from the crowd and . . . oh look, forget it, I know it'd probably embarrass you to have dinner with me and our friends would gossip and then people would judge you and you'd probably just do it for the novelty fac-

tor because you clearly wouldn't be interested in someone whose sex life has been so public and look, why don't we forget this conversation ever happened? I'll just grab that cab over there and be on my way . . .

I jest, but it's not far from reality. I've no idea how to move beyond my current fear. I would like to let Jay know that I find him interesting, enjoy his company and would be interested in getting to know him some more. I'd really like him to know that I find him attractive, but even though I'd love to jump into bed with him and fuck him senseless, I don't want to just add him to the Girl scorecard.

I'd like him to find out that I'm more than the sum of my book and my blog, that there are other parts of me and my life that are much more likeable than the ever-shag-loving Girl. And I really, really would like to ask him out on a date, but I don't know if I have the courage to do that. Yet.

// posted by thegirl @ 11:38:00 PM

Tuesday 7th November

After talking with my friend Tim about it on the phone, I've decided to bite the bullet and email Jay asking him out to dinner. It's just food, right? I sent the email past Tim first, to see what he thought and get some advice from him.

Me: Is it too flirtatious?
Tim: No. It's aggressive.

Me: Fuck. Really? Bugger.

Tim: You're the big bad Sex Blogress. You have no idea the impact you have on people. Even though you and I know you're just an average, normal girl, many guys will be intimidated by you.

Me: Oh Christ. I'm stuck, I really am.

Tim: You're not stuck, you're being neurotic. Snap out of it.

Me: Sorry, I can't help it.

And I can't. I'm still filled with such anxiety about dating: surely it should be simpler than this? All I'm asking is if he'd go on a date with me; should it really be that hard?

I trimmed the email down, under Tim's guidance, and sent it off. Fingers crossed I'll get a reply.

Girl's Guide to:
Being a 21st-Century Woman

1. Always pay for yourself on a date (or at least financially reciprocate another time). Otherwise, you are just exploiting a man for his money; this is old-fashioned and sexist behaviour and does not reflect the modern attitude of a financially independent 21st-Century Woman.

2. It is best to ensure that after a date, you have enough money to jump in a cab: a swift exit comes in handy should you need to escape quickly. Plus, if you are planning on getting to know your date a little more intimately, nothing kills the romance so much as having to travel on a London night bus: not exactly the greatest way to get you in the mood.

3. Make sure you carry condoms with you at all times, as you never know when the mood will, quite literally, arise. (And trying to find a local chemist that is open at 3 a.m. presents a frustrating challenge.)

4. Assert your needs: a 21st-Century Woman should enjoy herself in bed. Men are not mind readers: try to have the confidence to vocalize what you want, and you're more likely to get it. (And if all else fails, move their hand away and do it yourself: a guaranteed way to ensure mutual pleasure.)

5. Treat yourself. Forget having a spa or a manicure: go to a female-friendly sex shop like Ssh!, buy a decent vibrator and spend some quality time alone. You'll thank yourself for the enjoyable self-exploration later – and quite likely your partner/lover will too. Win/win.

Saturday 11th November

Jay did get back to me, and luckily he said 'yes' to a date. I almost leapt in the air with joy upon reading his email. But sadly, the date went really badly. It wasn't anything he said in particular, but it's what he didn't say that gave the game away.

Sometimes I hate being skilled in reading people's body language. I often wish I could look at a person's interaction with completely fresh eyes and not be able to interpret their interest, or otherwise, in me. It would be so nice to spend time with someone and wonder what their tapping foot meant; or their averted gaze; or the micro-expression produced with the quick downward turn of their mouth.

But instead, I absorb, analyse, acknowledge. My brain clickity-clicks into action and the motors of intuition instantly kick in.

I almost always know when someone enjoys my company: their body speaks volumes, even when clothed. And I almost always know when they don't: their body betrays whatever complimentary words they might say.

So rather than return home with a hope of potential interest from Jay tonight, I've already accepted that his body language made it clear he wasn't interested. I'm sure I won't hear from him again.

Oh well, another one down, right? Gutted. Still, stupid though it is, I can't help but find myself wondering: am I – or have I become – much more boring in person than I ever was online?

Sunday 12th November

I was trying to think of a way to write something on my blog, without, actually, you know, divulging anything; not saying anything that could be misinterpreted, taken too seriously, or, worse, make me sound like the neurotic twat that I really am.

Sometimes I look back at the archives on the blog and cringe; but it's the emotional vulnerability I've shared that embarrasses me far more than the sexual explicitness. It's much easier to openly say that I love cock than it is to state that I need emotional intimacy. Of course, what is available to read here is not the sum total of me: of course I'm more fragile than I appear; I have insecurities I do not voice; I have stupid, dumb moments where I am a total prat over something completely insignificant. But to share all those things on the blog now? I just can't. And, call me stupid, but I miss doing it.

Once upon a time I would type out my worries, knowing how irrational they might be, but feeling hugged by the impersonal arms of the Internet once I'd splurged my heart out to it. Now, with thoughts running round my head and no freedom to post them on the place that was once my cathartic outlet, my neuroses have no place to go; I end up feeling devoured by them.

In an IM chat with a friend earlier, I mourned not being able to voice these aspects of myself on my blog any more: too many people in my life read it, and worse, perhaps, men who I want to get to know better read it too. 'While a little bit of crazy is attractive and vulnerable,' said my friend, gently, 'we don't want them to know how ACTUALLY crazy we are until we know they can deal with it.' And of course my friend is right: there's a right time and place to show someone that amongst the cock-worshipping, self-deprecating humour and passion for life, you're also needy and demanding and insecure; but it's certainly not via the Internet.

So on days like today – where, for no justifiable reason at all, I'm filled with silly doubts; where I'm questioning things that are obvious; where I'm creating complexities out of the most simple situations – I long to be able to voice my thoughts so I can get some distance from them, and accept just how illogical they are. And I know that they are: as a glass-half-full optimist I always see the positive side of life.

But I have my weak moments and right now I guess I need some kind of validation, just so I know that, hey, it's OK to feel a little lost.

// posted by thegirl @ 10:22:00 PM

Monday 13th November

After the disappointing date with Jay, I feel like I'm back to square one with dating. Online dating's out for the time being; meeting men through work is long gone, given I'm no longer employed in the film industry; mutual friends are clearly a no-no. What other options do I have any more?

I don't know. But I'm aware that alongside my current desire for sex lies another more emotional need that is unfulfilled. It really is time I met someone special.

In the meantime, though, I could just do with spending the

night with someone who I trust. I've decided to get back in contact with Jamie. We were lovers, briefly, a year prior to my being outed, until he got back with his ex, and not only is he single again, but he knows about all the book stuff and is cool about it: he's just not the judgmental sort. I don't know if things could pick up again from where they left off, but I do know that lying in his arms again would make me very happy right now.

From: Jamie
To: Zoe
11:03 a.m.
Hello! Of course I'm up for getting together, tomorrow would be great. Are you not likely to be in pain shortly, though, given you're about to get your period? Should we rearrange?

I am not trying to get out of it, as I am looking forward to seeing you. Just thinking about you sitting there with a brave face on, feeling pants and wanting to be on your couch under a duvet with a hot water bottle . . .

From: Zoe
To: Jamie
11:07 a.m.
My period's due any time between now and Friday, hence my suggestion to meet up in tomorrow (but I wanted to warn you just in case). Most likely it'll arrive Thurs/Fri, so my pain is only going to increase throughout the week, not get any better, sadly.
My weekly breakdown for you (being a man):
Monday (not bleeding): mild pain (breasts, stomach), low mood, horny

Tuesday (not bleeding): mild pain (breasts, stomach), low mood, extremely horny

Wednesday (not bleeding): moderate pain (breasts, stomach, calves), depressed mood, wanking necessary to relieve mood

Thursday (possibly bleeding): bad pain (breasts, stomach, back), painkillers needed, bad mood, wanking necessary to relieve mood

Friday (bleeding): agonizing pain (stomach, back), maximum daily dose of painkillers ingested, wanking necessary to relieve pain

Saturday (bleeding day 2): excruciating pain (stomach, back, head), maximum daily dose of painkillers ingested, hot water bottle on tummy, under duvet, drinking whisky, crying, can't wank: in too much pain

Sunday (bleeding day 3): moderate pain (stomach), occasional painkillers taken, drinking cups of tea, happy wanking

Thus, you can see I'm not in agony now (unlike when I actually bleed), just feeling swollen and sore. So if you don't mind my tits and stomach looking a bit ballooned, let's stick with the meet tomorrow, OK?

From: Jamie
To: Zoe
11:12 a.m.
Heheheh.
I lived with a woman for seven years: I know bad periods.
Tomorrow is cool. And swollen breasts? I think I can cope.

From: Zoe
To: Jamie
11:17 a.m.
I'm sure you'll cope just fine with my boobs. I, however, am more

worried about the fight I will have trying to get them to fit into my bra. If I'm late meeting you, that will be the reason why. Well, either that, or my last-minute wank before leaving the house . . .

Tuesday 14th November

We both stared at the large wet patch on the bed.

I frowned. 'What the hell is that?'

Jamie shook his head. 'I don't know.'

'Did you spill on the bed? Naughty boy,' I said, smiling flirtatiously.

'That wasn't me. I'm still wearing this.' He pointed to the condom wrapped around his penis. 'Anyway, I didn't come.'

'You didn't?'

'No. You ejected my cock when you squeezed down by coming so hard, remember?'

I bit my lip, feeling embarrassed at the strength of my climax, recalling that the last time we had had sex a year ago I had done exactly the same thing. I suddenly felt very selfish. What a way to thank someone after a good shag!

'Sorry about that, we'll have to rectify that.' I reached over to him and stroked his hip with my fingertips.

'Will we now?'

I grinned. 'Yes.'

He leaned down to my face and kissed me.

'Anyway, even if I had come, there is no way I could make that much mess.'

He patted the dark area on the duvet cover beneath me. I moved off my stomach and sat back on my feet, looking at the duvet. The wet patch was huge, almost a foot across and a foot long. I placed my hand on it and was shocked to discover how wet it was: the material was drenched, soaked through the duvet feathers to the sheet below.

'What the fuck?'

'What?'

'Feel it. It's soaking.'

He pressed his hand onto the wet patch. 'Wow!'

'Hold on . . . ' I had a sudden thought and looked between my legs. No blood: it wasn't my period starting. Then I had another thought: 'You said you spilled some water, right? God, you are clumsier than me – you managed to get it all over the cover!'

'I did spill some water, but not on the bed. I knocked over a glass, see?' He motioned down to the floor and I peered over the bed. There was a small pool of water on the tiles below; the glass, now empty, stood adjacent to the liquid.

'Are you saying that you didn't spill the water on the cover?'

'That is exactly what I am saying.'

'Seriously?'

'Seriously.'

'So how did the water get there?'

'I think it was you squirting.'

'Bollocks.'

'Come on! There is no other explanation!'

'No way.'

He bent down to sniff the wet patch. 'Well, it's definitely not pee, if that's what you were worried about.'

I cringed and shifted to smell it for myself. I was surprised to discover that it had no odour at all. It was as if someone had poured half a glass of water onto the bed and soaked it. I suddenly became suspicious.

'You're not fucking with me, are you?'

'What do you mean?'

'I mean, trying to freak me out by secretly pouring your glass of water on the duvet cover.'

He sighed. 'No, I am not fucking with you. Why would I do that? And how could I do that? You haven't moved from the bed.'

I shrugged. 'I don't know. Promise me this isn't some kind of wind-up.'

'I promise. Honestly, is it so hard to believe that you wet the duvet?!'

'Well, yes, it is, actually.'

'You squirted, there is no other way to explain it. What's the problem?'

'Well, for one, I don't believe in it. You know me, sceptical as ever. I just don't support the idea that women ejaculate.'

'Not even when faced with scientific evidence in front of you?!'

I shrugged.

'Look, it's in the exact spot where you were lying, see?'

He gestured for me to lie back down on the bed and I did, noticing that directly under my groin was the wet patch. It was like lying in one of those police outlines in a crime scene, except instead of chalk representing a death, there was a wet patch providing the liquid evidence of my climax.

I shifted back onto my knees and shook my head in disbelief.

'So you've never squirted before?'

'No! And believe me, I have tried: every fucking toy and finger action that you can imagine. Given I come very easily and often, I assumed squirting was either a myth dreamt up by porn producers, or that I was just physically unable to do it.'

'Well, you've been proved wrong on both counts.'

I looked at him sheepishly. 'I guess so.'

'That really was a very intense orgasm you had . . .'

I nodded, thinking back to half an hour before; my head buried in the pillow, my eyes blindfolded and my weeping uncontrollably.

'I can't believe you cried like that. I was worried that I was hurting you too much.'

'Well, you were,' I said, rubbing the painful raised welts on my arse from where he had repeatedly whipped me with the cane, 'but that wasn't why I was crying. I mean, there's no real reason for it.'

As I said it, though, I wondered: maybe there was something deeper in me that needed to be expressed. With Jamie – and for the first time in many months – I felt safe; I could relax, finally. But not just physically: emotionally. It was a powerful moment indeed.

'Well,' I continued, 'most likely it was just my body responding to the incredible – and much needed – release you gave me . . .'

' . . . by crying, ejecting my cock and squirting,' he sniggered.

'Evidently. God, this whole thing has been weird . . .'

'And enjoyable . . .'

'Totally.'

He pulled off the condom and clambered back onto the bed. I snuggled up to him and felt him harden against me.

Suddenly I realized where he was lying; I tried to pull him away from the soaked area of the bed. 'You're in my wet patch, aren't you? That's not very fair!'

'Nah, don't worry, it's fine.'

'You're such a gentleman. I get restrained, whipped, then hugely pleasured and I don't even have to sleep in my own wet patch: result!'

He laughed and we kissed some more.

'You do realize I will never do that again, don't you?'

'Why not?'

'Because unless the planets are in the correct alignment or something, the possibility of my repeating that is about zero to one.'

'Well, we can but try,' he said, pressing himself against me.

'Well, if you put it that way . . .'

Wednesday 15th November

I'm so glad that things went well with Jamie: it was as if no time had passed between us and we continued where we left off a year ago: having excellent sex. It's so nice to be able to curl up into his arms and be relaxed about it; unlike the recent guys I've ended up with, I actually trust Jamie. And right now I need that: I need to know I'm safe. So much of my life has been put on public display, it's nice to have something for me; something private and tender. It's also nice that Jamie's so good in bed: that certainly helps relax me.

The Girl's Guide to: Being a good lover

- **Cock size** – It's irrelevant. Seriously. I have had cocks as small as my thumb and almost as large as my forearm – and everything in between. Whilst the former was hard to feel and the latter hurt like hell, the rest fulfilled their job very nicely, thank you.

- **Beauty** – Skin deep, obviously. I have fucked men who my friends thought were as ugly as dogs, as well as men who modelled for a living. In bed there was no difference: a horny man is a horny man – his skills in bed aren't connected to his handsomeness.

- **Intelligence** – Depends on the person. I have shagged guys who were so boring that I couldn't wait to leave (after fucking them) and ones who were so fascinating, our conversation continued whilst in the missionary position. Both types were fun to fuck (but being boring won't result in a second shag).

- **Social class/career** – Unimportant. I've bedded men with differing fiscal status: from a street cleaner to a multi-millionaire ambassador's son. Their wealth, or lack of, had no connection to their abilities in bed.

- **Racial/religious background** – Open-mindedness is more important. I have had men of many nationalities, both here and abroad. The only difference between them was their ability to say 'I want to fuck you' with an accent (or not).

- **Personality** – Individual preferences are immaterial. I have slept with bold, outgoing, dynamic men as well as quiet, shy, nervous men; naked, in bed, they were all alike.

If these things are not factors in making a good lover, then what is?

Chemistry.

The buzz you get from someone when you're with them. They may have some of the 'qualities' that you find attractive, they may have things in common with you and you enjoy their company, but without that fizz – that excitement you feel in their presence – the sex ain't going nowhere.

Given the choice between the most skilled lover in the world and one that is clumsy with his hands, but who – when he whispers in my ear, 'God, you've got me so turned on' – makes me drip in anticipation of his touch, I know who I would pick – and it wouldn't be Mr Loverlover. I'm of the opinion that every man can be taught (if necessary) how to please a woman well; but if there's no chemistry there to begin with – forget it.

This might sound harsh but it's true. Every good lover I have had was someone I had chemistry with; the ones I didn't didn't make me come (as hard, as much, or even at all).

In conclusion:

I think guys (and girls) should relax about whether they are skilled enough in bed, and instead try to just enjoy the sex they have.

Because at some point – when they encounter that magical chemistry with someone – the sex is going to be so dazzling, it will knock both their socks off.

Thursday 16th November

I just remembered that Jamie licked my face the other night.

It didn't happen randomly on the street: we were both naked at his place at the time, so one would assume some saliva would be exchanged, naturally. Still, having his tongue rasping all over my face did come as a bit of a shock to me; I'm an open-minded and adventurous woman, and face-licking is not something I am familiar with, or even particularly enjoy.

In addition, the fact that he has endearing puppy-dog brown eyes, and that I was on all fours most of the night kind of threw me a bit.

But it helped that I was being kept distracted by his busy hands at the same time. And the fact that, after drooling all over my face, Jamie enthusiastically used his wet tongue elsewhere too.

Which was nice.

☉

Want to know where all the fit thirty-something men are?

Apparently they are all jogging in my local park of an evening.

Which is rather convenient.

True, a (possibly large) proportion of them are likely to be gay (and sadly not up for a MMF threesome were I to suggest it). It's also true that not many of them are likely to be single. But doing the maths (a girl needs to know the difference between probability and chance), the fact that I spotted over twenty sexy men jogging last night would lead me to calculate that out of those, at least three might be heterosexual, single and available: more than enough for any girl (simultaneously, one-on-one, whatever).

Problem was, it's a little bit difficult to stop and chat to a guy when:

1. You're running in the opposite direction to them.
2. You're red-faced and hot and sweaty.
3. You're caught up in your iPod.

So, to the sexy dark-haired bloke with glasses and the cute blond guy, sorry I didn't pause to chat: I was a bit preoccupied with finishing my run. But thank you both for stopping to smile at me and continuing to do so, even when I was some way in the distance: that boosted my ego a lot. I kind of need that right now.

And now I know just how many of you fit men are out there running in the early evening, I think you'll be seeing rather more of me. Same time next week, gentlemen?

// posted by thegirl @ 11:48:00 PM

Saturday 18th November

Incident number 958 in a recent series of embarrassing moments:

Having a telephone conversation with my mother that began with her saying:

'Please, explain BDSM to me.'

And ended with her concluding:

'Well, I guess if it's all consensual and there are mutual orgasms for both people, then that's fine.'

I'm not sure who was more shocked by our discussion, me, or her.

// posted by thegirl @ 8:14:00 PM

Sunday 19th November

Usually, after having sex, one does not expect to find blood everywhere. That's not to say that bleeding doesn't occur: what horny woman who is sure she has finished her period and can't wait to enthusiastically jump on a cock hasn't been suddenly surprised by a puddle of blood on the bed (or couch), post-shag? Or the specks of blood that might appear during a particularly hard whipping, perhaps? (Though I'd argue, for my own part, that if there are any more than a few light welts on my arse U R DOIN IT RONG.)

So when you wake up in the morning to find fresh streaks of blood on the sheets and duvet, and you're not due for your period for some weeks, and you've had no more than a firm hand spank you, and, after checking, you're sure that you're not bleeding from any orifice or bodily surface, it's fair to say that you might be a little confused. Well, I was, anyway; it was clear that something – someone – was bleeding.

'I think I've figured out where the blood came from,' Jamie hollered from his bathroom last night.

'Oh? Where?' I called out from under the duvet, still curled up snug in bed.

'My back,' he replied. 'You practically ripped one of my moles clean off.'

I pulled my hand out from the warmth of the duvet and looked at my fingers: my nails were pretty short, as they always are (all the better for wanking[*] – and for sticking up boys' bums), so how could I have caused him to be so badly injured?

'Really?' I asked, as he walked back into the bedroom.

'Yup,' he replied. 'No worries, I'm sure it'll be fine.'

I made him turn around so I could peek at his back and was dismayed to see what remained of one of his moles ragged and bleeding.

'Oh god, I'm sorry! It looks like it might fall off. Let me put a plaster on it, stop it getting infected.'

I returned a moment later, Band-Aid in hand, and attached it carefully to the small gash on his back.

'I feel awful,' I said. 'I can't believe I wounded you! How the hell did I do that?'

'I think you dug your nails deeply into me every time you climaxed.'

I frowned, confused. 'But surely it must have hurt? Why didn't you say something, or stop me?'

He smiled. 'It did hurt, but you seemed to be enjoying yourself so much it was worth it to suffer a little pain.'

I laughed. 'Thanks, I was definitely enjoying it. But I didn't realize I was hurting you!'

---

[*] Which is why I cannot stand porn that includes female performers who have long acrylic nails: they're the antithesis to real – good – sex, and a sign to me that what I'm seeing on screen is bullshit and fake.

He shrugged. 'Don't worry about it – heat of passion and all that.'

'OK,' I said, kissing him gently. 'But next time I'll try not to inflict any more damage.' Or leave the task of scrubbing the sheets with soda crystals to you, alone.

Tuesday 21st November

After practically ripping apart someone's back with my fingers, I was very conscious of being surrounded by others' attractive hands (attached to men, not disembodied) whilst at a book reading I went to tonight, in Islington.

I guess I find hands one of the most attractive parts of a man, after taking into consideration his face, eyes and mouth. This isn't due to any correlation between hand size and penis size, though. Besides it being a completely unfounded myth (trust me, I have done lots of research), I'm not really bothered or impressed by measurements: with shagging, I just want to be fucked how I want, when I want, and I'm happy.

But hands? Another matter entirely. I am a hand-phile: I love them. The size and shape and hairiness of a man's hands are enough to make me want to turn my head in complete disinterest (Leonardo DiCaprio: yuck), or otherwise want to jump on top of them (Zachary Quinto: yum).

I know I am very prejudiced in such matters – I'm only interested in large hands with long, solid fingers, and if they're hairy too then that's a bonus – but if a man has nice hands, it gets me hot, and I'll want his fingers inside me, pronto.

Anyway, sitting amongst this thirty-something crowd, I became aware of just how many men seemed to have gorgeous hands. All around me were blokes with large, strong hands; fingers that seemed perfect for penetration. I was shocked at the sheer number of decent hands in the room and it made me wonder: do bookish blokes have sexier hands? I know that of the men who have made me go weak at the knees, they were all guys who enjoy a good book or five, and their hands were gorgeous. So could there be a correlation between the type of man to turn up to a book reading and the size of his hands? Does a man need to have big fingers to be into books? Or am I just drawing a conclusion based on no real evidence? Perhaps I should investigate this further and find some empirical proof . . .

Probably best not to investigate on a first date, though: my asking a man what his preferred reading material is, alongside a demand to see his hands, might not cast me in the best light. Though, thinking about it, by getting blokes to talk about what books they enjoy, that might be a good way to quickly eliminate the tossers from my 'potential' list, because I guarantee, no fan of Jeremy Clarkson is ever going to bring me off – even if his fingers were supreme.

// posted by thegirl @ 10:08:00 PM

Wednesday 22nd November

'Social networking' can really be such a double-edged sword. After meeting, you become friends on Facebook. You follow one another on Twitter, add each other as Flickr contacts and share your Upcoming events info. Soon you're reading each other's blogs, and sharing links you think are interesting, or pictures you hope they'll enjoy. You view their private Tumblr with relish, and smile when you see they've posted something you suggested. They privately message you to comment about a nice Flickr picture of you. You drop hints in your blog, hoping they'll spot the secret reference just for them; and they do. You direct message each other on Twitter and save your @ replies[*] for other, less personal, acquaintances. You play a few games of online Scrabble and innuendo seeps into the miniature chat box. Your Facebook flirtations spill over into gmail and you end up IMing about life, love, sex. You spend months regularly chatting or messaging or Direct Messaging on Twitter or emailing or playing, and you're flirting, and it's fun and exciting and hopeful, and there is mutual attraction; and all these ways of communicating, of staying in contact, mean you're both interconnected, even if there are miles between you.

And it's wonderful – until the communication ends.

Where once you'd find an almost daily email, now there is none; your inbox lies empty. They don't log in to gmail chat any more (or they're 'invisible'); they're no longer making themselves available to IM with you. You see their tweets but no private, saucy DM from them awaits you. You notice

---

[*] Using the @ symbol plus a username is a way of speaking directly to a person on Twitter, but it also makes the content of your message to them public. Fine, if all you're doing is friendly conversation; not so good if you're using sexual innuendo because it'll be viewable – with your name attached – on Google forever . . .

they've updated Flickr but they don't comment on your photos any more. They've stopped sending you links and pictures and articles and now you hesitate to send them any. You drop hints about them in your blog that you hope they'll pick up on, but they fail to react. You spot their Facebook updates but no jokey messages from them are in your inbox. The Scrabble game you created goes unplayed.

Once upon a time, outside the social network of the Internet, you'd just shrug if someone stopped communication and accept that if they really wanted to stay in contact, they'd simply pick up the phone and say hello. But in the web of modern interactivity, where you get used to the regular loud chatter of the (false?) intimacy of the social network, the sudden distance and silence from someone you've connected with on a frequent and personal basis is – ironically – deafening.

It's been a week since I've heard from Jamie, and in Internet terms, that's the equivalent of a year: too long for people who are actively having sex together not to communicate with each other.

The Girl's Guide to Social Network Flirting

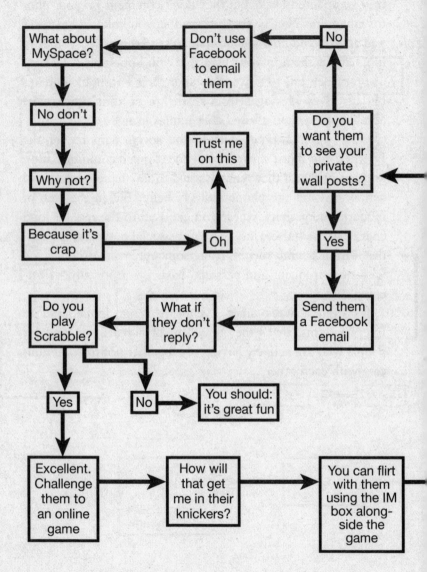

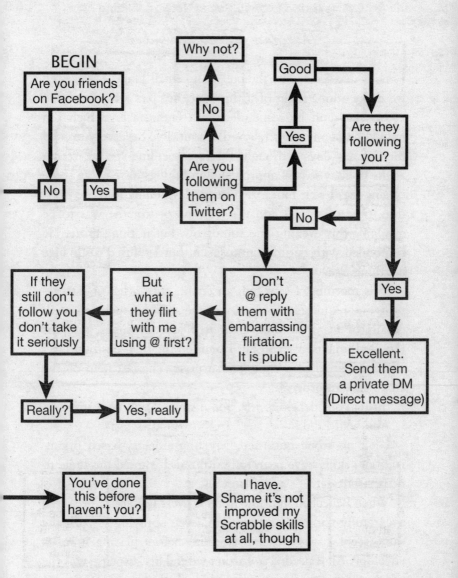

Thursday 23rd November

I finally decided to bite the bullet and email Jamie. I suggested we make a long night of it this time, not just a brief evening at his flat, and he responded with enthusiasm, which I'm happy (and somewhat relieved) about. I've been very excited the last few days: I thought I'd do something special, seeing as the holiday season approaches and things have taken some organizing. I sent him a text yesterday, telling him the location, time of arrival and the window of time he was to be available this evening and tomorrow, but nothing more. He responded with curious enthusiasm, but I refused to divulge anything else.

This morning, I sent him an email, with a list of instructions and requirements. A map of the area was included, with details of transport and estimated journey times, and his required time of arrival, but I omitted the final destination: I wanted that to be a complete surprise. The last item on the email was an order:

'Bring your delicious self, and a smile. I will be waiting.'

And wait I did.

I left no stone unturned. My film-industry-based organizational skills have been fully utilized: I wanted the stage to be perfectly set.

When I checked in at the hotel in west London, I prepared a carefully chosen card for him, even spraying it with the same scent I was wearing (vanilla) before placing it in its envelope. All it needed to further extend his suspense was the room number and key attached, with 'I'm upstairs waiting for you' neatly scribbled on it. I left the card at the desk, and smiled to myself as I walked down the atmospherically lit corridor, imagining his reaction when he was handed the envelope.

The room was impressive: soothing neutral blends of beige and brown; large windows stretching from floor to ceiling; and a bed so huge you could get ten people on it. But I wasn't planning a rampant sex orgy: it was just to be him and me.

I busied myself placing the champagne on ice, obtaining glasses and cooling the mineral water in the fridge. I lit my favourite incense (lavender) and placed bunches of the sticks to burn in the plant pots. I selected some soft music for the CD player, adjusted the lighting, fluffed the pillows and placed condoms and lube on both side tables, so they'd be within reach of either of us. We would not want for anything – I had covered it all – but there were still some finishing touches that needed to be made – to myself.

On the bed, I laid out a new matching black lace bra, pants and suspender set; alongside, a pair of sheer black stockings. On the floor, my only-for-very-special-occasions black leather peep-toe 'fuck me' heels: finally they get an outing! I picked up the bra, slinging the straps over my shoulders and attempted to squeeze my breasts into the cups. Damn it, they were now a little too small for me: overspill was the only option. Still, perhaps in this case, not a bad look – and the bra wouldn't be on for long, I was sure of that. Doing my utmost to be careful I then slid on the stockings, attaching them to my suspender belt. Next, the knickers – and a dilemma: should they go over the suspender belt and look stupid, but allow for them to be easily and quickly removed to be able to a) take a pee, and b) have sex? Or should they go under the suspender belt and a) look good, but b) make for frustrating finger/cock access? Oh god, why aren't there rulebooks for lingerie wearing? I felt like such a novice . . . (I ended up opting for the former, given I have a weak bladder – and a disposition for fucking.)

Wobbling in the high heels, I stood in front of the mirror and observed my reflection. I liked what I saw: the way the lingerie clung to my skin, highlighting and smoothing my body, made me feel sexy, horny and excited. But I also felt nervous for some reason. I was anxious that out of everything I had planned so carefully, this final piece of the puzzle might not fit; that somehow I wouldn't fit the situation. It wasn't that I thought he wouldn't like what he saw, or that we wouldn't have fun together. It was more that by the very fact that I had invited him to a hotel and was waiting for him whilst dressed so sexily, it made my desire to fuck him bla- tantly obvious. And this transparent need to have sex with him suddenly made me feel insecure. As I looked at my reflec- tion, I wondered if the confident, assertive, sexually desiring woman I saw was really me standing there, or instead an approximation: Abby Lee. And even though I am that person, with Jamie I didn't want to be her: I wanted to be me, Zoe.

Fuck it. It was too late for introspective psychoanalytical theorizing: this was not the time for self-doubt. I was horny and wanted to fuck him and I knew that very soon I would. Making a final adjustment to my stockings and suspenders, I lay back on the bed and waited. Soon I would hear the lock being turned and the door opening, announcing his arrival. Until then, my heart would beat in anticipation and suspense.

Friday 24th November

I can't believe it. Of all places to get recognized, it had to happen at the hotel I'm staying at with Jamie.

Early this morning, whilst Jamie was catching his breath (actually, he was crashed out: I think I exhausted him from jumping him all night), I popped out into the hallway to collect some ice, and bumped into one of the hotel receptionists.

We greeted each other with a polite 'hello' and I was just about to turn away and head back to the room when he said something else.

'Look, I have to say, I know who you are.'

'Sorry?' I turned back to look at him.

The hotel receptionist grinned at me sheepishly. 'You. I know about you.'

'About me?' What might he know? That I'm so clumsy I always trip up on my feet (even when I am not in heels or drunk)? How I tend to burp rudely when I've drunk too much whisky of a night? Or that I've just had a handful of orgasms and am now sexually sated? What did he know?

He slowly nodded at me. 'Yes, you, the book, everything.'

'Oh.' I bit my lip awkwardly, suddenly feeling uncomfortable as it dawned on me what he was saying. The irony of my standing there, post-coital, in nothing but a robe, didn't escape me. 'Um, how come you know?'

'I recognized your name from your booking!' he said.

'My name? But . . .'

'We read all the papers here. I knew I had seen your name somewhere before . . .'

'Oh. I see.'

'So then the manager and I Googled you,' he continued, 'and that's when it fitted into place. We read it all.'

I groaned and hid my face in my hands. 'You Googled me?! So then you know everything?'

'Ach, don't worry: we've seen it all here. You're fine. In fact, I think what you do is wonderful.'

Blushing, I lifted my head. 'Thanks, I'm just, er, a bit thrown that you recognized my name.'

'Well, we always check the list to see if we have anyone important staying. I knew your name was familiar and I was right.' He sounded almost triumphant.

'Evidently.' I shifted nervously and wondered how much of the blog he might have read – and what opinion he had reached about me from that.

'Anyway, I told my girlfriend, Carrie, that you were staying here and she was so excited: she has read your book three times and thinks it's brilliant.'

'Really?'

'Really. She asked if you would sign her book, but I won't be able to get it from her until tomorrow evening.'

'Well, I've got a spare copy in my room – I could sign that for her if you like.' (The recent bartender incident inspired me to carry a book with me all the time now.)

'Would you?'

'Of course. It'd be a pleasure. I'll be back in two ticks.'

I returned with the signed book a few moments later and handed it to him.

'She's going to be so happy about this: it'll really make her day.'

'Well, hearing that she's read the book three times has really made my day, if not my week, believe me.' I'm not sure he did, but I meant every word.

I never thought that my being a sexblogger would give other people pleasure; I feel honoured that it has.

⊙

After popping out to get the ice I needed some freshening up, so hopped straight in the hotel power shower. Lovely. When the strong jet had woken me up a bit, I headed back to the bedroom, towel draped over my arm and stumbling slightly, because my legs were sore – no doubt the result of spending hours with them wrapped tightly around Jamie's back.

Turning the corner of the room, I was surprised to see him sitting on the bed already, fully clothed; his jacket was zipped up and his overnight bag was packed.

'Um, look, do you mind if I go now?' he said, awkwardly. 'I really do need to get back.'

Caught off-guard by his request, I suddenly felt self-conscious about my nudity; ironic, given just minutes before, both our naked bodies were intertwined as the morning sunlight lit up our heated embrace. I crossed the room to the mirror and looked at our reflections in it: the juxtaposition of my nakedness and his covered-up body like some kind of analogy for us. Maybe I had got it all wrong. Maybe the crush he had on me last year had worn off.

I delayed for a moment, unsure of how to reply.

'Oh, right. Well then, OK,' I said, after I had momentarily collected my thoughts. I picked up my lingerie from the dresser and fidgeted with it, turning to face him; his expression showed mild relief. He immediately got up from the bed, walked over to me and then kissed me on the cheek before making his way to the door.

'See you soon,' he said, his hand already turning the door handle.

'Yup,' I replied, the forced smile on my face as uncomfortable as the atmosphere.

A moment later he was gone; I was left to check out of the hotel on my own.

Still naked, I looked over at the bed, the only evidence of our passionate night an imprint in the crumpled sheets and misplaced pillows. Part of me felt compelled to tidy the bed, as if by straightening the linen I could somehow neaten the situation. Then I realized I was still holding my pants and bra in my hands and decided to get dressed instead. I quickly slipped both on and looked at myself in the mirror again. As I cast my eyes over my semi-clad self and studied my reflection, I watched my chest expand and contract under the brassière as my breathing intensified. And with each heavy exhalation, I felt the anger in me increase. Running through my mind was this: He had left me with no more than a peck on the cheek; it was as if the all-night fuck-a-thon had never happened.

Now I wasn't expecting a romantic goodbye; our stay in the hotel had everything to do with shagging, and nothing to do with emotional ties. But his solitary kiss on my cheek had felt so cold and impersonal: just hours before, he had been passionate – his face buried between my legs, his fingers deep inside me, his lips on my breasts sucking with intensity – but now not even as much as an intimate kiss on my lips.

For me, it's rare for casual sex to end that way. Most lovers I've had will, at the very least, grab my arse whilst snogging me before departing. Or hopefully more than that: certainly if I was naked at the time, there might be a chance of a brief flick of their fingers in the right place, or perhaps a quick shag before we said goodbye. But to finish a long night of passion with just a brief peck on the cheek? Not a good sign. And, after knowing Jamie for more than a year, the abruptness of his exit left me fuming.

But it wasn't fury at him that I felt; instead it was directed inwards towards myself. When he exited the room and left me alone, I was disappointed – and feeling like that made me angry with myself.

It's not like I had any right to be upset by his leaving – this was casual sex, nothing more. But I really enjoyed his company: I wouldn't have fucked him, repeatedly, if I didn't. Partly this was because the sex we had was amazing. But he was also rather different to other men I have been with: he always showed another, deeper, sensitivity to his masculinity that I found very attractive. He had become a solace for me. He never judged me – he always accepted me for who I am. I didn't need to keep up a façade.

I have considered the romantic possibilities, of course, but I realize there are many reasons why we are not that well matched as a couple: we want very different things in life. I had still toyed with the idea of being more involved with him in the short-term, though: it'd be nice to be with someone for a few months. I guess, for the first time in ages, I had wondered if he'd be someone I'd like to have around; someone to invite into my life, messy flat and all.

Until he left me alone in the hotel room, I suppose I hadn't realized how much more I wanted and how disappointed I might be if he didn't want that too. Faced with the hard reality I had to accept that this want was one-sided.

As I looked at my reflection in the mirror, I felt stupid. Stupid for letting my guard down; stupid for allowing myself to have even considered being more than fuck-buddies with him; and more stupid for feeling rejected by him.

Standing there in my bra and pants, condoms and lube strewn all over the bedside table, my muscles aching from fucking him until the early hours, I finally saw the humorous absurdity of the situation, and laughed: it had been a great night, there was no doubt about that. I walked back into the bathroom and washed out sections of my dress, wondering how it managed to get so marked during our shagging.

After fixing my make-up and hair, and sliding on my shoes, I left the room. I made my way to the hotel lobby, which seemed filled with hordes of media types drinking coffee and reading the weekend papers. Signing out at the desk, I noticed a handsome thirty-something guy seated near reception, who was peering out from behind his *Guardian* newspaper. He smiled at me and I shyly grinned back. I was very tempted to go and say 'hello' to him, and perhaps under different circumstances I would have; he was certainly my type. But given the situation, my confidence had taken a knock, so I didn't feel up to flirting with a stranger.

Plus, I wasn't sure if I had got out all the stains on my clothes, and if there are any rules in 'The Game' I'd bet they damn well include not chatting up a bloke when you might have another guy's cum still visible on your dress. So I just

grabbed my bag, held my head high, and left the hotel with the sun shining brightly on my face.

Saturday 25th November

Recently, I've been trying to date on the sly. Actually, what I mean is that I've not written about it on my blog. Once upon a time, my blog was somewhere I wrote an extremely honest and open account of my romantic and sex life, but that's no longer possible – not with all my ex-lovers, friends, colleagues, acquaintances, but especially potential dates, quietly perusing my archives. So I've attempted some secret dating instead.

My first option – getting to know someone through friends – is still out, though. And now my fall-back method of meeting men – the Internet – is also proving a route fraught with anxiety and worry. I have had to back away from meeting men online, because too many of them recognized me as Girl with a One Track Mind. I guess the medium itself made it more likely: I may not get approached in the street, but a lot of geeks know my name or my face, because of my online 'notoriety'. So any time I've encountered someone who's spot-ted me as Abby, rather than just Zoe, I've immediately backed away; this has meant online dating has stopped working for me.

I am not suggesting that every man who looked at one of my online dating profiles put two and two together and guessed I wrote the blog and book, but the majority have: enough to make me yearn for my previous anonymity. Every time I've put a profile picture up on a dating site I have,

within a couple of days, received a handful of emails all saying the same thing:

'You're Girl with a One Track Mind! I knew I recognized you! I read about you online/in the newspapers/saw it on TV/heard about it on the radio!'

And I, feeling completely exposed, and open, and transparent, have immediately made my profile private and wept silent tears of frustration into my computer screen, resolving never to return to the website.

There have been a few occasions when a guy has emailed me and didn't mention my pseudonym, but that hasn't turned out well either. Yes, there might be mutual appreciation of profile pictures, some flirtatious emails, perhaps even suggesting meeting up for a drink one evening (finding out if they have Fuckability-Factor© is very important, so you need to meet in the flesh). There the conversation might flow, there may be good chemistry, heck, we might both wonder what the other looks like naked, but at some point, the inevitable happens:

Him: So, what do you do for a living?
Me: Oh, I write, it's nothing, really. Tell me some more about your legal/banking/sales/architecture/IT work.

[*A little time passes, during which a) I get to find out what sort of person he is and whether he lives to work, or works to live, and b) I feel relieved to have evaded talking about myself. But a short while later:*]

Him: What sort of stuff do you write, then?

Me: This and that; it's not very interesting. Hey, did you see *Charlie Brooker's Screenwipe* last night?

Him: I know.

Me: Sorry?

Him: I know: you're the Girl.

Me: What?

Him: Abby Lee. I've read the book and blog. I recognized you from your profile picture. I'm a huge fan.

Me (a rabbit in the headlights): Oh. I see.

Then follows a brief interlude where said man says very·nice things to reassure me, tells me how much he enjoys the blog and that he would like to see me again. Meanwhile I try not to appear like I am panicking, but am simultaneously planning the swiftest route to escape from the date.

Now, some might say I should embrace the situation: take advantage of the fact that there are cool, sexy, intelligent men out there who:

a) know about all the sex I've had and don't judge me on that;

b) are open-minded about sex themselves;

c) appear interested in getting to know me more intimately.

If I don't want to enter into anything serious with them, I should just mark them up on my shagging scorecard, right? A little casual sex with a book/blog-reader: what's wrong with that?

Two things really:

1. How could I ever feel relaxed in bed with someone if

I knew that he was purely interested in me because I've written about my sex life?

2. I expect the majority of guys might worry that they wouldn't be 'as good as the other men' I had written about. And I'd spend all night fretting over what an anti-climax I might be – literally – to whomever I'm in bed with, with his comparing me with my supposed sexual notoriety.

And as for romance, how could I ever be sure enough of their motives to build an equal, intimate relationship?

It's not that I've thought the men who have read my book or blog are odd in some way – the opposite is true, actually (excluding the hateful weirdos, that is) – but how could I trust the shared experience of learning and discovering about one another when a man can hold all that previous knowledge of me, and I none of him? Coming face to face with a guy whom, prior to even meeting me, knew almost my entire sexual history and all my thoughts and feelings about that, would leave me intimidated, not relaxed.

I have been very complimented by the fact that these guys enjoy the blog; I've felt honoured that they might think me interesting enough to want to get to know me some more. But recently I have felt so fragile and exposed trying to navigate my increasingly surreal life that I don't think I can cope with the shark-like prowling of the online dating world. This has all left me feeling like I'm going to be perpetually single, shagless and forever lacking any romance in my life. And by god, do I need some of that now.

There's a part of me that thinks I should perhaps move to

New York; I love the city and have spent increasing amounts of time there over the last few years. I doubt anyone there would have heard of my blog or book, so we would at least get off on the right foot. In addition, faced with a woman who's written about sex, I reckon Brit blokes are much more liable than a New Yorker to stare at the ceiling and nervously share their insecurities, rather than just getting stuck in, so to speak. Brits are a little hung-up about sex. We seem to stagger from a saucy, '*Carry-On*-ooh-matron!' type approach, to a stigmatized, disapproving and critical perspective with not much in between. I'm still stunned at the terminology the press – and others – used to describe me, just because I wrote about my sex life.

Contrast this to New York, and the difference is amazing. When I was last there, I happened to pick up a free paper on a street corner, and read something just as explicit as anything I had ever written. For a moment I was surprised, and then relieved: it showed a much more progressive attitude to sex than Britain; I can't imagine the London *Evening Standard* carrying an article advocating mutual masturbation.

The nicest thing about New York, though, are the men. In a city where people date in tandem, and only 'go steady' with one person when they're ready to be 'exclusive' to them, the guys naturally have a much more open-minded attitude to sex and dating.

Maybe I should book a flight to New York. It will be a new year soon, I have a new career: it's time I had a new man in my life, I think.

DECEMBER

Wednesday 6th December

This evening, I caught up with Sarah, an old friend from my early days in the film industry, whom I haven't seen since she had another child last year. So much has changed in our lives . . .

At some point in the evening, after plenty of wine and catching up on movie gossip, the conversation arrived at its natural zenith point: sex.

'So tell me,' I whispered conspiratorially to her, 'was there a big change in your sex drive?'

Sarah lifted her glass and took a large gulp of wine. 'Yes. Massive.' She grinned at me.

'Better, worse – what?!'

'Well, put it this way, we were fucking right up to me being in labour.'

I breathed a sigh of relief. 'Thank fuck for that; I was worried for a minute that you were going to tell me you were one of those women who lost their sex drive.'

'Oh god, far from it. I couldn't get enough, actually; I think I exhausted Arthur by jumping on him all the time.'

We both laughed and I refilled our glasses.

'I'm really relieved you said that,' I confessed. 'I was worrying that when – well, actually, if – I eventually get pregnant it would turn out to mean no sex – a terrifying thought for me.'

Sarah laid her hand gently on mine. 'Darling, knowing you, and after reading about your blog, I can guarantee that will never happen to you; your problem will be finding a man who will keep up with you, not the other way around.'

I giggled at Sarah's accuracy and suddenly felt sad. I realized that that's what I wanted now: someone who would want to settle down and have kids with me – as well as regularly fuck me rotten. Would I ever find someone like that?

Sarah pulled me out of my brief melancholy moment, by leaning over to me and whispering so quietly in my ear I had to get her to repeat what she said. 'Being pregnant makes you wet,' she cooed softly, with a triumphant tone.

'What?' I was a little confused. Was she talking about some kind of extra sanitary-towel daily usage? I frowned at her, mystified.

Sarah grinned at me. 'You get fucking wet,' she repeated. 'I was like a river!'

'Seriously,' she continued, 'I was continuously dripping 'cause I was horny all the time. Thank god Arthur loved it, otherwise I'd have been bashing my vibrator something rotten.'

We both laughed again and I took a swig of wine, which I proceeded to spit out all over my top as I giggled.

'So, that's good, right? I mean, the sex is still good?'

'The wetness made it great for him, but in all honesty, I would have preferred to be a bit drier,' Sarah confessed. 'No friction, see; he may as well have been sticking a finger in there for all I could feel during the last trimester.'

'So what did you do; how did you manage to climax?'

'Oh I just got him to fuck me spoon-style from behind or sideways on, and I used my Magic Wand at the same time. Don't worry: I always ensured I came!'

'Damn right. So what about after the birth – did you lose your sex drive completely?'

'Well, what with the stitches and a huge fucking thing the size of a watermelon coming out of you, it's kind of hard to feel anything down there – besides immense pain – for around a week.'

'And then?' I asked, getting slightly worried.

'Well, I wasn't really in the mood for penetration.'

My heart sank. So, it was true: if you became a mother, then you would lose your sex drive. Great; may as well sign my death sentence now.

Sarah took another swig of wine. 'But gentle hands down there were fine.'

I breathed out audibly. Thank god for that. 'So how long was it before you fucked – if you don't mind my asking?'

'About three weeks, I guess. Although that doesn't include all the blow-jobs I gave him during that time.'

I laughed again. 'You do realize, you are a girl after my own heart, don't you?'

I suddenly felt a surge of emotion for Sarah; we had bonded more deeply than ever. Out of all my friends, she is still the person I can talk about sex most openly with and I love her for it. It's just a shame that with her living outside of London now, we rarely get to see each other.

We carried on chatting for a while longer, until her husband Arthur came to pick her up. I watched her greet her sleepy baby in delight and I waved goodbye as they all bundled into the car. As I watched her young family drive off together into the night I felt a small pang of sadness in my heart.

Saturday 9th December

Kathy invited me to come and stay with her and David in the Norfolk cottage they'd rented for the weekend, and, gratefully accepting her offer, I travelled up here.

'How did you sleep?' she asked over breakfast this morning.

'Well, I had some extremely vivid dreams, but I did sleep well: it's so good to get out of the noise and grime of London and be somewhere quiet and clean for a change. Thanks so much for having me up here.'

'You're very welcome,' she smiled, pouring me a glass of orange juice.

I munched on my toast for a moment and then had a sudden flash of déjà vu.

'Oh my god, I'm remembering my dream. Sylar from *Heroes* was in it.'

'Sylar, eh?' Kathy grinned, no doubt recalling last night's drunken conversation where I had detailed my boy-boy crush on the characters Sylar and Peter Petrelli. I pondered for a moment as vivid memories flooded my head.

'Blimey.'

'What?' Kathy looked up from her coffee.

'That really was some dream . . .'

'Why? What happened?'

'Sylar was about to kill everyone – as he is wont to do –

and he was summoning all his powers to do that. I had to quickly find a way to distract him: people's lives were at risk.'

'What did you do?'

I blushed and looked to see where David was, embarrassed all of a sudden. Luckily he was still showering, so I could spill the details in full.

'Um, I convinced him he wanted to fuck me.'

Kathy laughed. 'Did it work?!'

'Well . . . I straddled him and felt his cock get hard under my crotch, so yeah, I think he was warming up to the idea.'

'And then?'

'He was in the midst of using his telekinesis, so objects were flying around the room and I knew it was just a matter of time before he killed me – and everyone else too. But somehow I managed to persuade him it wasn't in his interests to kill anyone.'

'How?'

'Er . . . By dry-humping him until he had an orgasm. He seemed plenty distracted by that.'

'Ha! I bet he was. And you?'

'Oh, I climaxed too – of course. And while I was grinding against him everyone else managed to escape, so all in all it turned out well.'

'That's some skill you had in your dream, managing to stop Sylar by dry-humping him and you to orgasm; like some kind of special power.'

'What, like one of the Heroes?'

'Yeah: your secret weapon against the evil forces.'

'Girl with a One Track Mind: saving the world, one fuck at a time. Ha! Some gift that would be!'

We both snorted out our orange juice and carried on sniggering until David entered the room wrapped in a towel. He looked at us both, raised his eyebrows in mock indignation and then departed once again.

We continued eating and laughing and I was filled with happiness: not only was I having the break that I needed but I was also, more importantly, finally able to be open and upfront about my thoughts and feelings about sex with my close friend. A seasonal gift indeed.

// posted by thegirl @ 11:49:00 PM

Girl's Guide to: Holiday Festivities

1. Leave present buying to the last minute. And laugh at others whilst they go mad buying into a consumerist nightmare.

2. Be thankful if you manage to avoid going to a work-related party. Yes, it means you miss out on all the drunken shenanigans and fun, but at least you don't end up shagging someone you wouldn't look twice at when sober – and then having to face them at the office again.

3. Watch in shock as people buy food like there is a war on, clearing the shelves of goods in a blind panic.

4. Saying that, think of all the delicious sweetmeats on offer . . .

5. Consider all the interesting things you could do with left-over Sellotape, bubble-wrap and scissors:

   a) Have someone strip naked.

   b) Cut required length of bubble-wrap.

   c) Coil the bubble-wrap around them, from armpits to shins (bubbles inward – obviously).

   d) Stick tape around their waist to prevent them wriggling.

   e) Squeeze tightly.

   f) Wait for their squeals of delight as the bubbles pop.

   g) Carefully cut appropriate hole in bubble-wrap.

   h) Fuck them through the hole.

   i) Unwrap them.

   j) Fuck them again.

N.B. Festive ribbon not necessary, but offers the fun option of removal by mouth if tied in an appropriate place.

Wednesday 13th December

I can't believe it: Harry's back in town! I got a call late last night from him saying he had to come over at the last minute for a few days' work. I'm so glad that he's here: I've missed him.

We met up for a quick coffee today, and he grilled me about what's been happening in my life and demanded to know when I would be visiting New York next. Very soon, I hope . . .

At some point, three coffees in, I think, I heard a text message arrive. Wondering who it might be, I scrabbled around my handbag to find my mobile.

'Two phones?'

Harry was peering into my bag.

'What the hell do you need two for?' he asked, somewhat incredulous.

'Ah. Well, this one's my personal mobile,' I said, pulling out my phone only to discover that the text was from my bank. 'I've had the same telephone number for fourteen years: how sad is that?'

'That's fine, but it's a bit chunky,' Harry remarked. 'Looks like a brick.'

I shrugged. 'But it has fast Internet access and instant email . . .'

'And the other one?'

I held up my other, smaller, mobile. 'Ah. Well this one's my "Abby" phone . . .'

'Your "Abby" phone?' he interrupted. 'What, like a

Bat-phone? When you get a call, Abby Lee springs into action?!'

I laughed. 'Yeah, something like that: it's now my work phone: this is the number media folk and journalists call to get in touch with me. But I've had the phone since my book deal surfaced and I became very nervous about protecting my anonymity: it was just easier dealing with publishers and stuff using two different phone numbers.'

'And two different identities.'

I nodded. 'It took me a while to get used to people calling me Abby. I felt so fake at first having that pseudonym, but nowadays I answer to it without a second thought.'

'Do you think it worked?'

'What?'

Harry pointed at the phones in my hands. 'Separating out those two parts of your life.'

I thought about it for a moment. 'For a while, yeah: I had the personal phone for my normal, private, day-to-day life and the Abby phone for my secret blogger identity. But when I lost my anonymity that all went arse-up: the press got hold of both my numbers – and my home phone – and then all my phones rang off the hook constantly.'

'I can't imagine how horrid that must have been.'

I nodded. 'It was. I was freaking out, I was so unprepared. Honestly, Harry, I felt like I was having a breakdown: not knowing who was calling me or whom I could trust. I eventually just stopped answering any of my phones at all.'

We both sipped our coffees silently for a moment.

'Actually . . . I even had three mobile phones at one point,' I admitted.

Harry raised his eyebrows. 'Pray tell, oh popular one.'

I pinched him lightly in jest. 'Well, I had a third identity for a little while too.'

Harry shook his head. 'Honestly, what are you like?!'

I continued. 'I also called myself "Katie" at one point.'

'"Katie"?'

'I became worried that people who I met, or dated, or shagged, might somehow figure out I was Girl with a One Track Mind, so I created another identity entirely. That way I could be completely anonymous and if I chose to write about them, and they then figured out they knew me from reading the blog, then they wouldn't have my real name or phone numbers, risking my anonymity.

'You paranoid freak.'

'Hey, fuck you, it kept me safe, plus it got me laid.'

'I suppose there are some advantages to having a secret life . . .'

'Well, for a while, but I ended up ditching "Katie" because it just got too confusing trying to keep up with all my different names and personas and lying to people all the time. Nowadays I've given up trying to keep it all separate. It's been bittersweet having everyone know all the details of my private life, but at least there is no more deceit on my part: I can relax in the knowledge that my friends and family know everything.'

Harry nodded in acknowledgement, and I felt a sudden pang of regret over hiding things from him for so long.

'You are such a geek,' he joked, pointing at the two mobiles I was holding aloft. I was grateful he changed the subject and broke the tension in the air.

'Yeah, well, I'd never profess to be a top tech-girl, but I scored 83 per cent Geek on a Facebook test, so that has to count for something, right?'

'Or,' he said, peering back into my bag, 'the fact that you appear to travel with two phones, a laptop and an iPod in your bag at all times . . .'

'And condoms too.'

'What, just in case you happen to meet a gorgeous geeky guy, when you're next in New York, who won't mind your being permanently connected to the web?'

'Absofuckinglutely.'

Harry knows me so well – and he's right. Especially about New York, I mean.

Sunday 17th December

Apparently – and I'm not sure when this happened: maybe I'm out of the loop, somewhat – it has now become acceptable for London blokes to say 'You look up for it!' when they are chatting you up, with no hint of irony, sarcasm or humour whilst doing so.

'Really?' I said, taking a physical step back from the man who decided to use that line on me at a do I went to with Fiona last night. This guy had manoeuvered himself to the point where I could smell his (bad) breath, e.g. less than one foot away from me. Too close, clearly, and certainly, when you've been speaking with someone for less than a minute, invading their personal, physical space is not the best way to make a good impression.

'Yes, really,' he continued, 'you do.'

The first thought that came to my mind was: But I'm wearing a modest dress and a long cardigan, how can that be perceived as being 'up for it'? My second thought was: It shouldn't matter what I'm wearing: you can't judge someone's sexual intent purely based on their sartorial choices (unless it's true that all guys showing man cleavage are trying to get laid?). My final thought was: I've not flirted with this guy in the slightest; I've given him no hints that I am interested in him sexually, or otherwise; the nametag pinned to my dress says 'Zoe', not 'Hi, I'm Girl with a One Track Mind and am feeling really horny right now, how about you show me some hot cock action?' Basically, how fucking dare he be so rude?

'Is that so?' I replied. 'That's a bit presumptuous of you, don't you think?'

'Well, I'm a man: what do you expect?'

For you not to be a dickhead, that's what, is what I wanted to say. I sighed, loudly. 'Yes, and I'm a woman. Your point is?'

'We all have needs,' he said, grinning, and took another step towards me.

'Yes, well, I need to go over there,' I retorted, and headed as far away from him as I could, muttering 'Wanker!' under my breath as I walked away.

Clueless fucker. But, you know, I'm really not that challenging to approach and chat with. If that bloke had just introduced himself and then asked, 'Angel or Spike?' he would have been right in there. (The answer, obviously, is: 'Both.')

But then London guys really don't have a clue, it would seem. I'm tired of them and tired of this city: time to book that flight, I reckon.

// posted by thegirl @ 9:13:00 PM

The Girl's Guide to Pulling . . . for Men

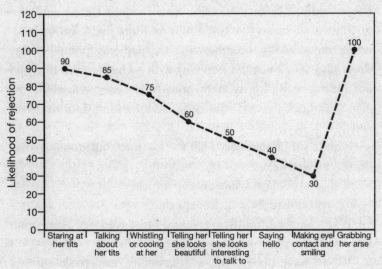

324

JANUARY

Wednesday 10th January

I'm writing this on an aeroplane bound for New York City. No surprises there: it was inevitable that I would have to make the trip to the city I love so much. I think I've begun to hate London – the UK, even. Maybe because the last few months have created such upheaval in my life that I need distance from it all; even walking through the streets of my hometown leaves me feeling aggrieved. It's no wonder, then, that my attitude to romance and dating needs a fresh, new outlook. I'm sure that that is impossible to achieve if I remain in London at the present time.

It may not be the men who need changing, so much as myself who needs to adapt, though. I mean, sure, I far prefer the attitudes, approach and outlook of New York blokes to London guys, but I think I'm self-aware enough to know that there are things I need to change about myself to give me the new start on life that I want.

This past year has been extremely hard for me, both emotionally and on a professional level, and what I have learned – about myself, and about my wants in life – is that honesty and openness are things that I value and need. Writing a secret blog and book about my sex life gave me the ability to connect with millions of people, and validated my feelings about sex, but the deceit involved also distanced me from my loved ones, and trying to reconnect with people – and regain their trust – has been a challenge.

I don't regret writing the blog or book, though: when I receive emails from women saying that my words have given them confidence about their own sex lives, it makes the struggles I've had all seem worth it; to know just one woman has an improved sex life as a result makes me incredibly happy. And amongst the turmoil, I've also had happiness: seeing my book displayed on the tables at WHSmith made my heart leap with joy. Knowing that my family feel proud of me for achieving that has been wonderful, too.

But losing the career I'd been working towards and having to reassess all my friendships has left me questioning what it is that I am seeking, what it is that I want and that is important to me. The experience of being 'outed' forced me to reflect on my life, and whilst that pushed me into a position not of my own choosing, it helped me to re-examine my thoughts on sex and relationships. I still don't subscribe to the view that women should solely seek an emotional connection in order for them to enjoy desirable sex, because I don't think that is true. And I also don't believe that pursuing romance and having to have the addition of a man in one's life is the answer to achieving happiness for women.

However, I think – actually, I know – I'm at a point where I now accept I have a need to be fulfilled emotionally as well as physically; I would like to share my life – my success, even, if you can call it that – with a partner: I feel ready to be with someone special for the long-term. I'm looking for Potential Husband Material©.

Whether I'll find him in New York, who knows, but what's important is that I know what I'm looking for now: an intelligent, honest, caring guy, who is open-minded enough to be comfortable with my Internet infamy; geeky enough to put up with all my gadgets (tech and/or sex toys); and horny enough to want to shag on a (very) regular basis. And if he was up for the occasional threesome, too, I wouldn't say no, obviously.

Well, a Girl can dream, can't she?

// posted by thegirl @ 5:14:00 PM

The Girl's Guide to her Ideal Man

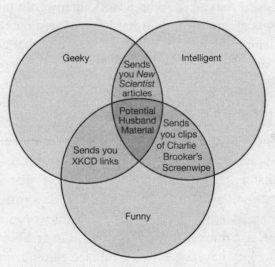

Still want more from Abby?

You can read her blog at:
http://girlwithaonetrackmind.co.uk

You can join her on Facebook at:
http://facebook.com/girlwithaonetrackmind

You can follow her on Twitter at:
http://twitter.com/girlonetrack

extracts reading groups
competitions books new
discounts extracts events
competitions extracts reading groups
books new extracts discounts events
events reading groups
extracts new books
new titles reading groups
interviews
books events extracts extracts
discounts events books
new books events events
events new interviews books extracts
discounts extracts discounts books
www.panmacmillan.com
extracts events reading groups books
competitions books extracts new